SURRENDER
INVITES
DEATH

SURRENDER INVITES DEATH

FIGHTING THE WAFFEN SS IN NORMANDY

JOHN A. ENGLISH

STACKPOLE
BOOKS

Published by
STACKPOLE BOOKS
5067 Ritter Road
Mechanicsburg, PA 17055

Printed in the United States of America

ISBN 978-0-8117-0763-3

*For my brother, Lyle English,
and our cousin, Superintendent Cecil Weigum,
Royal Canadian Mounted Police*

Table of Contents

Preface

Beyond the attraction of smart silver-trimmed black uniforms and trend-setting camouflaged battle smocks, I first became seriously interested in the Waffen SS as a fighting organization while arranging and conducting battlefield tours of Normandy for the Canadian Land Forces Command and Staff College. Since the Canadian Army had fought the 12th SS Panzer Division *Hitlerjugend* during the 1944 battle for Normandy, I took it upon myself to visit with the 12th SS's principal operations officer, Hubert Meyer, in his home in Leverkusen, West Germany, in March 1986. There, through his excellent series of maps and firsthand knowledge of the *Hitlerjugend*'s deployments in Normandy, I was able to gain a better understanding not only of the operations of the Germans, but those of Canadian forces as well. Meyer had labored for fourteen years to produce his history of the division, and we continued to exchange correspondence regarding the battle of Normandy after our meeting. In my 1991 book, *The Canadian Army and the Normandy Campaign*, I relied heavily on translated documentation and letters provided by Meyer. He was also kind enough to send me a personalized copy of his own book when it was first published in English in 1994.

Meyer's involvement with the *Hilfsorganisation auf Gegenseitigkeit der Waffen-SS,* a Waffen SS veterans association, prevented him from participating in the battlefield tour that I conducted for the staff college in 1989, but he selected former panzer commander *Sturmbannführer* Hans Siegel to attend in his stead. Awarded the Knight's Cross partly for his leadership in blunting a Canadian attack at Le Mesnil-Patry, Siegel greatly impressed the staff and students of the college during both the 1989 and 1990 battlefield tours. Especially appreciated were his insightful comments on German operations and the death of panzer ace *Hauptsturmführer* Michael Wittmann, whose remains had been unearthed near Gaumesnil in March 1983.

The likeable Siegel, who remained in contact with me for years after, also got along well with Canadian tank ace Brig. Gen. S.V. Radley Walters, who fought over the same ground. Together with fellow veterans Col. Tom Bond and Lt. Col. Bob Lucas of the Royal Canadian Artillery, Lockie Fulton of the Royal Winnipeg Rifles, Wing Commander "Papa" Ambrose (who flew Royal Air Force Typhoons), and Maj. William Whiteside of the Argyll and Sutherland Highlanders of Canada, they enhanced understanding of the hard-fought battle of Normandy. The recollections of experienced panzer leader *Oberst* Helmut Ritgen of the *Panzer Lehr* Division, who was also in attendance and with whom I had corresponded since 1984, gave balance to the German perspective. Lockie Fulton, who refused to forgive the 12th SS Panzer Division for the murders of Royal Winnipeg Rifles and other Canadian troops taken prisoner in Normandy, offered another view.

All that said, this work would have never seen the light of day without the active encouragement, support, and constructive criticism of editor Chris Evans and senior assistant editor David Reisch of Stackpole Books. I remain further grateful for the help and advice rendered by retired majors Mitch Kryzanowski and Bob Caldwell, both distinguished graduates of the Royal Military College of Canada's master of arts in war studies program; Col. John Selkirk of Reserves 2000; David Willis, chief librarian of the matchless Fort Frontenac Library; and Charles Messenger, close friend since the days of our service together in the Harz Mountains in 1966.

Introduction

The Waffen SS continues to hold a fascination long after it perished in the *Götterdämmerung* of the Third Reich. From a small black-uniformed guard initially assigned to protect Adolf Hitler, the force that became the Waffen SS first participated in combat operations in Poland wearing camouflage smocks. Numbering about 18,000 SS men at that time, this force was integrated and dispersed within formations of the German Army, which entered the Second World War on 1 September 1939 with 2,750,000 men in 102 divisions. By May 1941, the army had some 5,000,000 men in 209 divisions and the Waffen SS roughly 150,000 troops. In the middle of 1944, the strength of the Waffen SS stood at 560,000 within a total German armed force of 10,300,000 personnel. During the entire five and a half years of war, the Waffen SS grew to 38 divisions and a total strength of between 900,000 and 1,000,000 men. Of 910,000 at the end of 1944, 400,000 were Germans living within the Reich, 310,000 were *Volksdeutsch*, ethnic Germans living as nationals of other states, and 200,000 were foreigners. More than 300,000 Waffen SS soldiers never returned home.[1]

Originally conceived as Hitler's personal body guard and private party army with the motto *Meine Ehre heisst Treue* ("My honor is loyalty"), the armed SS under *Reichsführer* Heinrich Himmler assumed the role of National Socialist party police force and guarantor of the regime. Just as the German armed forces protected Germany from external enemies, the armed SS ensured the security of the Reich against internal enemies. Hitler and Himmler both feared, however, that even an elite police force would have difficulty in carrying out such a mission in wartime if it did not earn the respect of the population and the armed forces by sharing frontline duty. Only by shedding blood in battle at the front would the armed SS gain the moral right to shoot down rioters and antiwar protesters on the home front. Himmler also personally envisioned the armed SS as the vanguard of a National Socialist army that would infuse the traditional German army with a similar spirit. Hitler, for his part, remained more circumspect, realizing that he could not afford to dispense with army expertise and experience. The result was that despite his increasingly pronounced—and eventually total—mistrust of conservative generals, the Waffen SS never became a serious rival to the army.[2] Ironically, continuous service at the front further ensured that the Waffen SS never became a Praetorian Guard as occasionally portrayed; the attempted assassination of Hitler on 20 July 1944 was thwarted, much to Himmler's chagrin, by army rather than Waffen SS elements.[3]

The ten best Waffen SS divisions were formed before the end of 1943, the last being the 17th SS Panzergrenadier Division *Götz von Berlichingen*. The remaining seven established within this timeframe consisted of three divisions more notable for atrocities than fighting ability, two that enlisted Ukrainian and Latvian nationalists for the Eastern Front, and two with undistinguished records. Ironically, Himmler's vision of a purely Aryan organization transmogrified into a foreign legion. The eleven Waffen SS divisions nominally formed in 1944 tended to be of mixed caliber and reflected a degree of desperation. Two *Volksdeutsche*, one Estonian, and one Latvian were of division size; two Russian were of regimental strength; and two Muslim were never fully formed. The remaining three—one Italian and two Hungarian of unknown size—simply dissolved or disappeared eventually. The thirteen Waffen SS divisions formed in 1945 (three later dissolved) were of regiment size only, seven of which consisted of Dutch, Belgian, Italian, Hungarian, and French collaborators who feared retribution by local resistance movements. With no future in their homelands except trials for treason, they generally fought with great determination. Ironically, the last defenders of Third Reich Berlin included a doomed French battle group of the 33rd Waffen Grenadier Division of the SS *Charlemagne*.[4]

The Waffen SS divisions that fought the Allies in Normandy in the summer of 1944 were the finest of their kind and were concentrated in larger numbers than ever before. The Normandy invasion presented Hitler with a fleeting opportunity to stave off ultimate defeat by hurling the Allies back into the sea. With this accomplished, he could then have massed the bulk of his forces against the Russians to either destroy them or force a favorable German peace on them. For precisely this purpose, he sent the cream of his Waffen SS divisions to France. Of seven Waffen SS panzer divisions, he deployed five to fight the Allies. Only the 3rd SS Panzer Division *Totenkopf* and the 5th SS Panzer Division *Wiking* remained on the Eastern Front. In addition to his five Waffen SS panzer divisions, Hitler also sent an SS panzergrenadier division and two SS heavy panzer (Tiger) battalions to fight in Normandy. Collectively, these Waffen SS formations and units acquired a reputation for being the most fanatical and formidable opponents of the Allies.

Whether fanaticism produced superior performance is open to debate, however, as the Waffen SS divisions were larger and better equipped with materiel and weapons than many other German formations in Normandy. Arguably, army divisions like the *Panzer Lehr* and 2nd Panzer, which were larger and materially stronger than their Waffen SS equivalents, performed just as well or better. Then, too, Allied deployment mistakes related to such aspects as choice of ground, attack-force ratios, exploitation decisions, and even traffic congestion may have enabled Waffen SS troops to look better than they actually were. That is to say, the Clausewitzian concept of friction—the self-induced abrasion that prevents a force from even doing what it is capable of doing—worked more to the advantage of smaller, more maneuverable, but ultimately less effective Waffen SS battle groups than to the advantage of muscle-bound Allied forces falling over themselves. Whatever the case, the Waffen SS certainly showed that it was capable of exacting a high price in casualties for errors made by Allied forces at top or lower levels.

The reputation of the Waffen SS as an elite super soldiery capable of instilling terror in enemies was first earned on the Eastern Front, where both sides committed atrocities to an unprecedented degree. In this overtly racial and savage ideological conflict, killing prisoners happened routinely. Yet the Waffen SS had already demonstrated a penchant for doing so against British troops during the 1940 Dunkirk evacuation. In the 1944 battle for Normandy, the 12th SS Panzer Division *Hitlerjugend*, fighting for the first time, also killed prisoners of war. That some 12th SS officers and NCOs had fought on the Eastern Front only partly explains such conduct; after two years of combat in Russia, the 2nd Panzer Division went on to fight as clean a war in the West as the Afrika Korps' 21st Panzer Division and the more recently formed *Panzer Lehr* and 116th Panzer Divisions. Leadership and discipline surely played a role, for the 1st SS Panzer Division *Leibstandarte* did not commit atrocities like the 12th SS during the Normandy campaign, and when it did so during the Battle of the Bulge, the 12th SS did not. For whatever reason, the fact remains that Waffen SS divisions committed significant atrocities in the West, which prompted one Allied field army commander to urge his soldiers to fight harder by warning them that surrendering to German SS troops invited death.[5]

Waffen SS proclivity for committing atrocities contributed to its being lumped together with the rest of Himmler's SS and indicted as a criminal organization by the International Military Tribunal at Nuremberg after the war. The veterans of the *Hilfsorganisation auf Gegenseitkeit der Waffen SS* (Mutual Aid Society of the Waffen SS) ceaselessly argued, however, that Waffen SS troops were simply soldiers like any others and did not deserve to be stamped with collective guilt. Significantly, West German Chancellor Konrad Adenauer accepted this position in 1953.[6]

This naturally begs the question: who were the Waffen SS? This book will attempt to answer that in chapter 1. In this regard, the origins of the 3rd SS Panzer Division *Totenkopf* in particular are deemed to be highly pertinent and indeed critical to gaining a sound understanding of the Waffen SS organization as a whole. Given the overriding importance of the Eastern Front experience in the development and evolution of the Waffen SS, chapter 2 will be devoted to SS divisions fighting in that theater. Here again the role and performance of the *Totenkopf*, which Field Marshal Erich von Manstein rated the best of all the Waffen SS divisions he had seen, will be examined for the malignant influence it directly and indirectly exerted upon the rest of the Waffen SS.[7]

In subsequent chapters, the relative performance of British, American, and Canadian forces fighting the Waffen SS in Normandy will be assessed from an Allied perspective. The first Canadian encounter with the 12th SS Panzer Division *Hitlerjugend* will be covered in chapter 3 and the British encounter with *Obersturmführer* Michael Wittmann of the 101st SS Heavy (Tiger) Panzer Battalion in chapter 4; the "colossal crack" delivered by the Second British Army in Operation Epsom will also be discussed in the latter chapter. The tough business of capturing Caen will then be considered in chapter 5 and the "death ride" of the tanks in Operation Goodwood in chapter 6. The American breakout in Operation Cobra and the Canadian fight against the Waffen SS in Operation Spring will be juxtaposed in chapter 7. In chapter 8, the German counterattack on Mortain will be examined and, in chapter 9, the First Canadian Army's attack on Falaise. Finally, the struggle to close the Falaise gap will be considered in chapter 10, as well as Waffen SS efforts to keep it open for withdrawing German troops under Allied air and artillery fire that must have made them feel as though the sky was falling.

CHAPTER 1

Who Were the Waffen SS?

The fighting formations of the SS (*Schützstaffel* or "protection squad") encountered by Allied forces during the Normandy campaign belonged to the Waffen ("armed military") branch of *Reichsführer-SS* Heinrich Himmler's greater SS empire. Himmler's far-reaching SS bureaucracy and security service controlled all police forces within Germany and occupied areas, oversaw the concentration camp and forced-labor system, and set in train racial indoctrination, resettlement, and extermination programs. The growth of the Waffen SS followed the expansion of the *Allgemeine* ("general") SS, originally an adjunct of the *Sturmabteilung* (SA) brown shirts of the National Socialist party army formed in 1921. The SA itself sprang from volunteer paramilitary *Freikorps* of disenchanted anticommunist veterans of World War I who attributed German defeat to a stab in the back. The German Army, restricted to 100,000 troops by the terms of the Versailles Treaty, initially viewed the swaggering SA as a complementary means of buttressing German military strength. The SA was temporarily outlawed, however, after the abortive Munich *putsch* of November 1923 in which Adolf Hitler and his SA stormtroopers attempted to establish a National Socialist government by coup.

From this experience, Hitler decided to gain power through more democratic methods, but not so the SA under his lieutenant, Ernst Röhm, who continued to advocate the violent overthrow of the republic and the replacement of the army with a people's revolutionary militia. Hitler, on the other hand, saw that mindless bully tactics by the SA could well jeopardize the growing probability of National Socialist victory at the polls. He further feared that the army, recognized as the legitimate bearer of arms for the German state, might begin to look upon the nearly three-million-strong SA as a competitor rather than an avenue for desired army expansion and therefore act against it. Thus, while striving not to alienate his storm-troop supporters, Hitler came to view the SA as a liability and Röhm as a potential challenger.[1]

What Hitler needed was a counterforce, an internal party agency that owed complete allegiance not to some violent revolutionary creed, but to him and him alone. As a first step, Hitler reformed his armed personal bodyguard by establishing several *Stosstrupp* squads in cities he intended to visit. In January 1929, he also appointed his "Ignatius Loyola," as he called Himmler, to take command of this new organization of some 280 men. The ambitious Himmler in turn established the SS Security Service, the SD (*Sicherheitsdienst*), in 1931 and recruited Reinhard Heydrich in 1934 to head the branch. Under Himmler, the SS grew to 400 by January 1931 and to 52,000 by January 1933. Through intimidation and other maneuvers, Himmler and Heydrich asserted SS police control throughout Germany. In late 1933, Himmler also set up his own concentration camp at Dachau staffed by *Totenkopfverbände* ("death's head groups") guards commanded by *Standartenführer* Theodor Eicke, who would later, as *Gruppenführer* prison camp czar, extend the Dachau model to all of Germany. Eventually, the importance and membership of the fountainhead *Allgemeine* SS eroded as the SD, police, and Waffen SS grew in size and significance to become the three pillars of Himmler's empire.[2]

Himmler further established the black-uniformed *Stabwache* ("staff guard") headed by Sepp Dietrich, one of Hitler's original henchmen, and officered by Wilhelm Mohnke, Theodor Wisch, and Fritz Witt among others. In March 1933, Hitler ordered the *Stabwache* to assume the duty of guarding the Reich Chancellery in Berlin as *SS Sonderkommando Berlin*. In June 1933, two more *Sonderkommandos* were organized and trained at Jüterbog and Zossen army camps. In September, all three paraded together as a regiment under the new title *Adolf Hitler Standarte*. On 9 November 1933, on the tenth anniversary of the Munich *putsch*, the regiment, now renamed *Leibstandarte Adolf Hitler*, collectively took the oath, "I swear to you, Adolf Hitler, as Führer and Chancellor of the German Reich, loyalty and bravery. I pledge to you, and superiors appointed by you, obedience unto death, so help me God." Engraved upon their belt buckles were the words, *Meine Ehre heisst Treue* ("My honor is loyalty"). On their headdress, the men of the *Leibstandarte* wore the death's head badge traditionally common to many armies, but on their collars, they sported silvered Nordic lightning *Siegrunen* signifying victory.[3]

In February 1934, Hitler decreed that the armed SS, to be known as the *Verfügungstruppe* ("disposal force"), was to be organized and equipped in accordance with scales established by the army command. With the connivance of the army, he also settled his SA problem by liquidating Röhm and the top SA leadership during the "Night of the Long Knives" at Bad Wiessee on 30 June 1934. For the leading parts played by Himmler, Dietrich, and Eicke, who personally killed Röhm on Hitler's order, Hitler elevated the SS to the status of an independent organization within the National Socialist Worker's Party.

Buoyed by Hitler's confidence in the SS as a trustworthy force, Himmler now requested an increase in armed SS strength as the *Leibstandarte Adolf Hitler* remained only of regiment size at the end of the year. While Hitler looked upon this request favorably, especially since he harbored reservations about the loyalty of his conservative army generals, he was also aware that the surest way to erode that loyalty was to raise the specter of a another party army threatening to replace the traditional force and legitimate bearer of arms for the German state. In his announcement of conscription on 16 March

1935, Hitler compromised, stating his intention to increase the *Verfü-gungstruppe* to division size, but stipulating that it was to be incorporated into the army and subject to military law in wartime. Though funded from the Reich police budget, the *Verfügungstruppe* did not initially draw recruits from the *Totenkopfverbände*. Two of its regiments, the *Deutschland* and *Germania*, were raised instead from isolated SS units set up in major German cities during 1933, while the third regiment, *Leibstandarte Adolf Hitler*, retained a measure of autonomy owing to Dietrich's close friendship with Hitler.[4]

Himmler, who now privately inclined to Röhm's idea of replacing the traditional army with a more politically committed force, appointed *Brigadeführer* Paul Hausser in 1936 to head the *Verfügung-struppe*. Hausser had retired from the army in 1932 as a lieutenant general and, from 1935, set up SS cadet training centers at Bad Tölz and Brunswick to produce the future officers of the SS. Himmler envisioned turning the political soldiery of the SS into a modern version of medieval crusading orders and Jesuits of the Counter-Reformation. Ideological indoctrination accordingly figured prominently in the training system, which downplayed drill, except in the case of the *Leibstandarte*, and emphasized fighting skills, physical fitness, and live-fire exercises. The armed SS retained the SA rank structure and differed from the army in encouraging an egalitarianism among ranks. All ranks addressed each other as *kamerade*, and all officers had to serve first in the ranks. Educational requirements to join the armed SS were, however, lower than those of the army. Many men refused by the army thus joined the armed SS, which consisted largely of lower-middle-class or working-class German citizens. Not all who entered the ranks of the armed SS did so for ideological reasons. Some joined for more rapid advancement, others out of a desire for social prestige or belonging to an exclusive organization, and many for the glamour of wearing a smart black uniform. Once in, they also became members of a tight-knit brotherhood of arms.[5]

Under "Papa" Hausser, the father of the Waffen SS, the *Verfügung-struppe* continued to grow. On Hitler's specific order, the *Leibstandarte*

Adolf Hitler led the March 1935 reoccupation of the Saarland. The *Leibstandarte* also served under the command of Heinz Guderian's XVI Panzer Corps in the March 1938 annexation of Austria, which saw the incorporation of a fourth Austrian SS regiment, named *Der Führer*, into the *Verfügungstruppe*. Following these successes, Hitler on 17 August 1938 proclaimed himself commander of all armed forces and declared that he would decide the disposition of the *Verfügungstruppe*, whether for special domestic political tasks or deployment under army tactical control in war. In preparation for the wartime role, it was to be armed, trained, and organized as a military formation in army field grey uniform with SS badges and runes. Responsibility for administration, peacetime control, and recruitment continued to rest with Himmler, who retained command authority for dealing with internal threats. Service in this force also counted as fulfilling the obligation to perform military service, which membership in the *Totenkopfverbände*, though it was trained to army standards, did not. In the event of war, however, older SS personnel were to take over concentration camp guard duty from the *Totenkopfverbände*, thus releasing them for either internal policing or transfer to the *Verfügungstruppe* as combat replacements.[6]

In keeping with his pronouncement on the use of the *Verfügungstruppe*, Hitler decided that it would participate in Case Green, his planned invasion of Czechoslovakia. Once again, the *Leibstandarte* was placed under the command of Guderian's XVI Panzer Corps. As a result of the September 1938 Munich Agreement, however, which recognized Germany's right to annex Czech Sudetenland without a plebiscite in return for calling off the invasion, the XVI Panzer Corps moved peacefully into the Sudetenland at the beginning of October. In March 1939, the *Verfügungstruppe* participated in the occupation of Bohemia and Moravia, now proclaimed a German protectorate.

The following June, Hitler authorized the *Verfügungstruppe* to become a full field division, replete with regimental artillery and ancillary units. In a previous decree of 18 May 1939, he had also authorized the *Totenkopfverbände* to expand to a 25,000-man ceiling in a future mobilization. To protect this force from having its manpower poached by the army, he further decreed that all personnel who had joined *Totenkopfverbände* units on or before 20 September 1938 would receive credit for having fulfilled their military obligation.

Under Eicke, the *Totenkopfverbände* had meanwhile become a highly reliable paramilitary party formation imbued with a sense of uniqueness, egalitarian camaraderie, and esprit de corps. Eicke's ruthless insistence on absolute obedience and treatment of prisoners as inferior, implacable enemies of the state also produced a hardened and ruthlessly determined brotherhood that obeyed orders instinctively. Inured to the brutalities they inflicted, they remained completely indifferent to the sufferings they caused. To show mercy was to show weakness, almost as bad as cowardice. Obsessed with racial purity, Eicke viewed his *Totenkopfverbände* as a super racial elite within the elite SS, an instrument ready and capable of acting in accordance with Hitler's will.[7]

In the German invasion of Poland, Case White, the *Verfügungstruppe* did not fight as a division. The *Der Führer* remained in reserve at Prague while the *Germania* was attached to Wilhelm List's Fourteenth Army in East Prussia. The *Deutschland*, along with the divisional artillery and reconnaissance battalion, served as part of Werner Kempf's composite panzer division in Kuchler's Third Army. The *Leibstandarte Adolf Hitler* came under the command of the XIII Corps in Johannes Blaskowitz's Eighth Army covering the northern flank of Walter von Reichenau's Tenth Army in Army Group South. The only motorized element in the XIII Corps, the *Leibstandarte* eventually transferred to Georg-Hans Reinhart's 4th Panzer Division in the XVI Corps of the Tenth Army and finally to the XV Corps.

From all reports, none of the *Verfügungstruppe* performed outstandingly in field operations. Swashbucklers too eager to fight, they recklessly exposed themselves to risks. Officers led, but did not command. To army observers, the casualties incurred by the armed SS seemed unnecessarily high and disproportionate to their achievements, which they attributed to unskilled leadership and a poor standard of training. A common view held that inadequate training rendered them something of a liability, but placing them in reserve would have been unacceptable to Hitler, who took a personal interest in the progress of the *Leibstandarte*. Neither would he likely have countenanced the court-martial of Dietrich on charges brought against him by Blaskowitz alleging looting, indiscriminate shooting, and the burning of Polish villages by *Leibstandarte* troops.[8]

Eicke's *Totenkopfverbände*, relieved of concentration camp guard duty, also served in Poland. In the wake of the German advance, they carried out cleansing and security tasks aimed at exterminating all elements of Polish leadership and resistance. Three *Totenkopfverbände* regiments—the *Oberbayern* from Dachau, the *Brandenburg* from Sachsenhausen, and the *Thüringen* from Buchenwald—were deployed on Himmler's authority as independent security service *Einsatzgruppen*. The *Oberbayern* and *Thüringen* followed in rear of the Tenth Army and the *Brandenburg* in the rear of the Eighth Army. Heydrich's *SD Einsatzgruppen III*, operating behind the Eighth Army, was also placed under Eicke's direct command.

Until withdrawn from Poland in early October, the three *Totenkopfverbände* regiments and units of the SD under Eicke assumed supreme police powers in the provinces of Poznan, Lodz, and Warsaw as they were released from direct army control. In this role, they hunted down Polish army stragglers, expropriated farm produce and livestock, and tortured and murdered large numbers of Polish political leaders, bureaucrats, businessmen, professionals, mental patients, priests, and Jews. In their ruthless pursuit of Hitler's war aims, they ushered in a terrible creed of war that shocked and disgusted responsible senior officers of the army. Blaskowitz considered the *Totenkopfverbände* loathsome, and horrified by their excesses against the Poles, he protested their crimes in a formal letter to the commander-in-chief of the German Army. On being informed of the matter, Himmler promised that such activities would cease, but no further action was taken.[9]

In the first week of October, shortly after the conquest of Poland, Himmler obtained Hitler's authorization to form two new SS field divisions for the projected western campaign against the French and British. Together with the *Verfügungstruppe* division and Hitler's pet *Leibstandarte*, which was to be enlarged to a fully motorized infantry regiment, this force was officially designated as the Waffen SS in March 1940.

The problem Himmler now faced was finding enough trained personnel to fill these new divisions. Volunteers alone were insufficient, and the demands of the army, navy, and air force had resulted in a national manpower allocation ratio of 66 to 9 to 24, respectively, with no provision for the Waffen SS. As young recruits grudgingly released by the army also required training, they provided no immediate solution. Himmler therefore turned to conscripting older-age constables from the uniformed *Ordnungspolizei* national police in order to form the *SS Polizei* division. His other expedient was to incorporate Eicke's *Totenkopfverbände* into the Waffen SS as the *Totenkopf* Division, the establishment of which—with its death's head collar tabs instead of *Siegrunen*—critically changed the character of the armed SS.

Structured around the *Oberbayern*, *Brandenburg*, and *Thüringen* regiments, with *Heimwehr Danzig* providing most of the men for the artillery regiment, the *Totenkopf* Division filled its other units with new recruits and SS men from the *Verfügungstruppe*, the *Allgemeine* SS, the *Ordungspolizei*, and new *Totenkopfverbände* regiments that had been created by Eicke. Significantly, by decree of 17 October 1939, SS field formations were also granted judicial independence. Although theoretically subject to the same military law as the army, SS men were henceforth to be tried by special SS courts rather than by court-martial. Himmler had demanded this judicial separation as a result of a specific atrocity committed in Poland, when two SS men shot fifty Jews and the army demanded a trial and stiff penalties.[10]

By the spring of 1940, the *Verfügungstruppe* Division and the *Leibstandarte* Regiment were fully equipped and motorized with the best of German weapons. The *Totenkopf* and *Polizei* Divisions, in comparison, had to make do with requisitioned Czech armaments. Although the *Totenkopf* received a full complement of motor vehicles, the *Polizei* remained a marching formation with horse-drawn artillery and transport like the bulk of the German Army. Because the division retained police rank insignia and experienced training difficulties because of fitness and age, it remained for a long time something of a second-class formation.

Eicke, who once described the *Ordnungspolizei* as fat, complacent, and petty officials, was similarly held in outright contempt as a police general by army personnel who disliked the former concentration camp guards of the *Totenkopf*. Owing to his sheer toughness, ruthless determination, and talent for organization, however, Eicke was able to bring his division up to a combat-readiness standard that greatly impressed his experienced army superior, Maximilian *Freiherr* von Weichs, who, as a devout Catholic and aristocrat, was no friend of the SS. In his basic approach, Eicke reflected a view of many other Waffen SS commanders—that the army doctrine of speed and surprise could be enhanced by concentrating an even larger mass of troops and firepower in forward attack echelons and, by reckless and zealous pursuit, annihilate or force an enemy to surrender. Eicke had neither learning nor the slightest interest in more sophisticated theories of motorized operations. His main objective was to exterminate his foe; his uncomplicated method was to bring every available means to bear at the front and then smash away with relentless fury until the enemy crumbled. Indeed, it was upon this limited tactical approach that he directed the *Totenkopf* in battle until his death in Russia in 1943.[11]

For the attack in the West, Case Yellow, the *Polizei* Division joined Army Group C for mostly static duty opposite the Maginot Line. The pariah *Totenkopf*, much to Eicke's chagrin, remained in high command reserve along with three new infantry divisions in Weichs's Second Army. The *Leibstandarte* and the *Der Führer* Regiment of the *Verfügungstruppe* Division, in contrast, deployed with the first waves of the Eighteenth Army, attacking into Holland and Belgium, while the other two regiments of the division remained in Army Group B reserve.

Under the command of the 227th Infantry Division, the fully motorized *Leibstandarte* distinguished itself with a lightning advance along the Ijssel River above Arnhem, covering some 135 miles on the first day of the campaign. It then pushed on to Rotterdam and The Hague. The *Der Führer*, under the X Corps, stormed the Grebbe Line, which ran south between the Ijsselmeer and River Lek west of Arnhem, and pushed through to Amsterdam and Haarlem. The main body of the *Verfügungstruppe* Division followed the 9th Panzer Division over the Maas at Gennep to Tilburg and Breda northeast of Antwerp. Meanwhile, the *Deutschland* Regiment, in a tough struggle, fought its way through the flooded and well-defended Beveland Peninsula to occupy Flushing on the North Sea. The division was then withdrawn and redeployed through Belgium to take up a position on the western side of the Dunkirk pocket. As part of Georg-Hans Reinhardt's XXXXI Panzer Corps, it participated in heavy fighting against the British Expeditionary Force on the River Lys and La Bassée Canal in the vicinities of Estre and Aire. Under Hausser, the *Verfügungstruppe* Division appears to have performed well in its first actions.[12]

The *Leibstandarte*'s dazzling performance was somewhat marred, however, by the accidental wounding of Kurt Student of the 7th Air Division, which had parachuted into the Rotterdam area. As the *Leibstandarte* dashed into the city, trigger-happy elements opened fire on Dutch troops in the process of surrendering to Student, who was also hit. Following the capitulation of Holland on 14 May, the *Leibstandarte* came under the command of Guderian's XXIX Panzer Corps and took up a position on the western edge of the British Dunkirk perimeter near Watten. At this point, Dietrich tightened up on discipline as some of his men were wearing civilian clothes and had loaded their vehicles with all types of loot. In advancing toward Wormhoudt, the regiment also ran into the British 48th Division, which proved to be a much more formidable foe than any the *Leibstandarte* had yet encountered. As Dietrich deployed to attack, he was hit with an enemy spoiling attack. Once launched, the *Leibstandarte* progressed so slowly that Guderian was forced to commit the 2nd Panzer Division to the battle.

On a personal reconnaissance with Max Wünsche, Dietrich also came close to being captured. His vehicle was shot up, and he had to be rescued from a ditch. Eventually, his 2nd Battalion fought its way house by house into the center of Wormhoudt. In the process, the battalion commander was severely wounded, and *Hauptsturmführer* Wilhelm Mohnke, the senior company commander, took over. According to British reports, the *Leibstandarte*, supported by tanks, attacked in large numbers, shouting, "Heil Hitler!" and was mown down. Many SS men wore civilian clothes and British, French, and Belgian uniforms.

The battle for Wormhoudt constituted the hardest-fought action for the *Leibstandarte* in the West, and the combination of stiff resistance, the rumored capture of Dietrich, and the wounding of a battalion commander may have given rise to a thirst for revenge. On 28 May, in contrast with Dietrich's claims to have presented some captured British officers armbands and flashes as souvenirs, another ninety British prisoners were herded into a barn by Mohnke's men and taken out five at a time to be shot, allegedly on his order. After ten fell, the remainder refused to come out, whereupon the SS fired into the barn until they assumed no one was left. In fact, four prisoners survived to tell the tale, but the information leaked out only in late 1943 following an early prisoner exchange.[13]

Meanwhile, the speed of the German advance resulted in an earlier-than-anticipated commitment of Eicke's *Totenkopf* Division. On 19 May, it joined forces with Erwin Rommel's 7th Panzer Division and moved on to the Arras area, where both received a rude shock from counterattacking British armor, which panicked some *Totenkopf* troops into flight. After helping to blunt this attack with costly infantry assaults on enemy tanks, the *Totenkopf* was transferred to Erich Hoepner's XVI Panzer Corps, which also contained the *Verfügungstruppe* Division and the 3rd and 4th Panzer Divisions. Hoepner planned a full-scale attack across the La Bassée Canal on the western edge of the Dunkirk perimeter to prevent the British from digging in along this natural defense line. He assigned Eicke the task of advancing to the town of Bethune and probing the waterway for a suitable crossing place. Eicke decided instead to put a battalion across immediately, without reconnaissance, only to find the British strongly dug in. Caught by surprise in the open, the SS men withdrew in haste under heavy fire. Then Eicke, pistol in hand, personally led another crossing that succeeded in gaining a bridgehead. When ordered to withdraw to the south bank and assume the defensive as a result of a halt order from Hitler, he was enraged, especially since murderous British artillery fire rendered orderly withdrawal impossible. SS men simply raced for the canal, jumped in, and swam across, scrambling for cover on the south bank. Casualties were frightful. Shortly thereafter, Hoepner, who disliked the Waffen SS and retained doubts about the *Totenkopf*, reprimanded Eicke in front of his own staff and allegedly called him a butcher to his face.[14]

On 26 May, Eicke received orders to cross the canal again, by which time the British had greatly improved their defenses. The SS attack launched the next morning consequently produced the most savage and bitter close-quarter fighting that the *Totenkopf* Division experienced during the French campaign. By early afternoon, the entire division was stopped in its tracks. In the course of the struggle, which saw one battalion cut to pieces, the principal operations officer collapsed under the strain, doubtless aggravated by Eicke's ranting. To make matters worse, one of his best battalion commanders was killed by a British sniper near Le Paradis.

On 27 May, in the area of this village, 100 British soldiers barricaded themselves in a farmyard and pinned down an attacking *Totenkopf* company for more than an hour. When the British ran out of ammunition, they raised a white flag, threw down their arms, and put their hands on their heads, expecting to become prisoners of war. They were instead lined up against a barn wall by frustrated and maddened SS troops and cut down in the crossfire of two heavy machine guns. The company commander, *Obersturmführer* Fritz Knochlein, then had his men bayonet and shoot any who showed signs of life. Two British soldiers survived, however, as the SS hastened to press British rearguards covering the Allied withdrawal on Dunkirk. In a renewed attack around Estaires on 28 May, fierce enemy resistance limited the *Totenkopf*'s advance to less than a quarter of a mile. Another attack the following day again saw the division stopped cold by British artillery.[15]

As the British Army embarked from Dunkirk, the French vainly attempted to organize a cohesive defense in depth based on the Somme and Aisne River. On 5 June, Reichenau's Sixth Army, with Waffen SS elements under its command, attacked across the Somme at Peronne. After fighting through Ham, La Fère, and the Laon area, the *Leibstandarte* crossed the Marne west of Château-Thierry and the Seine south of Provins. Thereafter, it pushed through Sens and Auxerre to Nevers. South of the Loire, it attacked Moulins and struck south to Clermont-Ferrand and thence southeast to St. Etienne, southwest of Lyon, to assist the Italians attacking into the French Riviera.

Meanwhile, the *Verfügungstruppe* Division went into action first with Hoepner's XVI Corps and then with the XIV Motorized Corps under Gustav von Wietersheim, advancing through Soissons on the Aisne and across the Marne to the area of Troyes, thence south to Le Creusot, northeast of Moulins. The *Totenkopf*, also under the XIV Corps, advanced from Troyes to Chatillon, Chaumont, Dijon, and along the Rhone to Tarare, northwest of Lyon.

The *Polizei* Divsion had in the meantime advanced to Neufchâteau, northwest of Chaumont. The last heavy fighting against the French occurred on 16 June. On 21 June, the *Verfügungstruppe* Division, followed by the *Totenkopf*, moved via Orleans, Tours, Poitiers, Angoulême, and Bordeaux to Biarritz and the Spanish frontier on 27 June. On the conclusion of the French capitulation, both divisions took over the defense of the Bay of Biscay and the demarcation line of Vichy France.[16]

The fighting performance of the Waffen SS in the battle of France was on the whole acceptable, but not brilliant. The *Polizei* Division appeared much poorer than the others and certainly did not shine in operations against good-quality French defenders. Still, army reports showered no accolades upon any Waffen SS formation. The odium cast upon the Waffen SS in military circles as ugly rumors about atrocities spread was also pronounced. As early as 24 May, Hoepner heard that Eicke's men were seriously mistreating prisoners and issued a special order warning that killing prisoners in reprisal would be considered murder by an army court-martial. He also received a number of reports that *Totenkopf* troops had engaged in extensive looting in Bethune. On learning of the Le Paradis massacre, he apparently ordered a full investigation that, if ever undertaken thoroughly, had no visible effect on Eicke or his division. No charges were laid against Knochlein, and the atrocity was soon forgotten after Eicke explained away the incident to Himmler by claiming that the British had been using banned soft-point dum-dum bullets that expanded on impact.

Later, on encountering French Moroccan troops near Dijon, *Totenkopf* soldiers simply refused to take prisoners as they were considered racially inferior. The daily report of another engagement with French troops on 21 June near Lentilly simply read that the fighting resulted in "twenty-five French prisoners and forty-four dead Negroes."[17] Obviously, not all prisoners were killed by *Totenkopf* troops; the war diary claimed a total of 4,000 taken between 15 and 17 June and another 6,088 between 17 and 19 June. It does appear, however, that murdering defenseless prisoners was a natural outgrowth of the concentration camp roots of the *Totenkopf* Division and the fanatically harsh and vicious leadership approach of Eicke, who was used to treating prisoners as enemies of Germany.[18]

Eicke's battle performance additionally appeared amateurish insofar as his impulsive sledgehammer tactics produced heavy losses in men and equipment. Between 19 and 29 May, the *Totenkopf* suffered 1,140 casualties, including 300 officers, whom an irritated Himmler replaced with an equivalent number of half-trained cadets from the Bad Tölz *Junkerschule* just to keep the division in the field. In fighting the British on 27 May, the division incurred 155 dead, 483 wounded, and 53 missing while inflicting what Eicke estimated to be 300 casualties on the enemy, excluding the Le Paradis murders that day.

By way of comparison, the *Verfügungstruppe* Division, in advancing through the thick and tangled forest of Nieppe north of the *Totenkopf*'s sector, also encountered heavy British resistance. By mid-afternoon on 27 May, it had lost nearly every Waffen SS officer in two of its battalions. The reckless bravery, if not the calculated brutality, that appeared to be the hallmarks of Eicke's division also appeared to be characteristic of troops of the *Verfügungstruppe* Division despite Hausser's greater military experience. That both divisions had participated in some of the toughest fighting further supports the conclusion that they performed in acceptable fashion. The fact that Waffen SS formations were larger and better equipped than other divisions additionally increased their fighting value. Being motorized and hence always committed in the wake of the panzers further ensured their overall worth and potential for prominence in action. Hitler also lavishly showered them with medals.[19]

Between the capitulation of France on 22 June 1940 and the invasion of the Soviet Union on 22 June 1941, the Waffen SS underwent an enormous expansion. Hitler rewarded the *Leibstandarte* for its performance in the French campaign by decreeing that it would be expanded from regiment to brigade size. He also authorized Himmler to field another Waffen SS division. While Himmler was obviously ecstatic about promoting an ideologically committed fighting force, he once again faced the problem of finding sufficient manpower to carry out the expansion. Young conscripts permitted by the army high command to volunteer for the Waffen SS were for the most part needed as replacements for the field divisions.

On 15 August 1940, Himmler consequently ordered the incorporation of reserve *Totenkopfverbände* regiments into the Waffen SS. Up to this point, they had been Eicke's almost private manpower pool of replacement personnel for the *Totenkopf* Division alone. Two additional artillery batteries were also taken from the *Totenkopf* to enlarge the *Leibstandarte*, thus ensuring the infection of the concentration camp creed throughout the entire Waffen SS. The continual exchange of Waffen SS and concentration camp personnel henceforth continued throughout the war.

Himmler further sought to attract volunteers from *Volksdeutsche* (Germans living outside the Reich) and from racially acceptable nations such as Norway, Denmark, Holland, and Belgium. In short order, he found sufficient volunteers to form two new regiments: the *Nordland*, half composed of Danes and Norwegians, and the *Westland*, largely of Dutchmen and Flemish-speaking Belgians. By December, their training standard warranted combining them in a new division, the *Wiking*, with its third regiment, the *Germania*, coming from the *Verfügungstruppe* Division, which was renamed the *Reich* (later *Das Reich*) Division. In exchange for the *Germania*, the *Reich* Division received the *Totenkopfverbände*'s 11th SS Regiment, whose notoriously sordid behavior in Poland had drawn Blaskowitz's written protests. Another two *Totenkopfverbände* regiments were brigaded as *Kampfguppe Nord*, which later became the *Nord* Division. This left another five *Totenkopfverbände* regiments and two SS cavalry regiments still at Himmler's disposal for the attack on Russia.[20]

Hitler's decision to deny the Balkans to the British by shoring up his Axis ally, Benito Mussolini, delayed the invasion of the Soviet Union originally planned for 15 May. Mussolini considered the Balkans within Italy's sphere of influence and had been enraged by Germany's protective occupation of Romania's oilfields in October 1940. In response, he invaded Greece from Italian-annexed Albania in the same month but, in a humiliating reversal, lost a quarter of Albania to the counterattacking Greeks by the end of the year. During the same period, the British inflicted severe damage on the Italian navy at Taranto and put Mussolini's army in North Africa to flight. Britain's offer of support to Greece worried Hitler as both Italy and the Romanian oilfields could potentially be attacked from a British air base in the Balkans. To make matters worse, a coup in March 1941 took Yugoslavia out of the Axis camp. Having already dispatched German troops under Rommel to Libya in February, barely in advance of the arrival of British troops in Greece, Hitler now decided to invade

Yugoslavia as well as Greece. On 6 April, he struck with twenty-four divisions, nine of them panzer. Within eleven days, the Yugoslavs formally surrendered.

The *Reich* Division, under Reinhardt's XXXXI Panzer Corps, participated in operations against Belgrade, mopping up in the provinces of Banat and Batschka. An assault party under *Sturmbannführer* Fritz Klingenberg crossed the Danube in a motor boat and, after a hazardous journey, entered Belgrade, where he bluffed the mayor into handing over the city. For this action, Klingenberg received the Knight's Cross.

Meanwhile, the *Leibstandarte* crossed into Yugoslavia from Bulgaria at Kustendil and followed the 9th Panzer Division to Skopje. After fighting its way into Bitola, forty kilometers south of Prilip, it moved on to Monastir and linked up with the Italians to the west in Albania. On 9 April, after a tough fight against Australians, *Sturmbannführer* Fritz Witt's 1st Battalion group secured the Klidi Pass and beat off a counterattack by British armor. Like Witt, *Sturmbannführer* Kurt Meyer of the reconnaissance battalion distinguished himself in leading his troops from Klidi to seize the Klisura Pass and Kastoria, taking nearly 2,000 Greek prisoners. Significantly, *Stuka* dive-bombing contributed greatly to breaking general Greek army resistance.

On 20 April, at Katarra Pass, Dietrich received an offer of surrender from Greek Lt. Gen. Georgios Tsolakoglou, who considered the situation hopeless and wished to surrender to the Germans rather than the Italians, whom he had defeated. To forestall any possible change of mind, Dietrich decided to accept the offer of surrender and drew up lenient terms for a capitulation without humiliation. As the cessation of hostilities applied to the Italians as well, however, Mussolini strongly objected to the terms. This resulted in the Greeks signing a harsher protocol on 21 April, formalized by the Italians two days later. After receiving an admonition from Hitler, Dietrich spent the remainder of the month on tasks aimed at preventing the embarkation of British Commonwealth forces. Notably, as later reported by one British officer who had been captured, the *Leibstandarte* fought bravely and chivalrously in the Greek campaign.[21]

CHAPTER 2

Perdition on the Eastern Front

The spectacular Balkan *blitzkrieg* delayed Hitler's planned invasion of the Soviet Union. Operation Barbarossa opened on 22 June 1941, the anniversary of Napoleon's invasion of Russia, with Army Group North under Field Marshal Wilhelm Ritter von Leeb thrusting on Leningrad, Army Group Center under Field Marshal Fedor von Bock striking toward Moscow, and Army Group South under Field Marshal Gerd von Rundstedt cutting into the Ukraine. At the start, Leeb commanded twenty-six divisions, Bock forty-six, and Rundstedt forty-six. Four of the Waffen SS divisions that took part in these operations would eventually fight in Normandy.

In stark contrast with the war in the West, though not in Poland, four *Einsatzgruppen* SS security service task forces followed in the wake of German fighting forces and commenced the systematic extermination of Communist Party officials, partisans, Gypsies, and Jews through instigated pogroms and direct action. In July, Himmler ordered his two SS cavalry brigades, some 13,000 men, to deal with the threat of Jewish-Bolshevik subversion in occupied areas. In under a month, one brigade shot 25,000 Jewish men and women for aiding and abetting partisans; in three days in August, a second brigade killed another

23,600 men, women, and children. This was only the beginning. By the end of 1941, an estimated half a million Jews had been shot by SS and associated military and paramilitary groups who were also on their way to eventually executing 600,000 Soviet prisoners.[1]

The war on the Eastern Front, fought between two absolute dictatorships diametrically opposed to each other's ideology, brought out the worst of both awful systems. The racist and ideological overtones of the German campaign gave the Eastern Front an unparalleled nihilistic character. Nazi teaching and propaganda inciting fear and hate had so effectively dehumanized the Soviet enemy that German forces were morally anaesthetized from the start of the invasion. The Nazi soldier was to be the agent of a merciless racial concept in a life-and-death battle of annihilation against Jewish-Bolshevik commissars and Communist intelligentsia. The deliberate conflation of the racial extermination of Jews, not considered human, with the need for rear-area security against Slavic partisans, considered sub-human, further tended to negate major opposition to any abrogation of the civilized laws of war. Besides, the Soviet Union had not signed the 1929 Geneva Convention and could not be expected to wage civilized war.

On 10 October 1941, an order by army Gen. Walther von Reichenau noted that the SD and German police had been carrying out the necessary executions of criminal, Bolshevik, and mostly Jewish elements within his Sixth Army area. The same order warned that anyone in civilian clothes with short-cut hair was almost certain to be a Soviet soldier and should be shot. Civilians behaving in a hostile manner and especially those who gave food to Soviet soldiers hiding in woods were also to be shot. The soldier on the Eastern Front—the ruthless standard bearer of a national ideal and the avenger of all the bestialities perpetrated on the German people—had to fully appreciate the necessity for the severe but just retribution meted out to Jewry.

To Panzer Gen. Hermann Hoth, the annihilation of Jews who supported Bolshevism and its murderous partisan organization was a measure of self-preservation. Field Marshal Wilhelm Keitel's order of 6 June 1941 calling for all Soviet political commissars to be shot immediately on capture because they were the originators of barbaric Asiatic methods of fighting thus struck a responsive chord. His jurisdiction order of 13 May had also exonerated soldiers for crimes committed against Russian civilians. Only a few German generals, like Bock and Karl Strecker, quietly instructed their officers to ignore orders to kill commissars and civilians as they were incompatible with international law and considered dangerous to discipline. More than 3 million out of 5.7 million Soviet soldiers died in German camps. As the war went on and word of German atrocities spread, however, Russian outrage grew along with a terrible desire for revenge. Partisans freely attacked German hospital trains, and few Soviet pilots or gunners spared ambulances and field hospitals.[2]

As the Soviet NKVD (Internal Affairs Commissariat) demonstrated in murdering 20,000 Polish prisoners in the Katyn Forest near Smolensk and other locations in the spring of 1940, Russians were just as capable of barbarism as the Germans. Even so, of some significance, less than a month after the German invasion, the Soviet Union vainly proposed a reciprocal adherence to the Hague Convention. Although the Soviet army published no formal equivalent of the illegal orders issued by the German high command, it was almost certain that members of the SS and others such as camp guards and German secret field police were summarily executed on being taken prisoner. Captured panzer crews as well as grounded Luftwaffe pilots also ran the risk of being lynched, though for the most part the Soviet shooting of prisoners was random rather than systemically calculated. Wanton acts of cruelty also tended to be localized and inconsistent as the Soviet authorities desperately wanted prisoners, especially officers, for interrogation.

Where Stalin's approach was systematic, however, was in the control and treatment of his own Soviet troops. In an order to his high command in August 1941, he decreed that anyone who removed his insignia and surrendered during battle would be regarded as a malicious deserter whose family would be arrested and stigmatized for his betrayal of the motherland. Reissued in essence on 28 July 1942 as Order No. 227 for all troops, it aimed to eliminate the retreat mentality, allowed for the firing of commanders who permitted the voluntary abandonment of positions, and branded anyone who surrendered as a traitor to the motherland. For a while, each Soviet field army also had to organize blocking detachments to shoot down any soldiers who attempted to run away. Zhukov implemented this order with tanks ready to combat cowardice by firing on any soldier who wavered. As this practice took troops from the front and had always been carried out efficiently by the NKVD anyway, it was shortly discontinued.[3]

The divisions of the Waffen SS deployed for Barbarossa with the *Totenkopf* and the *Polizei* attached to Army Group North, the *Reich* with Army Group Center, and the *Leibstandarte* (expanded to division size after the Balkan campaign) and the *Wiking* to Army Group South. Although bigger than standard army divisions, they were but a small part of the total Barbarossa force. Yet as large motorized divisions within a spearhead that included only nineteen panzer and twelve motorized divisions, they constituted an important element of German striking power.

Compared to the fighting these divisions had experienced before, however, war on the Eastern Front presented them with nightmarish challenges that fanatical will alone could not overcome. While spectacular advances outdistancing those of 1917 were made on the central and southern thrusts, the experience of the *Totenkopf* on the northern thrust told another story. As early as 27 June near Dvinsk, Latvia, following the remarkable 200-mile advance of Erich von Manstein's LVI Panzer Corps in four days, SS soldiers experienced the first shock of Russian infantry suicidal charges. The next day, they also clashed repeatedly with wandering groups of Soviet soldiers who consistently fought to the death rather than surrender. In the village of Dagda on 2 July, the Soviets dealt the *Totenkopf* Division its first setback by forcing them onto the defensive. Four days later, in an attack by Manstein's corps, the division punctured the Stalin Line along the old Latvian-Russian frontier and precipitated the most vicious fighting yet experienced. Gains were measured in yards as fortifications had to be blasted open and the defenders rooted out with flame throwers, grenades, or bayonets. Night brought no relief; the Russians threw in heavy armor and all available infantry reserves. Fighting only subsided on 11 July with the capture of the town of Opochka. Casualty figures over sixteen days amounted to 82 officers and 1,626 other ranks—nearly 10 percent of the division's combat strength, a figure that drew criticism from Manstein, who thought such losses excessive for the relatively modest gains of the *Totenkopf*.[4]

Up to the beginning of August, the Russian campaign weakened, exhausted, and dispirited the *Totenkopf*, which thereafter operated in an atmosphere of mounting fear in which little quarter was expected or given. Eicke, seriously wounded by a mine, had been replaced by *Brigadeführer* Georg Keppler from the *Reich*, who described his two months in divisional command as among the most difficult of his military career. Assigned the task of flank protection in a poorly mapped, swampy, forested area west of Lake Ilmen, the *Totenkopf* endured a prolonged and terrible agony. This terrain, crisscrossed by numerous rivers and streams and soggy roads unsuitable for a motorized division, clearly favored the Russians. The pattern of advancing by day and repulsing Russian counterattacks all night simply wore down the *Totenkopf* as it slogged slowly forward to the Luga Line, which ran from Lake Ilmen to the Gulf of Finland.

On 14 August, a force of eight Soviet infantry divisions and a cavalry corps swung round the eastern edge of the lake and drove west, hoping to cut off the rear of the German armies advancing on Leningrad. Leeb responded by sending Manstein's corps to Dno, southwest of Lake Ilmen, from which, in a well-timed counterstroke on 19 August, it smashed into the Soviet left flank with the *Totenkopf* and the 3rd Motorized Division. The Soviet drive quickly collapsed, leaving the *Totenkopf* to experience its single most successful day since the beginning of Barbarossa. On 21 August, the mass slaughter of the entrapped Soviet force commenced. As spectacular as Manstein's counterthrust was, it was at best only a local victory. Although not then apparent, the offensive initiative in northern Russia was passing permanently to the Soviets.[5]

Although Manstein spurred his divisions eastward in pursuit, they failed to prevent the Soviets from establishing strong defenses along the Lovat and Pola Rivers. As the exhausted *Totenkopf* Division prepared to assault beyond the Pola, it was counterattacked by Russians taking advantage of torrential downpours that turned the ground into a quagmire. When Manstein issued new orders for an attack on 30 August, Keppler told him bluntly that his division was in such bad shape that it could advance no farther. He also requested that the *Totenkopf* be withdrawn from the front for recuperation. Manstein sensibly called off the attack, but savage Russian counterattacks ensured that the *Totenkopf* got little rest. As early as 12 September, the Germans had to abandon offensive operations and entrench in a permanent defensive network to protect the right flank of Leeb's army group.

On 21 September, Eicke returned to take command and was shocked by the condition of the men, whom he described as emaciated wrecks in rags. Like Keppler, he immediately urged that the division, suffering an acute shortage of officers and NCOs, be given a rest. Three days later, however, waves of Russian infantry, supported by air and artillery, penetrated deeply into the *Totenkopf*'s defenses, which hinged on Lushno on the southern edge of Lake Ilmen. Lushno changed hands several times in three days of fighting that raged with an intensity never before and seldom afterwards experienced by *Totenkopf* soldiers.

As German antitank guns proved ineffective against new Soviet T-34 tanks, Eicke created "tank annihilation squads" of two SS officers and ten men armed with bags of satchel charges, mines, grenade, and gasoline bombs to attack tanks on foot. At Lushno on 26 September, one such squad destroyed seven Russian T-34s by these desperate means. The next day, the Russians threw in three divisions and more than 100 tanks against the *Totenkopf*, but despite constant fire, bone-chilling temperatures, and lack of food and sleep, Eicke's men continued to hold. Inured to hardship, contemptuous of death, and possessed by a fanatical fear and hatred of the Jewish Bolshevik enemy, the individual *Totenkopf* soldier fought with a ruthless determination and tenacity that earned his division the unqualified respect of first-rate professional solders such as Manstein. The SS man's ability to remain calm in the face of disaster, his willingness to fight on against all odds, his passion for killing Russians, and his readiness to perish rather than appear weaker than his perceived racially inferior enemy all enabled him to retrieve, momentarily, seemingly hopeless situations.[6]

At the end of September, the Soviets broke off their offensive and withdrew to regroup. The 2 October attack on Moscow by Army Group Center forced Army Group North to keep pace by providing flank protection, which saw the *Totenkopf* Division participate in the pursuit of Soviet forces falling back into the heavily wooded Valdai Hills. An attack on a new enemy defensive position east of Lushno on 17 October, however, stalled almost immediately in the face of stiff resistance. Casualties by this time approached 9,000, nearly 50 percent of established strength, with the result that morale had begun to suffer and the division could barely conduct defense. As the German line stabilized between Lakes Ilmen and Seliger, the *Totenkopf* dug in on the northern edge of the Valdai Hills, the backbone and hinge of Army Group North's right flank. Here, with limited replacements, it battled both winter and partisans, the latter dealt with through merciless cleansing actions.

Worse was yet to come, however, as the Soviets on 7 January launched the second phase of their 1941 winter offensive against the right wing of Army Group North. By 7 February, they had encircled two German corps of six divisions, including the *Totenkopf*, within a pocket centered on Demyansk. Under the command of the II Corps, the division formed two regimental battle groups of mixed SS and army troops, the largest under Eicke and the other under *Brigadeführer* Max Simon, for deployment to the two hardest-pressed sectors inside the cauldron. During the second half of February, in savage fighting with equally determined foes, both battle groups took fewer than 100 enemy prisoners. Not until 14 April did the situation permit Eicke's battle group to break back, under concentrated air support, to link up with a German relieving force on 22 April.

In seventy-three days of encirclement, the division incurred 6,674 casualties. The shocking state of those still standing reminded one SS doctor of the concentration camp inmates that he had seen. Yet, as Hitler deemed the *Totenkopf* critical to the continued stability of the Lake Ilmen front largely because of its performance in the Demyansk pocket, he repeatedly refused Eicke's impassioned pleas to allow the decimated division to withdraw from Russia for rest and refit. As a result, the division continued to absorb the massive Soviet blows rained upon the Demyansk salient from summer to fall. By the time of its eleventh-hour relief on 16 October 1942, the once-mighty 17,265-man *Totenkopf* paraded in only company strength. After eighteen months on the Eastern Front, it had to be rebuilt from scratch.[7]

The *Reich* Division had a comparatively easier introduction to battle than the ferocious resistance encountered by the *Totenkopf*. As part of Guderian's Panzer Group 2 in Army Group Center, whose ten panzer divisions represented the bulk of German armor, the *Reich* participated in a 250-mile advance in six days. The task assigned to Bock was to destroy Russian forces north of the Pripet Marshes and deliver the main thrust, with Guderian commanding the armor on the right and Gen. Herman Hoth of Panzer Group 3 leading the armor on the left. Guderian had three panzer corps under his command, with the XXXXVI Panzer Corps of Gen. Heinrich von Vietinghoff in the second wave controlling the 10th Panzer Division, the *Reich* Division, and the *Grossdeutschland* Regiment.

Reinforced with a battalion of Sturmgeschütz III 75-millimeter assault guns, the *Reich* forced the Beresina River on 6 July and provided infantry support for speeding panzers in the heady days of the great encirclement before Minsk, which netted some 290,000 Russian prisoners, and the even larger Smolensk pocket that bagged a further 350,000 prisoners. Wheeling through Gorki, the division received orders on 20 July to barricade the Smolensk-Yelnya road near Jaswino against enemy attempts to break the Smolensk encirclement. On 22 July, the division seized the hills east of Yelnya and received the full onslaught of eleven Russian divisions—two of them armored—bent on recapturing Smolensk. Here the Soviets deployed their T-34 tank for the first time. At the beginning of August, the *Reich* redeployed to another defensive position and ultimately, having suffered heavy casualties, went into rest and refit.[8]

The overwhelming successes of Army Group Center prompted Hitler on 21 August to redirect Guderian's Panzer Group 2 southward away from the drive on Moscow, now delayed until fall. Placed under the command of Rundstedt, Guderian subsequently linked up with Kleist's Panzer Group 1 on 16 September at Lokhvitsa, 100 miles east of Kiev. This trapped the Soviet Southwestern Front that was defending Kiev. The *Reich* Division had meanwhile moved south on 1 September and attacked across the Desna River three days later. On 19 September, the division received orders to assist the 10th Motorized Infantry Division in preventing Soviet forces from breaking open the Kiev pocket at Romny, where it had been closed. Here the *Reich* fought a series of fierce engagements as the Russians vainly attempted to escape the noose around them. The Kiev pocket entrapped more than half a million Soviet soldiers. On 24 September, the division returned north.[9]

At the end of September, the *Reich* came under Gen. Georg Stumme's XXXX Panzer Corps in Hoepner's Panzer Group 4, which had been reassigned by Hitler from Army Group North to participate in Operation Typhoon, the attack on Moscow. On 6 October, the division received orders to cut the Smolensk-Vyazma highway and complete the encirclement of Vyazma that, with the Bryansk pocket, bagged 650,000 prisoners. After three days of tough fighting under air attack, the *Reich* succeeded in accomplishing this task, and on 9 October, it captured Gzhatsk in a raging blizzard. Two days later, they broke through enemy defenses in front of the Mozhaisk Line eighty miles west of Moscow. In the course of the fighting, the division commander, Hausser, was seriously wounded, losing an eye, and was succeeded by Wilhelm Bittrich.

On the historic battlefield of Borodino between 16 and 19 October, a fierce tank battle developed between Soviet T-34s and panzers of the 10th Panzer Division, which suffered heavy losses. In the area of Schelkowka south of Rusa, *Reich* troops also fought off counterattacking Soviet rifle units from Siberia. On 22 October, Mozhaisk fell to elements of the *Reich* and the 10th Panzer Division. By this time, increasingly heavy rainfall of the *rasputitsa* that rendered roads temporarily impassable left the entire *Reich* Division stuck in the mud. Only the onset of winter and frozen ground enabled the German offensive to be renewed on 17 November. This saw the *Reich* advance via Rusa to take Istra on 26 November after a hard-fought battle against Siberian troops. By 4 December, despite heavy snowstorms and temperatures of minus thirty degrees, leading elements of the division fought their way forward to the area of Lenino, seventeen kilometers outside Moscow.[10]

On 5 December, the Soviets launched a major winter counteroffensive that continued for three months. The next day, the *Reich* Division, having lost 7,000 men and down to about 35 men per rifle company, received orders to withdraw behind the Istra River and take up a defensive position. On 8 December, Hitler halted Typhoon. Three days after being redeployed on the tenth, however, another heavy enemy attack left the *Reich* encircled. This necessitated a further withdrawal of thirty-five kilometers in knee-deep snow and icy cold to a defensive location west of the Rusa River. On 21 December, the totally exhausted men of the division occupied their new position and repelled repeated enemy attacks. In mid-January, as a result of a general withdrawal to shorten the front line, the *Reich* Division abandoned the Rusa position and moved north to help plug critical gaps in General Model's Ninth Army encirclement of Soviet forces in the Rzhev area. In temperatures approaching fifty degrees below zero, the understrength *Reich* Division managed to withstand continuous mass attacks that reached their high point between 28 and 30 January. By mid-February, the division had incurred 4,000 casualties. On finally being relieved, the *Der Führer* Regiment had only 35 men. This all but ensured that the *Reich* would leave the war until the beginning of 1943.[11]

The *Leibstandarte*, assigned to Rundstedt's Army Group South, did not take part in the spectacular Kiev encirclement. Initially placed under the command of Kleist's Panzer Group 1—five panzer and three motorized divisions, of which the *Leibstandarte* was one—it saw its first action on 1 July when called upon to repel fierce Soviet counterattacks holding up the rapid German advance. This enabled Kleist's armor to get moving once again, at which point the *Leibstandarte* came under the command of Gen. Eberhard von Mackensen's III Corps. By 8 July, Kleist succeeded in penetrating the Stalin Line in the area of Berdichev, and the 13th Panzer, with the *Leibstandarte* in its wake beating off Soviet counterattacks on the northern flank, advanced on Zhitomir. The last major town before Kiev, Zhitomir fell to the 13th Panzer on 10 July. Reinforced by the 14th and 25th Panzer Divisions the next day, it then drove on to reach the River Irpen within ten miles of Kiev.

By 17 July, Kleist's armor was in front of Kiev, with the *Leibstandarte* having suffered 683 casualties in three weeks of fighting. On being relieved by the Sixth Army on 24 July, Kleist continued his advance southward along the line of the Bug River. Now placed under the command of Gen. Werner Kempf's XXXXVIII Corps and flanked by the 11th Panzer on the left and the 16th Panzer on the right, the *Leibstandarte* spearheaded the drive on Uman. On reaching Uman on 31 July, the corps wheeled round to face west, trapping the Soviet Sixth and Twelfth Armies as they desperately sought to break out eastward. Here the *Leibstandarte* captured and firmly held Novo Archangelsk on the main escape route of the Soviet Twelfth Army. The exhausting week of fighting that followed yielded over 100,000 Russian prisoners.[12]

Panzer Group Kleist now continued to strike toward the lower Dnieper River, with the *Leibstandarte*, still under Kempf, advancing on Kherson on the Black Sea. In the course of this drive, a battalion of the *Leibstandarte* discovered 103 German officers and men of the 16th Infantry Division strung up in a cherry orchard along with the bodies of six other German soldiers who had clearly been shot after capture.

Allegedly, Dietrich or someone higher in the chain of command ordered the killing of 4,000 recently captured Russian prisoners in reprisal. They were apparently shot eight at a time on the edge of an antitank ditch. Although who ordered the mass killing is not conclusively substantiated, it is a fact that the *Leibstandarte* captured 4,283 Russians on 16 August and another 4,643 the following day and likely did the job. Regardless of who gave the order, the shooting of 4,000 prisoners in batches surely says something about the *Leibstandarte*, which pressed on to take Kherson by 19 August in a fiercely contested fight.

The next day, the division went into rest and refit. Reassigned to the Eleventh Army, which was then spearheading Army Group South's drive on the Crimea and the Donetz Basin, it came under the command of Gen. Erik Hansen's LIV Corps in the Berislav bridgehead. On 11 September, Kurt Meyer led the *Leibstandarte* reconnaissance battalion to bounce the Perekop Isthmus, the gateway to the Crimea, only to find it heavily defended. Manstein, who had just arrived to take command of the Eleventh Army, immediately ordered a frontal attack that produced fierce fighting between 24 and 26 September, but only a partial penetration of enemy defenses. At this point, Manstein had to suspend operations to deal with a Soviet counterattack that had torn a gap through the Third Romanian Army and threatened to cut off the Eleventh Army.[13]

Regrouped by Manstein as part of Gen. Ludwig Kubler's XXXXIX Mountain Corps, the *Leibstandarte* moved to the area of Melitopol, where it first contained the Soviet attack and then counterattacked to restore the German-Romanian line. At this juncture, Kleist's redesignated First Panzer Army, freed from the battle of the Kiev pocket, swept south behind the Soviet forces to link up with Manstein's troops at Orechov on 6 October. The following day at Berdyansk on the Sea of Azov, the *Leibstandarte* linked up with Kleist's armor. With this operation, the *Leibstandarte* gained a reputation for being a "fire brigade" to be called on to deal with critical situations, a development not lost upon Hitler. Possibly for this reason and the seemingly more glamorous operations of the First Panzer Army, he again reassigned the *Leibstandarte* to Kleist. Once more placed under the command of Mackensen's III Corps, the division captured Taganrog on 16 October and pressed on toward the key communication center of Rostov on the Don. By this time, growing Russian resistance, sickness, supply shortages, and increasingly foul weather conditions had taken a toll. Rifle companies were down to a third of their effective strength, and morale was beginning to suffer as covering great distances and taking numerous prisoners had no apparent end in sight.

On 17 November, with the temperature below twenty degrees Celsius, the *Leibstandarte*, reinforced with a regiment of the 13th Panzer Division, spearheaded the attack on Rostov. In conjunction with the 14th Panzer Division, it captured the city after a bitter close-quarter battle on 21 November. Rostov now came under heavy enemy artillery fire as growing Soviet pressure on the northern flank began to threaten Kleist's rear. Although the *Leibstandarte* valiantly beat off an assault by elements of two enemy Soviet divisions, the Rostov bridgehead ultimately proved too extended to be able to withstand sustained enemy counterattack. On 28 November, Rundstedt ordered Kleist to withdraw from the city to behind the Mius River. The action had decimated the *Leibstandarte*, which by Christmas held a defensive line with its right flank on the Sea of Asov, just east of Taganrog, where it remained until June 1942.[14]

When Hitler directed Guderian southward away from the Moscow drive and dispatched Hoth's Panzer Group 3 north to assist Army Group North, he also ordered the 5th Battalion of the *Leibstandarte*, under Hugo Kraas, to the northern front. His apparent intention was to stiffen, symbolically, the resolve of Gen. Georg von Kuchler's Eighteenth Army, which was charged with the capture of Leningrad. Immediately spotted by the Russians on its arrival, the unit was greeted with propaganda loudspeakers blaring, "We greet the *Leibstandarte*, think about Rostov! We'll smash you here as we did in the south."[15]

If the significance of the German withdrawal from Rostov was not lost upon the Russians, however, this first major German reverse on the Eastern Front positively infuriated Hitler. In short order, he replaced Rundstedt with Reichenau. Other sackings followed as his confidence in the fighting spirit and ability of his retreat-minded generals waned. On 19 December 1941, he also formally took active control of the army. Forced to accept the investment rather than capture of Leningrad, the defensive on the Moscow front, and the retreat from Rostov, Hitler now refocused the main German effort for 1942 on the capture of the Caucasian oilfields. Having noticed the ferocious fighting performance of Waffen SS divisions in seemingly hopeless situations, he also decided to increase their striking power by reconstituting them as completely motorized panzergrenadier divisions supplemented with half-tracked vehicles and integral panzer battalions.[16]

Hitler's distrust of the army further led him to look to an expanded Waffen SS to attain fighting success. In May 1942, he authorized the establishment of an SS corps headquarters under Hausser. Reflecting his intentions and his growing fear of an Allied invasion of Northwest Europe, the *Leibstandarte* and the *Reich* (now renamed *Das Reich*) redeployed to France in July to undergo refit and reorganization. The long-suffering *Totenkopf* followed in October, leaving only the *Polizei* and *Wiking* Divisions on the Eastern Front. *Kampfgruppe Nord* was also withdrawn as ideological conviction alone was not enough to prevent Waffen SS troops from fleeing in abject terror from Russian tanks at Salla, Lapland, on the Finnish front in July. Eventually reconstituted as the 6th SS Mountain Division, the *Nord* was sent back to that front in August 1942. The *Polizei*, which bore police rather than full SS insignia, remained a relatively undistinguished formation on the Leningrad front. The *Wiking*, in stark contrast, shone in the fierce battle for Dnepropetrovsk, but along with the *Leibstandarte*, it was thrown out of Rostov and condemned for the rest of the war to fight on the Eastern Front.

In the summer of 1942, Hitler agreed to the creation of the 7th SS Mountain Division *Prinz Eugen* and the 8th SS Cavalry Division

Florian Geyer for antipartisan operations in the Balkans and Russia. Recruited and conscripted from ethnic German and other Balkan nationalities in the former case and unsavory *Totenkampverbände* cavalry regiments in the latter, atrocities became their trademark. Brutal in search and reprisal, they could not stand up to trained troops in conventional battle. As a rule of thumb, their second-rate status as fighting formations was generally replicated with few exceptions by other Waffen SS divisions (many in name only) numbered twenty and above.[17]

They were certainly not in the league of the 9th *Hohenstaufen*, 10th *Frundsberg*, 11th *Nordland*, 12th *Hitlerjugend*, 16th *Reichsführer-SS*, and 17th *Götz von Berlichingen* SS panzergrenadier divisions authorized in the fall of 1942. Of the divisions that would fight in Normandy, the 9th SS, named after Hohenstaufen monarch Frederick Barbarossa, formed and trained in France around a veteran cadre under *Brigadeführer* Wilhelm Bittrich during 1943. Its sister division, the 10th SS, named after Georg von Frundsberg, who led renowned Landsknechte pike troops and distinguished himself in the 1504 Battle of Regensburg, also worked up in France under *Gruppenführern* Lothar Debes and Karl von Treuenfeld. As manpower was short, both divisions conscripted 70 to 80 percent of their strength from the eighteen-year-old cohort. Redesignated as panzer divisions in October, they together constituted Hausser's SS Panzer Corps at the end of 1943. Originally, the 17th SS Panzergrenadier Division, named after the imperial knight and mercenary, Götz von Berlichingen (1480–1562), who lost his right hand in battle and replaced it with an artificial iron fist, was to have been paired with the *Frundsberg* in a *Landsknecht* corps. Composed mainly of German and Austrian draftees and some *Volksdeutsch* volunteers, it also worked up in France from late 1943. The 12th SS Panzergrenadier Division *Hitlerjugend*, authorized by Hitler in February 1943 and activated in June in Beverloo, Belgium, under *Standartenführer* Fritz Witt, drew its recruits from senior Hitler Youth. Officered by a *Leibstandarte* and army cadre, the division became a full-fledged panzer division in October.[18]

In December 1942, Hausser's new SS Panzer Corps—with the *Leibstandarte*, *Das Reich*, and *Totenkopf* slated to come under its command—received orders to join Manstein's Army Group South on the Eastern Front. By this time, the Russians had permanently encircled the German Sixth Army at Stalingrad, and Hausser, subordinated to Army Detachment Lanz (after Gen. Hubert Lanz), assumed responsibility for the defense of Kharkov in the face of the ongoing Russian Uranus counteroffensive that was flowing well to the west around both sides of the trapped Sixth Army.

On 14 February 1943, with Kharkov nearly surrounded, Hausser signalled his intention to evacuate the city, but was told to stand fast in light of Hitler's order to hold Kharkov at all costs. As the Russians pushed well into the northwestern and southeastern sectors of the city by the next morning, however, he gave the order to withdraw to prevent the *Das Reich* from being cut off. A furious Hitler, determined to sack him, flew to Manstein's headquarters, where he instead replaced Lanz with Kempf, but continued to hold a grudge against Hausser. Manstein himself managed to withstand Hitler's urgings for the immediate recapture Kharkov, which enabled him to deliver a devastating counterstroke on 20 February that shattered two Russian armies. The SS Panzer Corps played a critical role in the counterstroke and, in four days of bitter fighting, captured Kharkov on 14 March. In a little over two months in action, the corps incurred more than 11,000 casualties for a local victory that left the *Leibstandarte* and *Das Reich* badly cut up from city fighting. On their recapture of Kharkov in August 1943, the Russians discovered several mass graves in the area, some containing 800 shot down in a Soviet army hospital, for which they blamed Dietrich and *Brigadeführer* Max Simon, who had taken command of the *Totenkopf* after the Russians shot Eicke's light aircraft out of the sky on 26 February.[19]

In April 1943, Hitler appointed Dietrich to command a second (but senior) SS panzer corps to be activated on 27 July in Berlin and designated as the I SS Panzer Corps, eventually with the *Leibstandarte* and the newly authorized 12th SS *Hitlerjugend* under its command.

Dietrich had been made into a national icon by Goebbels's propaganda machine, and his appointment largely reflected Hitler's irrational conviction that political loyalty and sheer will could achieve success on the battlefield. Dietrich had finished the Great War as a sergeant major and exhibited coolness and courage in dealing with communist toughs during Hitler's rise. His staunch support of his *Führer* further ensured his early ascendancy to high rank within the SS. Hitler himself described Dietrich as cunning, energetic, and brutal—redeeming characteristics in his view—and thought his swashbuckling appearance and earthy humor concealed true ability. Clearly, however, corps command lay beyond Dietrich's level of competence, and for lack of intellect, he remained uncomfortable in senior command positions. Bittrich had a low opinion of Dietrich's military ability and related how he once tried to explain a situation to him with the aid of a map, but gave up after an hour and a half as Dietrich comprehended nothing. The system partly compensated for Dietrich's limitations by giving him an army general staff officer, Fritz Kraemer, as his corps chief of staff. In many ways, Dietrich was like the uneducated, but street-smart Eicke, whose sheer toughness elicited awe. They both shared discomforts with their men, ate meager rations with them, and looked always to their welfare. For this, they retained the loyalty and even love of their troops. To a degree, the crude, conceited, garrulous, and humbly born Dietrich personified the Waffen SS, though, ironically, with his short, stocky, swarthy build, he looked more like a bar-room brawler than the idealized handsome blond superman.[20]

On 4 June 1943, Dietrich handed over divisional command to Theodor Wisch, who the next day led the *Leibstandarte*, buttressed by 2,500 drafted replacements from the Luftwaffe, into the battle of Kursk. The astounding German recovery from Stalingrad, which surprised even Stalin, had filled Hitler with hope that he could regain the strategic initiative by pinching off the Soviet salient at Kursk. What he failed to appreciate was that the Russians had by this time taken the full measure of *blitzkrieg*, which was essentially fair-weather war requiring good flying conditions and adequate road systems. Soviet commanders like Gen. Vasili Chuikov of the 62nd Army at Stalingrad saw that the success of German arms stemmed from the superior coordination of all arms, none in themselves of outstanding quality. As *blitzkrieg* was greater than the sum of its parts, Chuikov sought to separate the parts. Keeping Soviet troops as close as possible to the enemy restricted Luftwaffe strikes as they risked hitting German soldiers. Letting panzers roll over them also enabled Russian infantry to strip them of their protective panzergrenadiers, leaving the panzers vulnerable to antitank fire and tank-hunting teams in depth. Chuikov used such hugging tactics at Stalingrad with great effect and took advantage of darkness and foul weather to launch stealthy storm group attacks incessantly upon the Germans. Recognizing that the greatest enemy of the tank was the *unseen* antitank gun, the Russians also deployed multiple well-camouflaged antitank positions in depth, grouped as *pakfronts* under single commanders who concentrated the fire of all guns on one target at a time. This style of defense, designed to wear down attacking armor, is what the Germans encountered on a grand scale at Kursk.[21]

Pinning his hopes on fielding more of the newly introduced Panther and Tiger tanks hurriedly rushed into service despite teething problems, Hitler nonetheless unleashed Operation Citadel. On 5 July, Gen. Walter Model's Ninth Army struck with three panzer divisions from the north while Hoth's Fourth Panzer Army attacked with nine from the south. Under Hoth, Hausser's newly designated II SS Panzer Corps—still controlling the *Leibstandarte*, *Das Reich*, and *Totenkopf* and supported by Stukas underfitted with 37-millimeter antitank cannons—smashed through strong Soviet *pakfront* antitank defenses in depth to gain nearly thirty miles by morning on 7 July. Although Soviet resistance stiffened that evening, Hausser managed to throw the full weight of his entire corps against the last enemy line in a final heave on 10 July. Having captured Krasny Octyobar and forced a crossing of the Psel River southeast of Oboyan, the only natural obstacle between the Fourth Panzer Army and Kursk, the II Panzer Corps was ideally placed to strike into the Russian left rear.

With success seemingly at hand, Hausser on 11 July confidently regrouped some 273 panzers and assault guns to deliver a knock-out blow aimed at Prokhorovka. At mid-morning the next day, they collided with 850 tanks and assault guns of the reserve Soviet Fifth Guards Tank Army bearing down upon them. In a triangular area three miles square, the three SS divisions fought at point-blank range throughout the morning while the XXXXVIII Panzer Corps on their left struggled to reach them. In eight hours of fighting, the Russians lost half their tanks, including thirty to one Tiger commanded by Michael Wittmann of the *Leibstandarte*, but they stopped the Germans cold. They now unleashed their own massive offensive on both sides of the Kursk salient to recapture Orel, behind Model, and later Kharkov. After Kursk, which marked the end of German air supremacy, the initiative on the Eastern Front passed permanently to the Russians, who henceforth dictated when and where to fight German forces in general retreat.[22]

With the strategic initiative having slipped permanently from his hands, Hitler looked increasingly upon Waffen SS divisions as emergency "fire brigades" to be used singly or in combination to deal with frequent crises threatening to rupture German fronts in Russia, Italy, France, and the Balkans. Wherever the situation was the most critical and the prospect for German recovery least likely, the elite divisions of the Waffen SS were nearly always found offering suicidal resistance— but in most cases only temporarily mastering the crisis of the moment by vicious counterattacks that blunted enemy offensives. After the capture of Kharkov in March 1943, Hitler had crowed that Hausser's SS panzer corps was worth twenty Italian divisions, and he remained dazzled by thoughts of what might be accomplished with a corps or even field army made up of such formations. Ironically, his confidence in Hausser's three "classic" divisions soared to an even higher level after Kursk than it had in the euphoria of the capture of Kharkov. The cream of the Waffen SS had not only made the deepest penetration of Soviet defenses, but had also not buckled under massive enemy counterattack. All three divisions emerged from the decisive defeat of Kursk severely battered, but with their reputations and prestige enhanced. Henceforth, Hitler repeatedly castigated his army generals by pointing to the superior leadership and fighting capacity of Waffen SS divisions, which in his view refused through sheer willpower to admit defeat or surrender to a racially inferior foe. Accordingly, he came to rely almost exclusively on Waffen SS formations to shore up the most dangerous weak spots in the line and stay for a time the Soviets' relentless westward advance. It was thus in the capacity of crisis-retrieval specialists that Waffen SS divisions unlucky enough to spend the remaining twenty months of the war on the Eastern Front operated.[23]

The *Totenkopf*, so condemned and left to trudge pathetically back and forth between threatened sectors, never regained anything of the offensive power it projected at Kursk. With energetic leadership and heroism not being the exclusive province of either side, more than ideological commitment and willpower were needed to withstand sustained Soviet offensives. In fact, much of the successful battlefield performance of Waffen SS divisions resulted from the preferential treatment Hitler accorded them in manpower replacement and materiel. At Christmas 1941, for example, the Waffen SS received winter parkas before the army.

From 1942, expansion plans also called for equipping Waffen SS divisions with the finest and most recent heavy weapons. Over army objections, Hitler insisted on equipping them with Mark IV tanks, at first in battalion strength and later in regiment strength of two battalions, one eventually with Panther tanks. In November 1942, they even received Tigers that had just entered service in September. With one panzer and two panzergrenadier regiments, Waffen SS divisions were also bigger than ordinary German army divisions.

In April 1943, the *Leibstandarte* had 21,000 men, and in October, along with the *Das Reich*, *Totenkopf*, *Wiking*, *Hohenstaufen*, *Frundsberg*, and *Hitlerjugend*, it was redesignated as an SS panzer division. These seven formations constituted almost a quarter of the divisional strength of the German panzer force, but could have been converted into fourteen regular army divisions instead. The creation of such elite forces had the further adverse effect of lowering the quality of other formations by robbing them of critical equipment, leadership, and manpower. In Hitler's military, the existence of Luftwaffe parachute and special infantry field divisions compounded the problem. Incredibly, the Luftwaffe fielded 200,000 men in twenty unreliable infantry field divisions that mostly fell apart in action and had to be salvaged by army training cadres.[24]

Upon his cancellation of Citadel on 13 July 1943, Hitler turned his attention to Italy, where the Allies had invaded Sicily. On 17 July, Army Group South received orders to release the decimated II SS Panzer Corps for possible operations to shore up Mussolini and secure passes through the Alps. The mounting pressure of continuous Russian counteroffensives was such, however, that only II SS Panzer Corps headquarters and the *Leibstandarte* could be spared. During what turned out to be a highly questionable diversion of troops, the 3rd Panzergrenadier Battalion under Joachim Peiper shelled the Italian alpine village of Boves, killing thirty-four residents, in reprisal for the kidnapping of two NCOs.

At the end of October, Hausser's headquarters and the *Leibstandarte* returned to the Eastern Front to help stem the Soviet autumn offensive that had reached the Dnieper on 22 September, recaptured Smolensk three days later, and thrown the *Das Reich* out of Kremenchug on 29 September. Under the command of the XXXXVIII Corps, the *Leibstandarte* became embroiled in savage fighting around Kiev, which fell to the Russians on 6 November. In the area of Zhitomir, it gained breathing space for the sorely pressed *Das Reich*, which, reduced to a fraction of its strength after a difficult fighting withdrawal, was relieved in December 1943 and eventually transferred to France.

Still the Soviet offensive continued, trapping 56,000 Germans in seven divisions, including the *Wiking*, in the Cherkassy-Korsun pocket on 28 January 1944. In the ensuing struggle to open this pocket from which a badly battered *Wiking* barely escaped on 17 February, the *Leibstandarte* incurred crippling casualties in men and vehicles. Divisional armored strength reported for 6 March included only five Panthers, one Tiger, and three assault guns.[25]

To make matters worse, the Soviets on 27 March encircled the 200,000-man First Panzer Army in the Kamenetz-Podolsk pocket, 250 kilometers southeast of Tarnopol, Ukraine. They also swept in the *Leibstandarte* and a 2,500-man *Das Reich* battle group that was left behind when the main body of the division deployed to Bordeaux in February. In response, Hausser's II SS Panzer Corps—the 9th SS *Hohenstaufen* and 10th SS *Frundsberg* Panzer Divisions, hurriedly rushed from France—charged into action for the first time to break through to the First Panzer Army, which was breaking out toward German-held Tarnopol.

On 6 April, the II SS Panzer Corps linked up with its beleaguered Waffen SS comrades in the First Panzer Army at Buczacz. In the desperate defense of Tarnopol, which fell to the Russians on 14 April, both the 9th and understrength 10th SS, committed piecemeal, suffered heavy losses. While the 9th SS went into refit in late April, the 10th SS remained in the line for several weeks in defensive positions along the Bug River. Immediately upon its escape from the Kamenetz-Podolsk pocket, the largely burnt-out *Leibstandarte* deployed to Belgium, where, completely in need of reconstitution in personnel and equipment, it joined the almost combat-ready 12th SS *Hitlerjugend*. On 12 June, the battered II SS Panzer Corps also returned to counter the D-Day landings.[26]

It is difficult not to draw the conclusion that the Waffen SS experience on the Eastern Front was one long, dark night of strategic defeat occasionally illuminated by local tactical victories that were eventually, and often quickly, reversed. The divisions that went happily from the Eastern Front to fight in the West—the *Leibstandarte*, *Das Reich*, *Hohenstaufen*, and *Frundsberg*—though they may not have known it at the time, were essentially losers who never scored more than ephemeral successes within a larger landscape of defeat. There were simply not enough of them to exert the effect that Hitler desired, and relatively, they remained but a drop in the truly massive bucket of forces engaged on the Eastern Front. In the end, they were capable only of momentarily stemming the tide locally, never turning it decisively. Hitler's faith in magic weapons and elites to win his war was as misplaced as his expectation that ideological commitment and unconquerable will alone could triumph over the practical realities of mass and materiel effectively employed. The assignment of single divisions here and there to plug holes in eroding defensive lines also tended to be reactive and difficult to coordinate in respect of massing artillery support and movement, which often resulted in the piecemeal commitment of fighting elements. Restoring a critical situation even with a Waffen SS corps still represented dancing to the enemy's tune and surrendering the initiative. Normandy offered the promise of reversing this state of affairs through offensive action that would be decisive.

CHAPTER 3

First Clashes with the Waffen SS in Normandy

Acclaimed military historian John Keegan has suggested that in a very real sense, Normandy was a Waffen SS battle. With fifty-eight infantry divisions thinly deployed in static defense from the Hook of Holland to the Spanish border and along the southern coast of France, the Germans could not easily pull any out to counter major developing threats. The Normandy invasion therefore had to be fought by those infantry divisions in position backed up by reserve formations that could be quickly transferred into the battle area. This called for the commitment of motorized and panzer divisions controlled by Panzer Group West, but as the 11th Panzer Division had to be left in southern France, only eight were available. Of these, the Waffen SS provided four: the 1st SS Panzer Division *Leibstandarte*, the 2nd SS Panzer Division *Das Reich*, the 12th SS Panzer Division *Hitlerjugend*, and the 17th SS Panzergrenadier Division *Götz von Berlichingen*. In addition to these, the 101st SS and 102nd SS Heavy Panzer Battalions, formerly part of divisional establishments, were also sent west with their Tigers. Shortly after the battle for Normandy began, Hitler additionally dispatched Hausser's II SS Panzer Corps and its 9th SS Panzer Division *Hohenstaufen* and the 10th SS Panzer Division *Frundsberg* to fight in the theater. Although neither the *Hitlerjugend* nor

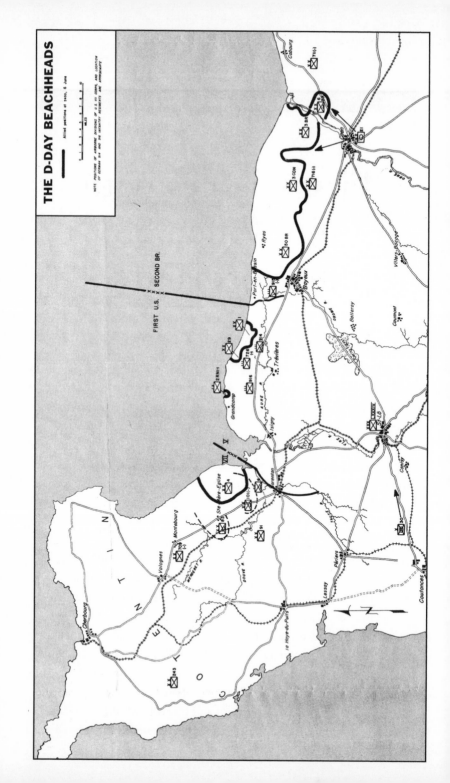

THE D-DAY BEACHHEADS

Allied positions at 2400, 6 June

MILES

NOTE: POSITIONS OF AIRBORNE DIVISIONS OF U.S. VII CORPS, AND LOCATION OF GERMAN 914 AND 916 INFANTRY REGIMENTS ARE APPROXIMATE

Götz von Berlichingen had fought before, the Allies faced a concentration of some of the best divisions fielded by the Waffen SS.[1]

German strategy in 1944 called for concentrating on defeating the anticipated Allied invasion in the West, while holding as well as possible on the Eastern Front and shoring up the Italian theater as far south as possible. This strategy took advantage of Germany's strong position in the West and offered the best prospect for a decisive turning point. The enormous risks of amphibious assault, which the Germans at the height of their 1940 successes never dared attempt on Britain, also appeared to play to Hitler's advantage. The British, having been kicked off the continent numerous times, certainly feared that a fourth failed attempt would be the end of the road for them. Ironically, original German plans for launching thirteen divisions against Britain in Operation Sealion may have helped confirm their initially mistaken belief that the D-Day invasion, with only five sea assault divisions, was at best a feint. In any case, German defeat of a major Allied landing in the West would have inflicted such losses in men and materiel that it would have been almost impossible to launch another amphibious assault in the short or even longer term. New German submarine models coming into service would also have helped prevent the Americans from being able to mount a second invasion. Such a triumph would at the same time have released German forces in the West for a major counteroffensive against already taxed Russian troops on the Eastern Front. Of course, the Soviets might still have prevailed and conquered all of Germany to the detriment of the Allies. On the other hand, this last German opportunity to turn the tide may conceivably have led to the defeat of the Soviets or, alternately, forced them to sue for peace.[2]

Hitler's deployment in strength of his prized Waffen SS divisions to Normandy aimed directly at throwing the Allies back into the sea in a decisive struggle. In the spring of 1944, few Germans believed that the invasion would succeed, and from Hitler on down, the leaders of the Third Reich remained confident that the Allies would be smashed on the beaches as they had been at Dieppe in August 1942.

Strategically, defeating the Allied invasion of Western Europe was Hitler's last chance for either victory or a draw based on a negotiated peace with the Soviet Union. After Stalingrad, the Soviet High Command felt confident that the Red Army could expel the Germans from Russian soil, and after Kursk, they knew that they could defeat Germany by themselves. The only question was at what cost and how long it would take, especially in light of the uncertain Allied invasion of Europe being delayed until 1944.

The shock of German military revival after Stalingrad signalled a difficult road to Berlin and led Stalin to contemplate a possible separate peace with Germany. Leaving the British and Americans to fight the Germans and Japanese was not necessarily bad for the Soviet Union and would have paid the West back for the 1938 Munich Agreement that appeared to turn Hitler on the Russians. Contacts between the Soviets and Nazis through intermediaries in Stockholm occurred most extensively in the summer of 1943, but continued into the fall. The Soviets demanded a German evacuation to the 1941 border and, after Kursk, to the 1914 Russian border, but Hitler insisted on retaining Ukraine, knowing that this was unacceptable to them. These negotiations, coupled with the withdrawal of Soviet ambassadors from London and Washington in June and intelligence showing that the Japanese were urging a Nazi–Soviet peace, nonetheless left the British and American governments apprehensive.[3]

The battle for Normandy was a closer-run affair than commonly thought, and Allied victory was not preordained. The British—and Churchill in particular—viewed the invasion with a certain amount of trepidation, fearing that it might become another Gallipoli or, worse, another Dunkirk or Dieppe. The strongly contested landings at Salerno and Anzio had also created serious doubts about the likelihood of amphibious operations producing success. On learning of Nazi–Soviet peace feelers, the British further feared that the Russians might stop at their border after pushing the Germans out, leaving the Allies alone to carry on the fight in the West.[4] At the 1943 Quebec Conference with the Americans, the British reluctantly accepted the principle of a cross-channel invasion, Operation Overlord, but with the reservations that the German fighter force be reduced in strength and that no more than twelve German divisions be held in reserve to oppose the attacking invasion force.

Yet with the ink barely dried on the agreement, the British began chipping away at the concept of Overlord, Churchill himself cursing what he called the "bloody second front" and suggesting that the folly of Overlord be thrown overboard. Although not openly flouting the publicly agreed strategy, the British began advocating other peripheral courses of action. Ironically, it was left to Stalin, flushed with victory from Kursk, to force the issue of launching a major invasion of Western Europe by demanding at the Tehran Conference of November 1943 both a fixed date for Operation Overlord and the appointment of an Allied supreme commander to carry it out.[5]

The problem facing Overlord planners was how to win the race, with roughly thirty-seven Allied divisions against about fifty available German equivalents, to create a lodgement on the continent from which to conduct further operations into the heart of Germany. Of course, the progressive destruction of the Luftwaffe in Operation Pointblank bombing raids over Germany had all but guaranteed overwhelming Allied air supremacy for the invasion. As *blitzkrieg* depended largely on air support for its early successes, this boded particularly ill for German forces in the West.

The German Army was also by this stage of the war an old-fashioned one compared to fully motorized British and American ground forces. The mobility of the German Fifteenth and Seventh Armies defending the English Channel coast from the Pas de Calais to Normandy depended largely on 67,000 horses. German supply trains as well as howitzers in standard infantry divisions were usually pulled by horses. A German artillery battery was supposed to have 126 horses, a battalion 516. Some coastal defense divisions, like the German 716th at Caen, had no horses at all, which essentially left their gun positions fixed. German marching infantry divisions also lacked sufficient anti-tank and antiaircraft weapons to be able to ward off determined ground and air attack.[6] Given such circumstances, the importance of mobile German armored formations, especially Waffen SS panzer divisions, can hardly be overestimated.

With substantial panzer and artillery complements, Waffen SS formations constituted a disproportionate share of the armored mobile reserve. Heavier in integral infantry—with six instead of four battalions standard for ordinary panzer divisions—they were also well suited to fight the grim, primarily infantry, struggle that developed in the restricted terrain of the Norman countryside.[7] That said, with 97 Mark IV panzers, 86 Panthers, 40 tank destroyers, and a company of King Tigers, the elite army *Panzer Lehr* Division was the strongest in France in June 1944. All of its grenadier battalions had semitracked armored personnel carriers, an equipment level unmatched by any panzer divisions in the West, including the 1st SS Panzer Division *Leibstandarte*. The next strongest formation was the 2nd Panzer Division, with 94 Mark IVs, 67 Panthers, and 41 tank destroyers. The 12th SS Panzer Division *Hitlerjugend*, with 91 Mark IVs, 48 Panthers, and 44 tank destroyers, followed in third place. The *Leibstandarte* had 42 Mark IVs, 38 Panthers, and 44 tank destroyers. The 21st Panzer Division, with 98 Mark IVs and 111 tank destroyers, had no Panthers at all, and the 10th SS Panzer Division *Frundsberg*, with 32 Mark IVs, had neither Panther nor tank destroyer battalions. The 9th SS Panzer Division *Hohenstaufen* possessed 41 Mark IVs and 30 Panthers but had no tank destroyer battalion initially. The remaining panzer divisions averaged 45 tanks per Mark IV panzer battalion and, for the divisions that had them, 35 Panthers each. Some of the tank destroyer battalions equipped with Sturmgeschütz III assault guns were later upgraded with more fearsome Jagdpanzer IV tank hunters.[8]

Waffen SS panzer divisional establishments in Normandy included a panzer regiment with Panther and Mark IV battalions and two panzergrenadier regiments of three battalions each, with four companies per battalion. One panzergrenadier battalion in each regiment was equipped with Schützenpanzerwagen 251 semitracked open-topped armored personnel carriers while the other two battalions moved in trucks. A division also had an assault gun or tank hunter battalion, a reconnaissance battalion, a pioneer battalion, a Flak battalion with three antiaircraft batteries of 88-millimeter and one or two batteries of 37-millimeter guns, and a Nebelwerfer battalion with three or four batteries of 150-millimeter towed multibarrelled mortars.[9]

The divisional artillery regiment consisted of three artillery battalions: one self-propelled with two or three batteries of 105-millimeter Wasps and one battery of 150-millimeter Hummels; another with two or three batteries of 105-millimeter towed guns; and a third with two or three batteries of 150-millimeter towed guns and a battery of 100-millimeter towed cannons. Each panzergrenadier regiment also had an infantry gun company with six 150-millimeter self-propelled Hummels, a Flak company with twelve 20-millimeter towed guns, and a pioneer company. The Waffen SS panzer division fielded 7,000 panzergrenadiers as compared to 3,400 and 3,000 infantrymen, respectively, on the establishments of British and American armored divisions. They also held an edge with sixty medium and heavy mortars as compared to twenty-four in Allied armored divisions.[10] In fact, Waffen SS panzer division organization bore greater resemblance to an Anglo-Canadian infantry division supported by an armored brigade.

The Germans possessed a huge defensive advantage over the Allies with their superior panzers. Hardly any ground fire could knock out Panthers and Tigers that were properly sited in hull-down positions, and nothing on the Allied side could withstand their fire. Even the Mark IV, the work horse of German armor, had a better gun than the upgraded 76-millimeter of the Sherman. While the 75-millimeter Sherman gun could penetrate the frontal armor of the Mark IV at 1,000 meters, the Mark IV long KwK 40 could kill any Allied tank at 1,500 meters. For the forty-five-ton Panther and its 75-millimeter KwK 42 main armament, this range increased to 2,000 meters and, for the 88-millimeter KwK 36 of the fifty-five-ton Tiger, in excess of 2,500 meters.

The 75-millimeter Sherman could not kill a Tiger unless it closed to 100 meters or hit the rear of the turret or vertical plates on the flank. The only way to kill a Panther from the front was to hit the lower part of its mantlet. Both entailed great risk as German panzers tended to work in twos or with an assault gun, one protecting another, with Panzerfaust-armed infantry in support. The Panther, which actually had larger dimensions than the Tiger, could also out-maneuver the Sherman in wet or muddy terrain and had a better magnification sight and a low-flash firing signature. The primary danger to these Eastern Front leviathans came from the undue reckless-ness and aggressiveness that their sheer imperviousness produced in crews, who often maneuvered fully exposed on forward slopes. So long as they fought prudently from hull-down positions, however, they could shoot down Allied tanks like sitting ducks.[11] Their longer range also provided an inestimable advantage in defense as they could fire enfilade at great distance across a wide front.

The Sherman's 75-millimeter gun could not pierce the frontal armor of a Panther and could deal with a Tiger only from the rear or point-blank from enfilade. The American 76-millimeter tank gun introduced later was not much of an improvement, and 90-millimeter rounds bounced off the Tiger's front at 1,200 yards. Fortunately for their offensive capacity, the British possessed the only Allied tank capa-ble of taking on Panthers and Tigers. The Firefly, a Sherman variant to which the British 17-pounder antitank gun had been fitted, could eas-ily penetrate the frontal armor of the Tiger with armor-piercing dis-carding sabot shot from up to 1,800 yards. By far the best Allied tank of the war, the Firefly was initially issued on a limited scale of one per four tank troops. Montgomery planned to offer one Firefly per tank platoon to the Americans once the British possessed two per tank troop, then build the British up to three per tank troop. Although the Firefly had to wait for a good high-explosive round, it proved a formi-dable enough weapon for the Germans to seek it out as a prime target. Crews loved it, and the Firefly enabled the Anglo-Canadians to take on a weight of German panzer might that less well-gunned tanks could hardly have handled over open ground. Firefly engagements with the Tiger tended to take the form of both tanks—the Tiger with its hand-cranked turret—jockeying for kill positions while the three other Shermans worked round for rear shots.[12]

While a critical dimension of the Waffen SS's field performance obviously reflected superior equipment and supply priorities that emanated from Hitler himself, training also counted. The 12th SS Panzer Division *Hitlerjugend* went into battle for the first time in Normandy, but gave a good account of itself as the scourge of Canadian arms throughout the Normandy campaign. Derisively called a baby division with a milk-bottle badge by a disparaging Allied press, the division had been formed in June 1943 almost entirely of youths around seventeen years of age. This was a consequence of *Reichsjugendführer* Arthur Axmann's Hitler Youth project, approved by Hitler after Stalingrad, to induct senior *Hitlerjugend* with some military training into a volunteer division. On passing the test of war, this formation would serve as a model for the incorporation of additional volunteers into other German divisions.

In June 1943, *Oberführer* Fritz Witt of the *Leibstandarte* assumed command, and with other veteran officers and noncommissioned officers from the Waffen SS and army, he instituted a vigorous training program that stressed fitness. One suspects that easier access to better training areas than the Allies had in Britain also enabled them to conduct more realistic field exercises, including live fire. The training philosophy of the *Hitlerjugend* appears to have been innovative, with great importance attached to inculcating a sense of responsibility, self-sacrifice, and comradeship. Only eighteen-year-olds were allowed cigarettes; younger soldiers were issued candy. The relationship between battle-hardened veterans and inexperienced youth has been likened to that between older and younger brothers.

For nine months, despite certain equipment shortages, the 12th SS conducted thorough battle-oriented training. Fieldcraft—in particular camouflage techniques learned from the Russians—received special attention. Marksmanship training focused on shooting not on formal gallery ranges, but exclusively in the field using silhouette targets. Physical fitness was attained mainly through playing sports and running obstacle courses rather than route marching. Parade square drill took a back seat to training under as realistic combat conditions as possible. Panzer battalions concentrated on their basic skills, which included repair and maintenance, driver training, radio operation, and gunnery. As cross-training was an unaffordable luxury by 1944, new crewmen learned only one of these jobs. Formation training from early 1944 consisted of live-fire and large-scale tank exercises that stressed the cooperation of arms within the panzer battle group. By April 1944, the division had already suffered fifteen dead, presumably the result of training accidents. When the 20,540 soldiers of the 12th SS Panzer Division (two panzergrenadier regiments of three infantry battalions each and one panzer regiment with Mark IVs and one Panther battalion) went into action, they were considered excellently trained—as well trained as scarcely any other division had ever been—so that their operational employment could be fully justified. This, more than just will and fanaticism, was surely their great forte.[13]

The first encounter between Allied and Waffen SS formations occurred on 7 June, the day after Gen. Miles Dempsey's British Second Army stormed Sword, Juno, and Gold Beaches. While Lt. Gen. John Crocker's 1 Corps assaulted Sword with the 3rd British Infantry Division Group and Juno with the 3rd Canadian Infantry Division Group, Lt. Gen. Gerard Bucknall's 30 Corps assaulted Gold with the 50th (Northumbrian) Division Group. The task of Crocker's corps was to secure a lodgement that included Caen and the important high ground around Carpiquet airfield, while Bucknall's 30 Corps drove seven miles inland to Bayeux. The 2nd Canadian Armoured Brigade of the 3rd Canadian Infantry Division Group was meanwhile to make a rapid fifteen-mile thrust to secure the high ground around Evercy, southwest of Caen.

Although the quick capture of Caen and Carpiquet remained a high-priority objective for Crocker, the location of the 21st Panzer Division southeast of Caen meant it was capable of intervening on D-Day. In the event the enemy forestalled the capture of Caen, Crocker's plan called for avoiding costly frontal attacks and instead seizing the high ground to its north and masking the city until the 51st (Highland) Division and the 4th Armoured Brigade became available to participate in a concerted attack. In fact, the 21st Panzer did counterattack the 3rd British Division on D-Day and, though staunchly repulsed, managed to delay the advance on Caen. The dash by other 21st Panzer elements to Lion-sur-Mer further opened a dangerous two-mile gap between the 3rd British and 3rd Canadian Divisions, a vulnerability exacerbated by the continued resistance of German strongpoints near Douvres-la-Délivrande.

On the afternoon of 7 June, the 25th Panzergrenadier Regiment of the 12th SS Panzer Division *Hitlerjugend* delivered an additional shock by counterattacking the 3rd Canadian Infantry Division Group, which was advancing inland on Carpiquet airport. Commanded by Maj. Gen. Rod Keller, the 18,000-strong all-volunteer Canadian division comprised three lorried infantry brigades, each of a headquarters and three infantry battalions fielding four companies each for a total of twelve rifle companies. The division also had a machine-gun battalion and reconnaissance, antitank, and light antiaircraft regiments of battalion size. The reinforced divisional artillery consisted of ninety 105-millimeter self-propelled Priests and medium guns. Supported by the 2nd Canadian Armoured Brigade of 3,500 men and seventy-nine Sherman tanks in three armored regiments of three nineteen-tank squadrons each, the divisional group had trained hard for a year in amphibious operations.

After landing at 0730 hours on D-Day with the 7th Infantry Brigade Group to its right and the 8th Infantry Brigade Group to its left, the division fought through to beyond Cruelly, Pierrepont, and Colomby-sur-Thaon by 2000 hours. The reserve 9th Brigade then passed through to Villons-les-Buissons, where mounting resistance indicated that the final objective line along the Caen-Bayeux railway could not be reached before dark. The division accordingly dug in to form a firm base for resuming operations in daylight. The next day, the 7th Brigade dashed for the final objective line, with the Royal Winnipeg Rifle Battalion securing Putot-en-Bessin and the Regina

Rifles the villages of Bretteville-l'Orgueilleus and Norrey-en-Bessin. On the left, in the van of the 9th Brigade, the North Nova Scotia Highlanders Battalion, supported by the 27th Armoured Regiment (The Sherbrooke Fusiliers), fought its way into Buron and Authie by early afternoon.

The 9th Brigade advanced with its left flank open as a result of the D-Day counterattack of the 21st Panzer Division that slashed between the 3rd Canadian and British 3rd Division. Although the German counterattack by more than fifty panzers received a rude shock when thirteen of their number were knocked out by a Firefly tank squadron of the Staffordshire Yeomanry anchoring the British 3rd Division's right flank, a small tank-infantry battle group slipped through to the coast at Lion-sur-Mer before turning back. On the whole, the 21st Panzer Division, deployed astride the River Orne and committed piecemeal, had been largely ineffective on D-Day, losing more than 50 out of 127 tanks, but it had managed to block the approaches to Caen.

When the British 3rd Division pushed on to Caen on 7 June, its 9th Brigade, on the right, was held up at Cambes, thus leaving the advancing Canadian 9th Brigade's left flank unavoidably exposed. Worse yet, as the Canadian brigade advanced with Stuart light tanks and a company in thin-skinned armored universal carriers leading, supporting artillery failed to keep pace and provide effective liaison and communications. A combination of beach congestion and enemy mortar fire delayed battery movement, even though the 105-millimeter self-propelled Priest was protected with heavy armor. According to the commander of the divisional artillery, this was essentially an organizational and gun area problem that should have been solved by good planning. In short, there was no excuse for Canadian artillery not being able to provide support within range. The next day, the army commander, Gen. Miles Dempsey, reminded Keller of the importance of getting his artillery and armor properly under control.

Kurt Meyer's 25th Panzergrenadier Regiment had meanwhile appeared on the scene, with the 1st Battalion deployed between Epron and La Folie, the 2nd in Bitot near St. Contest, and the 3rd southeast of Franqueville. At 0900, Meyer established a command post in the Ardenne Abbey, from which he observed the Canadian advance roll across his front. With him were his heavy artillery battalion commander and Max Wünsche, commander of the 12th Panzer Regiment, who had fifty Mark IV panzers in his 2nd Battalion. Another forty had still to arrive, and his 1st Panzer Battalion with forty-eight Panthers remained east of the Orne, stranded for lack of fuel.

Although the 12th SS's commander, *Brigadeführer* Fritz Witt, had planned to launch a coordinated attack in conjunction with the 21st Panzer at 1600 hours to throw the enemy back into the sea, he also told Meyer to deny the Carpiquet airfield to the enemy at all costs. Meyer had ordered his men to hold fire, but after a tank fight developed south of Authie around 1400, resulting in the loss of three Mark IVs to the Sherbrookes, he felt compelled to attack early. As the Canadian vanguard passed Franqueville just north of Carpiquet, Karl-Heinz Milius's 3rd Battalion and twenty panzers suddenly lashed out, completely surprising the Canadians, who fell back on Authie. The Sherbrookes engaged panzers at close quarters, losing three Shermans, while the North Novas defended Authie for an hour before being overrun. At 1500 hours, Meyer's other two battalions and remaining panzers joined the fray, destroying ten Shermans.

While the 2nd Battalion drove on Buron, the 1st Battalion took St. Contest and clashed with British troops attacking Cambes. The British lost three Shermans but claimed five Mark IVs before falling back on Le Mesnil. Meanwhile, Canadian antitank guns shooting from 1,500 to 2,000 meters poured out a withering fire that destroyed five panzers. After a bitter see-saw struggle for Buron, the 9th Brigade's commander, unwilling to risk the security of his brigade to rescue the vanguard, ordered the North Novas back to dig in around Villons-les-Buissons.[14]

Meyer's counterattack cost the Canadians 110 dead, 64 wounded, and 128 prisoners. The Sherbrookes had twenty-one Shermans knocked out and seven more damaged, but Meyer also lost seventeen tanks and 86 dead, 216 wounded, and 27 missing. The cost to the 12th

SS in terms of reputation was even higher. During and after the battle for Authie, between 27 and 33 Canadian prisoners were murdered. Some wounded were bayoneted to death; others were kicked and shot. One corpse was propped up with a hat on his head and a cigarette pack stuffed in his mouth. Many dead were intentionally thrown into the streets to be overrun by tanks. For six days, French civilians were not allowed to remove their bodies, four of which were so mutilated they could not be identified. In the fight for Buron, several North Novas were also shot out of hand as they surrendered. Milius, who had never commanded more than a platoon and had not seen combat for four years, was indicted for these war crimes after the war, but was never brought to trial.

The remaining Canadian prisoners were taken to regimental headquarters at the Ardenne Abbey, where another eighteen were murdered, seven by shots to the back of the head. Kurt Meyer, who allegedly said prisoners only consumed German rations and henceforth were not to be taken, was later court-martialed and sentenced to death for inciting his men to deny quarter to Allied troops. Meyer later said that such deeds were not committed by his young soldiers, but by noncommissioned elements that had become brutalized by years of fighting. The Waffen SS's egalitarian creed of rarely discouraging men from committing excesses may also have exerted an influence. On the other hand, a desperate shortage of officers—the division lacked between 144 and 208—could simply have compromised discipline and allowed troops who had never fought before to run wild as though they were on drugs.[15]

Whatever the case, the murder of Canadian prisoners of war at this early stage of hostilities on the Western Front cannot possibly be construed as reprisal killings. Of course, moral relativists might argue that it was payback for the firestorm bombings of German cities, which certainly drove Propaganda Minister Joseph Goebbels "mad to think that some Canadian boor, who probably can't even find Europe on the globe, flies here . . . to bombard a continent with a crowded population."[16] The fact remains, however, that no strong evidence exists of German Army divisions committing such crimes in Normandy. In stark contrast with the Eastern Front, the German Army in the West generally behaved with marked correctness. The highly respected *Panzer Lehr* Division was even considered a formation of gentlemen fighters.[17]

Although Meyer, in typical Waffen SS fashion, managed to blunt the Canadian advance by pushing them back two miles, he did not succeed in throwing the "little fish back into the sea" as he earlier promised to do. While one can perhaps understand that seeing small Stuart reconnaissance tanks and tiny Universal Bren gun carriers, as compared to T-34s, may have confirmed to Meyer that Canadians were indeed "little fish," he appears to have been surprised by the defensive resistance they offered. With artillery support, they would have withstood him. In retrospect, the piecemeal attack forced on him by the Canadian advance that threatened to outflank his regiment turned out to be counterproductive in the long run as it greatly reduced the chance of mounting a larger German attack.

This was certainly the view of *Sturmbannführer* Hubert "Marmalade" Meyer, principal operations staff officer of the 12th SS Panzer Division, who would have preferred to wait in order to launch a full-strength attack by the entire 20,000-man division.[18] This would have gained much more than Kurt Meyer's local success, which really had little effect on the bridgehead battle as a whole. Granted, the Canadians would not recover the ground lost for a month, but they fought Meyer to a standstill. The battle of Buron, fought with Canadian artillery in range, drew from him the observation that he had never before experienced such a concentration of fire. Forced into a defensive posture, the 25th Regiment could not now easily extricate itself for another assault, which was a major reason why the 21st Panzer was unable to attack in conjunction with Meyer. As historian Carlo D'Este observed, apart from the failure to commit the 21st Panzer promptly on D-Day, the unnecessary absence of the 12th SS Division from Caen constituted the greatest German mistake.[19] Even Gen. Bernard Montgomery admitted to Field Marshal Alan Brooke on 13 June that for all Allied advantages, had Rommel been able to mount strong assaults from mid D-Day against forces still in a confused state on the beaches, the Allies could well have been defeated.[20]

D-Day was an unmitigated disaster for the Germans. Largely because of an inability to predict the main Allied landing site, Field Marshal Gerd von Rundstedt, Supreme Commander West, had established Panzer Group West as a concentrated mobile reserve ready to counterattack an invasion of either the Pas de Calais area (defended by the Fifteenth Army) or the Normandy area (defended by the Seventh Army). This left Field Marshal Erwin Rommel, commander of Army Group B, which controlled the Fifteenth and Seventh, without the means to carry out his plan of defeating the Allies on the beach by employing armor forward to avoid air interdiction. Since the commander of Panzer Group West, Gen. Leo *Freiherr* Geyr von Schweppenburg, fundamentally disagreed with this approach, Rommel appealed directly to Hitler for control of all motorized and armored formations. Hitler first agreed, then changed his mind on Runstedt's protests. This resulted in a compromise: transferring the 2nd, 21st, and 116th Panzer Divisions to Rommel while leaving Panzer Group West with the 1st SS, 12th SS, 17th SS, and *Panzer Lehr* Divisions, which could be released only by Hitler.

When Rundstedt, early on 6 June, alerted the 12th SS, 17th SS, and *Panzer Lehr* and asked for their release to deal with the invasion, his request was denied. By the time Hitler authorized the movement of the 12th SS and *Panzer Lehr* in the afternoon, it was too late. Indecision at Army Group B—in the absence of Rommel, who was away at the time—over the commitment of the 21st Panzer Division east of the Orne to deal with the British airborne landing there and then west of the river exacerbated the situation. Had the Germans in the early days of battle opted to reinforce Normandy rapidly with divisions from Panzer Group West and the Fifteenth Army, backed up by the 2nd and 116th Panzer, they might have turned the tide in their favor. The Fifteenth Army remained deployed in the Pas de Calais area until late July, however, owing to the preconception that the main landing would occur there and to the effectiveness of the Allied deception plan that reinforced this mistaken view.[21]

Dietrich's I SS Panzer Corps, subordinated to the Seventh Army on the afternoon of 6 June and set up near Falaise that night, had attempted to coordinate the attack by the 12th SS and the 21st Panzer Divisions. Originally, the Seventh Army had directed Dietrich to launch a three-division attack including the *Panzer Lehr*, but that division had been ordered to move in daylight on 7 June and had been severely mauled by devastating Allied air attacks. Given the urgency of the situation, Dietrich, now again under Geyr von Schweppenburg, decided to launch without the *Panzer Lehr* and ordered an attack for 1000 hours on 8 June north on the Caen-Douvres axis, with 12th SS left and 21st Panzer right. Rommel countermanded this order, however, and redirected the main thrust north and northwest of Caen using all three divisions.

As only leading elements of the *Panzer Lehr* had arrived in position near Tilley-sur-Seulles during the night of 7 June and with the 21st Panzer astride the Orne still fighting off the 3rd British Division, the 12th SS Division alone was left to comply. This, too, proved difficult as the 26th SS Regiment under Wilhelm Mohnke was just coming into line on Meyer's left flank. Despite his lack of tank support, Mohnke ordered his battalions to attack before dawn on 8 June, directing the 1st against Norrey, the 2nd on Putot, and the 3rd on Brouay to link up with the 12th SS Reconnaissance Battalion, which was screening the division's left flank. In the event, they attacked piecemeal. Launched across open fields after 0330, the attack on Norrey shattered against a well-prepared Regina Rifles' fortress defense supported by massive artillery fire and was called off at 1100 hours.[22]

The 2nd SS Battalion's attack against Putot fared better although it was hastily launched later off the line of march. Around 0630 hours, three assaulting panzergrenadier companies began infiltrating between three companies of the Royal Winnipeg Rifles, which were poorly deployed along a railway line. In the ensuing firefight, the Waffen SS soldiers managed to cut off and surround the defending Winnipeg companies, the remnants of which withdrew under cover of smoke behind the reserve company east of Putot after 1330. The Winnipegs incurred some 256 casualties, including 105 dead, largely because the Germans possessed an advantage in machine-gun power. The Canadian companies had one Bren light machine gun per section for a total of nine, whereas SS companies fielded almost twice that number of MG 42 general-purpose machine guns. The belt-fed MG 42 fired 1,200 rounds per minute compared to the Bren's 500 rounds a minute, giving a clear edge to Germans in such infantry-on-infantry clashes. The Winnipegs reported that they had been attacked by tanks, but the 26th Regiment employed only half-tracks with 75-millimeter guns in the 3rd Battalion's attack on Brouay, where they went to ground on encountering a lead battalion of the *Panzer Lehr* Division that had been ripped apart by Allied air and naval gun fire.[23]

Three days after the German attack, British troops found evidence of 12th SS atrocities in the area of the Château d'Audrieu, southwest of Brouay. Here on 8 June, twenty-six Canadian prisoners were murdered after interrogation at the command post of *Sturmbannführer* Gerhard Bremer's 12th SS Reconnaissance Battalion. Seven more were murdered in Mouen by the 12th SS Engineer Battalion. Another thirty-five were murdered en masse by automatic fire while being escorted to the rear from the headquarters of the 2nd Battalion of Mohnke's 26th Panzergrenadier Regiment at Le Mesnil-Patry. Five escaped to tell the tale after being recaptured by another German unit that evacuated them to prison camp. The day after this massacre, another three Canadians being treated for wounds at the 2nd Battalion's first-aid post were shot. In the same area on 11 June, another three Canadian prisoners were executed and another five at Les Saullets near Le Mesnil-Patry. The commander of the 2nd Battalion, Bernard Siebken, and his orderly officer, Dietrich Schnabel, were both tried by British military court in Hamburg, found guilty, and hanged on 20 January 1949 for the murders at the first-aid post.[24]

On learning of the loss of Putot, the 7th Canadian Infantry Brigade's commander, Brig. Harry Foster, decided to take it back. At

1700 hours on 8 June, he ordered his Canadian Scottish Battalion under Lt. Col. F. N. Calbeldu to mount a counterattack. Supported by a squadron of the 6th Armoured Regiment (1st Hussars) and the massed fire of five artillery field regiments, Cabeldu assaulted behind a creeping barrage at 2030 hours. In spite of fierce opposition, the left forward company was on its objective within half an hour, and by 2130, the battalion was mopping up. The Canadian Scottish suffered 125 casualties, but the counterattack showed that they possessed a clear edge over the Germans in coordinating effective artillery support. Compared to an attack launched by Meyer at 2200 hours that night, it was also a brilliant success.

To support a second assault on Norrey by Mohnke's 1st Battalion, Meyer launched two Panther companies (about thirty tanks) and infantry against the Reginas defending Bretteville in a night shock attack in order to avoid Allied air attack. In the ensuing melee around Bretteville, the Reginas, backed up by concentrated artillery fire, destroyed six Panthers using hand-held antitank weapons and 6-pounders firing new armor-piercing discarding sabot ammunition. According to Meyer, such shock tactics worked in Russia, but they failed miserably against well-disciplined Canadian troops with antitank weapons cleverly sited in depth. Unfortunately for Meyer, Mohnke's 1st Battalion attack at Norrey also failed with heavy casualties. Meyer tried again after lunch on 9 June by ordering a single panzer company of twelve Panthers to charge the Reginas in broad daylight over open ground. Seven Panthers never returned, partly because the Reginas had been reinforced with tanks that morning. One Firefly knocked out five Panthers. Wünsche, who saw the burning tanks, later wrote that he could have cried with rage and sorrow.[25]

Significantly, neither Meyer nor Wünsche had fought at Kursk, where, despite German local air superiority, Russian antitank defenses came into their own and exacted a terrible toll on panzers. At Kursk, Soviet rifle divisions of about 10,000 men on a primary approach defending a frontage of six to nine kilometers usually formed nine to twelve antitank strongpoints throughout an eight-kilometer depth.

Protected by engineer defenses, these antitank strongpoints integrated antitank fire with the fire of infantry and artillery. Known to the Germans as *pakfronts*, they had the collective effect of drawing enemy panzers into a web of enfilade fire. The normal composition of an antitank strongpoint was four to seven antitank guns, six to nine antitank rifles, two to three heavy machine guns, and three to four light machine guns. Garrisons of up to company strength and engineers with antitank mines supported the antitank gunners in each strongpoint. Rifle regiments covering main attack axes usually formed three to four antitank strongpoints, which, in areas of greater threat, were combined to form a larger and more durable antitank region. Deeper in depth, rifle divisions and rifle corps created independent antitank regions around the nuclei of artillery battalions. Virtually all Soviet artillery—whether howitzer, gun, or antiaircraft weapon—participated in antitank defense. In addition, tanks and self-propelled guns assigned to forward battalions strengthened antitank defense.[26] The Regina and Canadian antitank defense largely reflected the same deployment, though on a much smaller scale.

Schweppenburg observed the start of Meyer's last abortive charge as he happened to be visiting that morning to explain his plan to launch an attack with all three divisions of the I SS Panzer Corps on the night of 10 June. Extricating the now heavily committed divisions remained a problem, however, since the British continued to push through Tilly-sur-Seulles toward Villers-Bocage and the Canadians through Rots toward Cheux. To Rommel, the timeframe was unrealistic, and he ordered a return to the defensive, postponing the counterattack until preparations could be completed. Just before dawn on 10 June, Mohnke nonetheless ordered a further counterattack on Norrey by the 12th SS Panzer Pioneer Battalion, which had recently been attached to his 26th Regiment. The battle went on throughout the day, but ended as another costly disaster. Four attempts to capture Norrey had failed.

At 2030 hours that evening, rocket-firing Typhoons of the Royal Air Force accurately struck Schweppenburg's Panzer Group West headquarters, which the British located through Ultra intelligence. A subsequent raid by seventy-one medium bombers completed the total destruction of the headquarters, leaving Schweppenburg wounded and his chief of staff and other key staff officers dead. As a result of this attack, the I SS Panzer Corps reverted to the command of the Seventh Army, with responsibility for the Caen sector and the highly elusive multidivision counterattack. Dietrich made no attempt to carry out the attack.[27]

On 11 June, the pressed 12th SS still skillfully managed to throw back coordinated attacks by the British in the area of Audrieu and Les Hauts Vents and the Canadians around Le Mesnil-Patry. The Canadian attack mounted by the 2nd Armoured Brigade to move via Le Mesnil-Patry around Cheux to seize the high ground to the south proved especially tragic. From intercepted wireless traffic, the Germans knew the Canadians were coming and reinforced Mohnke's regiment with Mark IV tanks from the 2nd SS Panzer Battalion. The Canadians overran a company of the 2nd SS Panzergrenadier Battalion, but the German counterattack that followed cost the 1st Hussars thirty-four Shermans and three Fireflies. The Queen's Own Rifles infantry company supporting them incurred ninety-six casualties, half of them missing.

After being personally interrogated by Mohnke at his headquarters, three Canadian prisoners were murdered that day while he and some of his officers watched. Mohnke, who allegedly ordered the killings, had lost a foot in Yugoslavia and developed a morphine addiction that exacerbated an already explosive temper. There is much evidence to show that Mohnke was directly and indirectly behind all the killings carried out by his men.[28] At the time of the better-known Malmedy Massacre perpetrated by the 1st SS Panzer Division *Leibstandarte* during the Battle of the Bulge in December 1944, there may have been a German shortage of morphine. In any case, wherever Mohnke went, atrocities seem to have followed. Surrendering to troops commanded by him did indeed seem to invite death. In all, the 12th SS murdered 156 Canadian prisoners. Between 6 and 11 June, one out of seven Canadians killed did not die in combat.[29]

CHAPTER 4

Tiger Shock and "Colossal Cracks"

While the Germans vainly planned to deliver a multidivision counterattack, the British were hatching plans of their own. Montgomery planned a double encirclement of Caen with the 51st Highland Division and 4th Armoured Brigade executing a short hook east of the city via the Orne bridgehead and the 30 Corps to the west continuing its attack down the Seulles River Valley to capture Villers-Bocage. Corps elements were then to turn east to link up with the 1st British Airborne Division, to be dropped around Noyers and Evercy. RAF objections scratched the parachute operation, however, and the 21st Panzer and *Panzer Lehr* Divisions both counterattacked to stall, respectively, the east and west British pincer movements. The discovery of a gap in the German front on the Aure River three miles west of Tilly-sur-Seulles, however, offered the possibility of a wider flanking movement on Villers-Bocage.

On 12 June, Dempsey went to the 30 Corps' sector to see for himself what could be done to regain the initiative. At the 7th Armoured Division's headquarters, he seized on the suggestion of Maj. Gen. Bobby Erskine that it might be possible to outflank the *Panzer Lehr* by driving on Villers-Bocage from the west, leaving the 50th (Northumberland) Division to hold the German formation in

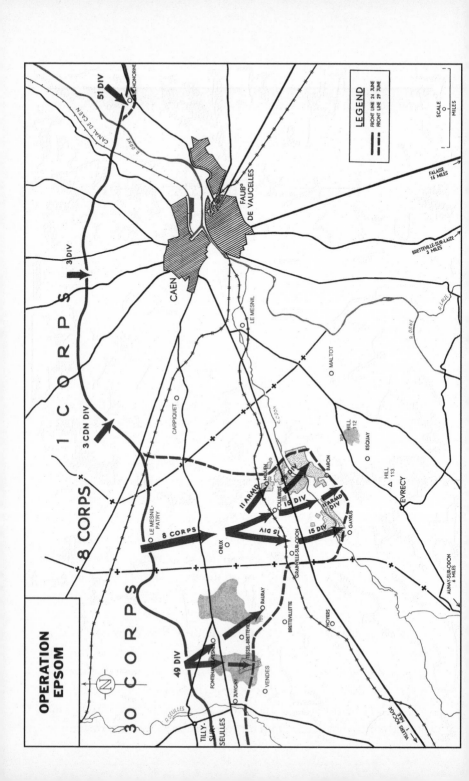

OPERATION EPSOM

LEGEND
FRONT LINE 24 JUNE
FRONT LINE 29 JUNE

SCALE
MILES

30 CORPS

8 CORPS

1 CORPS

CANAL DE CAEN

R. ORNE

51 DIV

STE-HONORINE

3 DIV

3 CDN DIV

CAEN

FAUB° DE VAUCELLES

FALAISE 15 MILES

BRETTEVILLE-SUR-LAIZE 3 MILES

LE MESNIL

R. LAIZE

CARPIQUET

MALTOT

R. ODON

R. ORNE

HILL 112

ESQUAY

HILL 113

EVRECY

LE MESNIL-PATRY

8 CORPS

II ARMD

COLLEVILLE

MOUEN

15 DIV

11 ARMD DIV

BARON

15 DIV

GAVRUS

GRAINVILLE-SUR-ODON

AUNAY-SUR-ODON 6 MILES

CHEUX

49 DIV

RAURAY

BRETTEVILLETTE

NOYERS

FONTENAY-LE-PESNEL

TESSEL-BRETTEVILLE

JUVIGNY

VENDES

R. SEULLES

TILLY-SUR-SEULLES

VILLERS BOCAGE 8 MILES

place. Correctly sensing that Erskine had identified a weak spot in the German defense along the Aure River, Dempsey directed him and Bucknall to immediately execute the movement with all speed.[1]

That afternoon, Erskine's 7th Armoured Division, primarily equipped with Cromwell tanks, started moving. Brig. Robert "Looney" Hinde's 22nd Armoured Brigade, with two armored regiments and two infantry battalions, spearheaded the drive through the gap, followed by Brig. Michael Elkins's 131st Infantry Brigade, which had one tank regiment and two infantry battalions. By late evening, Hinde's formation had reached Livry, five miles west of Villers-Bocage. There, owing to uncertainty about enemy strength in the latter village, he wisely decided not to undertake further movement that night.[2]

In the early morning of 13 June, a battle group of the 4th County of London Yeomanry tanks and a motorized company of the 1st Battalion of The Rifle Brigade advanced virtually unopposed into the town. While attempting to secure the key high ground northeast of the town, the battle group encountered the 2nd Company of the 101st SS Heavy (Tiger) Panzer Battalion.[3] The company was commanded by the already legendary tank ace *Obersturmführer* Michael Wittmann, who, in short order, cut a swath of destruction along the strung-out British armored column, his single Tiger destroying six Cromwell tanks, two Shermans, a Firefly, and numerous infantry carriers. By the time the action finished, Wittmann and his four other Tigers and Mark IV Special had knocked out around thirty British tanks and an equal number of armored vehicles. Although Wittmann later lost three Tigers and the Special to 6-pounder and hand-held antitank weapon fire in attacking Villers-Bocage itself, he went on to coordinate the deployment of nine more Tigers from the 1st SS Heavy Panzer Company and fifteen Mark IVs from the *Panzer Lehr*. Significantly, however, three more Tigers were knocked out in the town, which was defended from 1000 hours by Hinde's 2nd Infantry Battalion from the Queen's Royal Regiment.

The shock of the Wittmann attack not only threw the British onto the defensive, but also trumped good tactical sense. When the

Queen's commanding officer asked to be reinforced in Villers-Bocage, he was told by a visiting Elkins that the situation looked hopeless. Erskine, on the other hand, recognized the urgent need for more infantry and gave Hinde another Queen's infantry battalion from Elkins's 131st Brigade. Just before this battalion began to arrive in Villers-Bocage, however, Hinde, with Erskine's approval, ordered a withdrawal to the high ground two miles to the west of the village. Had he not done so, Villers-Bocage could have been turned into a fortress by the two Queen's battalions and the bulk the Rifle Brigade motorized battalion. Conceivably, such a fortress defense could have been made stronger than those effectively established by the Regina Rifles at Bretteville and Norrey. In addition, Erskine still had at his disposal 155 operational tanks and the last infantry battalion of the 131st Infantry Brigade to defend the high ground west of the village.

In any case, spooked by Ultra reports of the imminent arrival in area of the 2nd Panzer Division, the entire 22nd Armoured Brigade withdrew from Villers-Bocage to tighter positions around Point 174 a mile to the west, near Tracy-Bocage, by 2000 hours on 13 June. Arguably, Ultra intelligence appears to have worked against tactical effectiveness in this case by encouraging excessive caution. In fact, the first of the 2nd Panzer Division's tanks did not arrive in the area until 18 June. Most German attacks launched against the British in Villers-Bocage also appear to have been mounted by *Panzer Lehr* scratch forces and only leading elements of the 2nd Panzer Division, most notably reconnaissance battalion troops, reinforced by the few remaining Tigers of the 1st SS Heavy Panzer Company.

Notwithstanding decisions made by Hinde and Erskine, primary responsibility for the failure of the Villers-Bocage turning movement must be laid at the feet of the corps commander, Bucknall. On the night of 13 June, after committing his last infantry battalion to Hinde, Erskine warned Bucknall that without additional infantry reinforcement, the 22nd Armoured Brigade could not continue to hang on between the *Panzer Lehr* in the north and the 2nd Panzer in the south. If Bucknall provided such reinforcement, however, Erskine was confident Hinde could hold out and keep threatening the German flank. Instead of reacting quickly to Erskine's request by dispatching his reserve 151st Infantry Brigade or an infantry force from the 50th Division through the still-open gap to reinforce the 22nd Armoured Brigade, Bucknall opted to continue the 50th Division's drive south in the hope that it could break through the *Panzer Lehr* to relieve Hinde.

At the time, Hinde's positions astride the Caumont–Villers-Bocage road around Point 174 were defensible against anything short of concentrated attack, but by the morning of 14 June, Bucknall recognized that the 50th Division would be unable to break through the *Panzer Lehr* and provide additional reinforcement. Deciding that the 7th Armoured was now at unacceptable risk, he obtained Dempsey's permission to have it withdraw to new positions east of Caumont. At no time, apparently, had Bucknall ever considered asking Dempsey to divert recently landed infantry brigades of the 49th (West Riding) Division to Erskine. For his part, Dempsey was furious that the 7th Armoured had withdrawn from Villers-Bocage without his permission. In his view, he had told both Erskine and Bucknall what to do, and they should have complied. Without the stunning intervention of *Obersturmführer* Wittmann and his Tigers—which seemed to change the entire dynamic of the battle in favor of the Germans—they might well have succeeded. A fleeting opportunity to roll up the I SS Panzer Corps' flank and envelop Caen from the southwest was thus lost.[4]

Dietrich had ordered the deployment of the 101st SS Heavy (Tiger) Panzer Battalion to occupy reserve positions west of the Odon on 12 June. The 1st Company, with nine Tigers, took up a position behind the 12th SS Panzer Division near Noyers-Bocage while the 2nd Company, with five Tigers, fortuitously occupied the very ground northeast of Villers-Bocage that the lead battle group of the British 7th Armoured Division had attempted to secure. By this time, Dietrich had given up hope of being able to launch a coordinated panzer counterattack. Within his I SS Panzer Corps, from left to right, the *Panzer Lehr*, 12th SS Panzer, and 21st Panzer Divisions remained fully committed to holding the line and plugging gaps as best they could against constant Allied pressure. Each had experienced 50 percent losses, and the 716th Infantry Division had been all but destroyed. By 16 June, the 12th SS had incurred 1,149 casualties, including Witt, who had been killed two days earlier, and the division fielded only fifty-two Mark IVs, thirty-eight Panthers, and ten 105-millimeter and five 150-millimeter self-propelled artillery pieces.

In response to his pleas for infantry divisions to relieve his panzer formations, Dietrich received assurances that the 16th Luftwaffe Field Division and the 276th Infantry Division would be made available to replace the 21st Panzer and 12th SS Panzer Divisions in line. On 12 June, Hitler had hastily recalled Hausser's II SS Panzer Corps and directed the speedy western deployment of the 9th SS Division *Hohenstaufen*, 10th SS Panzer Division *Frundsberg*, and 102nd Heavy (Tiger) Panzer Battalion. At the same time, he ordered the *Leibstandarte* to be united with the *Hitlerjugend* as soon as possible. Having been diverted to Bruges on 9 June to oppose a threatened Allied landing in the Pas de Calais area that never materialized, the *Leibstandarte* commenced its move from Belgium on 17 June. Between 23 June and 6 July, the division assembled in the Foret-de-Cinglais between Caen and Falaise.[5]

Following the failure of the turning movement on Villers-Bocage, Montgomery decided to launch what Dietrich could not—a full-fledged multidivision attack against German defenses on the west side of Caen. This attack, Operation Epsom, launched through the 3rd Canadian Division's front would turn out to be the first of a series of "colossal cracks" delivered west and east of the city with the object of shaking Caen loose. Montgomery fully intended to retain the initiative through such smashing body blows. Intelligence that the II SS Panzer Corps and the *Leibstandarte* would soon be arriving on the front increased the urgency to attack in order to draw in enemy armor rather than let it be committed at a time and place of the Germans' choosing.

Operation Epsom opened on 26 June, with Lt. Gen. Sir Richard O'Connor's 8 Corps striking southeast toward the Orne on a four-mile front between Carpiquet airfield and Rauray with three fresh divisions, the 15th (Scottish), 43rd (Wessex), and 11th Armoured. Assisted by supporting attacks from the 30 Corps on the right and 1 Corps on the left, O'Connor had at his disposal 60,000 troops, 550 tanks, and more than 700 artillery pieces, plus the fire of three Royal Navy cruisers and fighter-bombers of the 2nd Tactical Air Force. Preliminary operations commenced on 25 June with a 30 Corps attack by the 49th (West Riding) Division to seize Rauray, the high ground around it, and Noyers on the Caen–Villers-Bocage road. Although the 49th, aided by heavy air support, tore a three-mile-wide gap along the *Panzer Lehr*–12th SS boundary, the Germans refused to surrender Rauray.[6]

The 12th SS Panzer Division, now commanded by Kurt Meyer after the death of Witt on 14 June, played a key role in defending the I SS Panzer Corps' front against British preliminary and main thrusts. While the 25th Panzergrenadier Regiment, newly headed by Milius, held well-reinforced positions from Franqueville to Epron, north of Caen, Mohnke's 26th Panzergrenadier Regiment held the front from Carpiquet airfield to Fontenay-le-Pesnel. They were backed up by 58 Mark IV tanks (plus 18 under repair), 44 Panthers (plus 10 under repair), 233 half-tracks and scout cars, and 17 heavy antitank guns (with 55 under short-term repair). Although the eighteen-kilometer front could not be held in depth because of personnel losses, all tanks had reconnoitered alternate positions from which to shoot. The preliminary attack by the British 49th Division, supported by the 8th Armoured Brigade, nonetheless put the 12th SS's defense to the test. Advancing behind a wall of barrage fire from 250 guns, the 146th Brigade, supported by tanks from the 24th Lancers, secured the Bas de Fontenay and western portion of Fontenay-le-Pesnel by 0915 hours. In the early afternoon, a battalion of the King's Own Yorkshire Light Infantry occupied the Tessel Woods north of Vendes in the *Panzer*

Lehr's sector. These attacks cost the British 263 casualties, but their three-kilometer penetration posed a serious threat to Mohnke's western flank. A local counterattack by the 3rd SS Panzergrenadier Battalion, supported by Mark IVs, failed to dislodge them.

Both Dietrich and Meyer realized that a dangerous gap had developed between the *Panzer Lehr* and 12th SS and ordered Wünsche's 12th Panzer Regiment to plug it. By 2230 hours, with three companies of Panthers and supporting infantry, Wünsche had established contact with the 3rd SS Panzergrenadier Battalion, which was still holding most of Fontenay-le-Pesnel, but he failed to link up with the *Panzer Lehr* via the Tessel Woods. Dietrich therefore gave up Fontenay-le-Pesnel and ordered Meyer to fall back on a line running from Le Haut du Bosq, south of Cheux, through Rauray to Le Manoir, from which junction was made with the *Panzer Lehr* at Vendes. Dietrich then ordered a counterattack for early morning on 26 June by both the *Panzer Lehr* and the 12th SS to restore the original front line. Meyer protested that he had insufficient forces for the task, but assembled all available 12th SS panzers, less one company defending Carpiquet, along with supporting infantry during the night of 25 June.

The next morning, this battle group, commanded by Wünsche, ran headlong into tank-infantry elements of the 49th Division, which was attempting once again to capture Tessel-Bretteville, Le Manoir, and Rauray in order to secure the right flank of Operation Epsom. Meyer immediately halted Wünsche's attack and made him responsible for the defense of Rauray. At the same time, he ordered all Mark IV panzer companies to return to their fighting positions behind Mohnke's 26th Regiment, which was defending Cheux and St. Mauvieu.[7] Once more, Dietrich's I SS Panzer Corps was left only to conduct a desperate defense, totally unable to mount a major coordinated panzer counterattack.

The main Epsom attack opened at 0730 hours on 26 June with an awesome artillery barrage by 344 field and medium guns advancing ninety meters every three minutes. Unfortunately for the British, bad weather limited the effectiveness of air support when the 8 Corps' attack kicked off. Spearheaded through Norrey and Le Mesnil-Patry by the 15th (Scottish) Division and 31st Armoured Brigade with the 43rd (Wessex) committed on the left, the attack aimed at capturing bridges over the Odon five miles to the south. With the Odon breached, the 11th Armoured Division was then to pass through and drive southeast to seize a bridgehead over the Orne. Resistance by the 12th SS Panzer Division *Hitlerjugend* proved so tough, however, that by noon, only modest progress had been made. The attack on St. Manvieu by the 44th (Lowland) Brigade of the 15th (Scottish) Division took all day to eject the 1st SS Panzergrenadier Battalion. Flame-throwing Churchill tanks helped eliminate the last enemy resistance. The 46th (Highland) Brigade's thrust on Cheux met similar resistance and more from Wünsche's Panthers firing from the high ground at Rauray, but by 1130 hours, the 2nd Glasgow Highlanders gained a foothold and, at a cost of 200 casualties, cleared and held the village.

As the 15th (Scottish) Division gained St. Manvieu and Cheux and now threatened Mouen and Verson, Meyer appealed to Dietrich for reinforcements. This resulted in the early-evening deployment of the 101st Heavy Panzer Battalion to the Grainville area and the dispatch of panzers and assault guns from the 21st Panzer Division. Meyer's fears proved well founded as O'Connor, shortly after midday, had unleashed the 11th Armoured to seize crossings over the Odon. In trying to advance beyond heavy congestion in Cheux, however, the division almost immediately incurred the loss of two Cromwells and eight Shermans. At 1800 hours, the 15th (Scottish) Division committed its 227th (Highland) Reserve Brigade to clear a path for the 11th Armoured, but Panther and Tiger fire, along with that of newly arrived Mark IVs from the 21st Panzer Division and Meyer's own, soon checked the British advance. By the end of the first day of Epsom, the 15th Division had gained only four miles, while the 49th Division in Bucknall's 30 Corps still lay short of Rauray.

Dietrich nonetheless considered the threat to the center of his I SS Panzer Corps serious. Wünsche was down to seventeen Panthers facing the 49th Division while twelve Tigers and other Panthers were

in the area of Grainville and Verson. The 2nd SS Panzer Battalion—
roughly thirty Mark IVs as well as some tanks and assault guns
detached from the 21st Panzer Division—backed up Mohnke's regiment. Although Dietrich had 88-millimeter guns of the 4th Flak
Regiment farther to the rear, he required further reinforcement. As
leading elements of the *Leibstandarte* were not expected before 28
June and Hausser's II SS Panzer Corps the day after, Rommel authorized transferring a tank battalion from the 2nd Panzer near St. Lô and
a battle group from the 2nd SS Panzer Division *Das Reich*, which had
just arrived in that area. Dietrich directed their immediate deployment to attack the flank of the British 8 Corps.

In the event, the *Das Reich* battle group never arrived to help stem
the 27 June attack by the 227th (Highland) Brigade to seize crossings
over the Odon at Gavrus and Tourmauville. The too-hasty flank counterattack launched by seventeen Panthers from the 2nd Panzer Division also went in without infantry support and resulted in the loss of
five of their number to tank and antitank fire. Fortunately for the
Germans, they were able to stop the British attack on Gavrus, but the
Argyll and Sutherland Highlanders, supported by Churchill tanks of
the 23rd Hussar, 11th Armoured Division, managed around 1900
hours to attain a bridgehead at Tourmauville reaching out to the lower
slopes of Hill 112. Three hours later, two battalions of the 159th
Infantry Brigade of the 11th Armoured and its motorized infantry
battalion began to cross.

Meanwhile, in the late afternoon, the 70th Infantry Brigade of
the 49th Division finally captured Rauray. The British bridgehead
south of the Odon forced Meyer to pull back along a concave line
running from Carpiquet to Haut de Verson, across the Odon to Hill
112, thence to Esquay, Gavrus, and back across the Odon to Grainville.
He redeployed most of Wünsche's panzers to the area of Hill 112.[8]

At this point, Dietrich placed *Sturmbannführer* Albert Frey's newly
arrived 1st SS Panzergrenadier Regiment of the 1st SS Panzer Division *Leibstandarte* at Meyer's disposal. Frey had only his 1st and 2nd
Battalions available and awaited the arrival of his 3rd Battalion and

other regimental units, but Meyer immediately ordered him to attack at midday on 28 June with the aim of cutting off the head of the British salient. In response to Frey's complaint that he lacked heavy-weapon support, Meyer allocated him some Panthers from the 12th SS, a few Tigers, and a composite Mark IV group based on 21st Panzer elements. Striking southwest from Verson astride the Caen road to Villers-Bocage, Frey's formation was to link up with the previously promised *Das Reich* battle group that had instead ended up attached to the *Panzer Lehr* Division. Deployed along the line of Grainville-Rauray-Tessel and commanded by *Sturmbannführer* Otto Weidinger, the *Das Reich* battle group consisted of two panzer-grenadier battalions and pioneer, infantry gun, reconnaissance, and flak companies of his *Der Führer* Regiment.

When Frey requested a delay of his attack until the *Leibstandarte*'s artillery came up, Meyer promised him that the 12th SS's artillery would provide fire support. Incredibly, however, Frey received no artillery liaison when he started his attack at 0600 hours on 28 June, and as a result, the 12th SS's artillery did not provide effective fire support, which Weidinger noted, too. In the heavy fighting that followed, Frey's two battalions managed to reach the areas of Mouen and Tourville, but at 1945 hours, the Highland Light Infantry, supported by tanks from the City of London Yeomanry, slammed into his right flank. The ensuing battle lasted throughout the night and prevented Frey from linking up with Weidinger, who passed the day fending off attacks by the British 49th Division.[9]

While this overly hasty and poorly mounted attack was taking place, the German high command reacted to the British attainment of a bridgehead over the Odon with alarm and panic. In the absence of Rundstedt and Rommel, who had been summoned to Berchtesgaden by Hitler, the commander of the German Seventh Army, Gen. Friedrich Dollmann, frantically ordered Hausser at 0810 hours on 28 June to attack immediately with his II SS Panzer Corps to clear out the British breach south of Cheux. When Hausser refused to carry out this ill-conceived order on the grounds that his corps would not be ready to attack before the next day, Dollmann, already fearful of incurring Hitler's wrath over the loss of Cherbourg on 26 June, committed suicide. Ironically, in the early afternoon, Hausser changed his tune, telling the Seventh Army that he could, if necessary, mount a counterattack on 28 June, though he preferred to wait and deliver one properly coordinated.

Hausser had barely started to organize such an attack, however, when Hitler appointed him Seventh Army commander with supreme authority to act in the absence of Rundstedt and Rommel. This, in turn, meant handing over counterattack planning to the new commander of the II SS Panzer Corps, *Gruppenführer* Wilhelm Bittrich of the 9th SS Panzer Division *Hohenstaufen*. The reactivation of Panzer Group West at 1700 hours, with responsibility for the Caen sector, further saw Geyr von Schweppenburg confirm the order for the II SS Panzer Corps to counterattack immediately from the line Noyers-Evrecy to seize Grainville, Mouen, and Cheux north of the Odon and Gavrus, Baron, and Hill 112 south of the river. At 1800 hours, the II SS Panzer Corps reported that it would be ready to attack at 0600 hours on 29 June. British artillery and air bombardment of German troop concentrations proved so heavy, however, that the attack had to be postponed until later that afternoon. Hubert Meyer later wrote that vulnerability to enemy air and massive artillery concentrations, coupled with the lack of adequate preparation, doomed the counterattack to failure.[10]

As Ultra intelligence had pinpointed the movements of the II SS Panzer Corps, Dempsey decided to shore up his bridgehead and take measures to withstand a major counterattack. He therefore ordered the 11th Armoured Division not to cross the Orne, but rather expand the bridgehead while the 15th (Scottish) and the 43rd (Wessex) Divisions cleared and widened the salient. By the time the II SS Panzer Corps' counterattack went in at 1400 hours on 29 June, the 11th Armoured had captured Hill 112, and the 43rd Division had taken Marcelet and Mouen. The counterattack of the II SS Panzer Corps astride the Odon looked more like two separate division attacks than a unified and coordinated corps attack. Neither had the necessary artillery support that might have powered success. *Standartenführer* Thomas Müller's 9th SS Panzer Division *Hohenstaufen* attacked through hedgerows on the left, north of the river, toward Cheux, while *Brigadeführer* Heinz Harmel's 10th SS Panzer Division *Frundsberg*, which lacked its Panther and tank destroyer battalions, attacked at 1430 hours on the right, south of the Odon, toward Gavrus and Hill 112. Advancing in daylight, they were both smothered with air interdiction and artillery fire so intense that they quickly foundered.

The 15th (Scottish) Division not only stopped the 9th SS's counterattack with concentrated artillery fire, but also turned it into a rout. From this, Dempsey drew the erroneous conclusion that it was not the main counterattack, which he anticipated would come elsewhere. He therefore ordered O'Connor to pull the 11th Armoured back behind the Odon to meet the expected threat to the 8 Corps, which at that time lacked sufficient depth and striking power to defeat a strong armored counterattack. In fact, the two German divisions attacked again at night and continued to do so up to 1 July, but finally gave up as their efforts became hopeless. Dempsey's understandable, though regrettable decision proved the turning point of Epsom, which Montgomery terminated on 30 June.[11]

Epsom confirmed the powerful strength and capability of the British artillery system that had evolved since the disaster of Dunkirk, which focused attention too exclusively upon panzer successes rather than the inherent weaknesses of *blitzkrieg*. Events in France convinced many that fighting by divisions was too slow and cumbersome in light of fast-moving panzers and dive-bombers rendering the vast array of Allied towed artillery impotent. A British committee investigating the lessons of Flanders consequently recommended basing the tactical handling of the division on a brigade group of all arms.

This more mobile formation penny-packaged artillery, however, and undermined the system for massing artillery fire. This practice reached its apogee in the Western Desert with the employment of "Jock columns," a concept of gunner Brig. J. C. "Jock" Campbell that progressed from minor to major tactical status possibly because of his reputation as a bold and aggressive fighter. Originally intended to lend artillery weight to forward screens and to harass the enemy, Jock columns were little more than mobile field artillery batteries escorted by motorized infantry and often some tanks, but they really represented the ultimate fragmentation of British tactics. This situation was only reversed by 1943 with the restoration of commanders of reserve artillery formations and the positions of corps and divisional artillery commanders within a functional artillery chain of command.

Largely through the efforts of Brig. H. J. Parham, the Royal Artillery after Dunkirk perfected a highly efficient gunfire control system capable of delivering, in a matter of minutes, a massive weight of fire on organized enemy defenses. Unlike Stukas, the artillery could also attack targets by day or night in all kinds of weather. A faster communications network separate from the normal hierarchical chain of command additionally permitted quicker responses to requests for gunfire. The pursuit of extreme accuracy was in these instances forsaken in favor of bringing overwhelming fire rapidly to bear. Under the Parham system, designated artillery officers could order the fire of all guns within range. To a call prefaced by "Uncle target," the entire divisional artillery responded. Similarly, a "Victor" called for a corps shoot, and a "William" for a response by all available field army guns.

When this system fully evolved by mid-1943, gunner commanders were integrated at every level and linked together by an efficient wireless network. Along the front, junior troop commanders serving as forward observers ordered massed gunfire on their own. Eventually, artillery batteries with two four-gun troops were intimately affiliated with armored regiments and infantry battalions. Artillery regiments were in turn affiliated with brigades, with the gunner commanding officer acting as artillery adviser to the brigade commander, from whom he was inseparable. At higher levels, divisional and corps artillery commanders performed a similar role and controlled the movement and allotment of guns. Behind the corps artilleries stood reinforcing army artillery brigades called Army Groups Royal

Artillery. Of no fixed composition, they usually consisted of three medium and one or two field and heavy regiments in proportions considered most suitable to the mission assigned. To gain maximum effect from the longer range and greater throw weight of medium and heavy guns, they were employed as single-fire entities and not in penny packets along a front.[12]

While Epsom did not attain its territorial objectives and resulted in the return of Hill 112 to enemy hands, the Germans had been forced to commit all available reserves to stem the British onslaught. Rommel had not wanted to employ the II SS Panzer Corps, which is why he allocated battle groups from the 2nd Panzer Division and 2nd SS Panzer Division *Das Reich* to meet Dietrich's reinforcement needs. Like Rommel, Schweppenburg also preferred to husband the II SS Panzer Corps for eventual use in a coordinated night counterattack with Dietrich's I SS Panzer Corps striking at Bayeux and the sea along the Anglo-American boundary.

British pressure forced the Germans to abandon these plans, with the result that the premature commitment of the II SS Panzer Corps dashed any realistic hope of launching a decisive counterstroke against the Allies. Hausser's brilliant land-air riposte of Kharkov was not repeated by Bittrich in the *bocage* of Normandy. Montgomery had retained the initiative and not suffered any serious setback to prospects of victory. From this point on, Waffen SS formations replayed their Eastern Front defensive role, dashing here and there to momentarily stem the tide by counterattack, vainly trying to mount effective offensive attacks, but always dancing to the enemy's tune. By 30 June, Rundstedt, Rommel, Geyr, and Hausser all agreed on the necessity of withdrawing German forces to a new line of defense running from Caen south through Villers-Bocage to Caumont. This proved totally unacceptable to Hitler, who on 2 July replaced Rundstdt with Field Marshal Günther von Kluge and Geyr with Gen. Heinrich Eberbach the next day.[13]

The II SS Panzer Corps' counterattack to stem Epsom was a costly venture in men and materiel that succeeded in pushing back, but not eliminating, the Odon bridgehead. The price paid by the British in five days of fighting was high—over 5,000 casualties—but if casualty figures were any indication of fighting determination, then the British demonstrated that they were as willing as the Waffen SS to die for a cause. If relative losses reflected superior fighting skill by one side over another, on the other hand, the 12th SS did not have too great an edge over the British divisions, especially as the latter attacked and the former defended from well-prepared positions with superior armor. Compared to the 15th (Scottish) Division's losses of 2,720, the 12th SS's casualties of 1,244 for Epsom certainly seem light, but when set against the 49th (West Riding) Division's losses of over 1,000 and the 11th Armoured and 43rd (Wessex) Divisions' combined 1,256, they appear roughly equivalent. Of course, assessing the significance of casualty figures is highly problematic. Ironically, too, Waffen SS troops prided themselves on their willingness to die for the *Führer* and take high casualties through daredevil recklessness. Mohnke's 26th Panzergrenadier Regiment finished Epsom terribly battered, if not beaten, and the *Panzer Lehr* Division, having lost 3,407 men and fifty panzers, had ceased to be a viable divisional formation. Total 12th SS casualties approached 2,662. Indeed, all three divisions of Dietrich's I SS Panzer Corps—the *Panzer Lehr*, 12th SS, and 21st Panzer—were in dire need of rest and reconstitution, and Dietrich felt compelled to withdraw his logistical installations farther east.[14]

CHAPTER 5

A Tough Business

Operation Epsom originally called for the capture of the Carpiquet area, but this action had to be postponed in light of the limited ground gained by the British 8 Corps. Crocker's 1 Corps now produced a revised plan for the 3rd Canadian Division, supported by the 2nd Canadian Armoured Brigade, to seize both the airfield and Carpiquet village as a prelude to their participation in a three-division assault directly on Caen. Planned for 4 July and code-named Operation Windsor, the Carpiquet attack was to be launched by Brig. Ken Blackader's 8th Canadian Infantry Brigade, augmented by the Royal Winnipeg Rifles and supported by the 10th Armoured Regiment (The Fort Garry Horse). Roughly 760 divisional and army group artillery pieces from one heavy, eight medium, and twelve field regiments provided indirect fire support. The 16-inch guns of HMS *Rodney* and the 15-inch guns of the Royal Navy monitor HMS *Roberts* assisted with preparatory bombardment of the objective area. Additional maneuver support included the 4.2-inch heavy mortars and Vickers medium machine guns of the Cameron Highlanders of Ottawa's machine-gun battalion and three squadrons of special armor, including tanks with chain flails for beating paths through minefields, flame-throwing Crocodiles, and engineer assault vehicles designed to

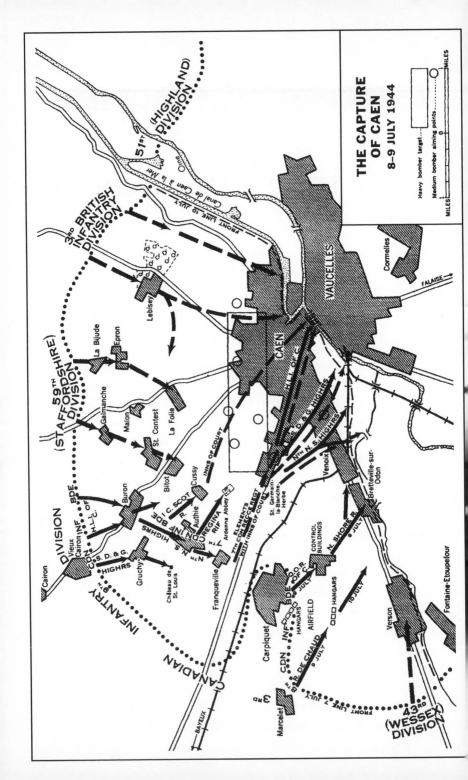

THE CAPTURE
OF CAEN
8-9 JULY 1944

Heavy bomber target
Medium bomber aiming points
MILES

hurl petards against strongpoints and provide armor cover for soldiers engaged on demolition tasks. Two squadrons of tank-busting Typhoon fighter-bombers were also on call to the brigade.[1]

The powerful support accorded Operation Windsor recognized the fact that the 12th SS Panzer Division *Hitlerjugend* defended the Carpiquet area from well-prepared positions. After Epsom, Dietrich's I SS Panzer Corps had also been reorganized as Hitler wished, with only the 12th SS and the still-arriving 1st SS Panzer Division *Leibstandarte* under his command. The depleted *Panzer Lehr* Division had been placed under the XXXXVII Panzer Corps, together with the 2nd Panzer Division, while the 9th SS Panzer Division *Hohenstaufen*, 10th SS Panzer Division *Frundsberg*, and Weidinger's *Das Reich* battle group constituted the II SS Panzer Corps. All three corps, plus the LXXXVI Corps (21st Panzer, 16th Luftwaffe, and 711th, 346th, and 716th Infantry Divisions) made up Eberbach's Panzer Group West, roughly facing the Second British Army.

Specifically, Milius's 25th Panzergrenadier Regiment of the 12th SS Panzer Division defended a line running from just below Cambes, north of Caen, through Buron, Gruchy, and Authie to Franqueville. Southwest from Franqueville, Mohnke's severely mauled 26th Regiment held Carpiquet village and airfield and a southwest line that linked up with Frey's now-complete 1st SS Panzergrenadier Regiment of the *Leibstandarte*, defending from Les Jumeaux to Eterville. Mohnke's 1st Battalion defended the western edge of the village, supported by two infantry guns in the east end, as well as the southern edge of the airfield, supported by five Mark IVs at the southeast corner. Part of a Panther company remained in reserve at Bretteville-sur-Odon and a battery of 88-millimeter guns of the 12th SS Flak Regiment in St. Germane-la Blanche-Herbe covered the eastern portion of Carpiquet. The 3rd SS Panzer Artillery Battalion and elements of the 83rd Werfer Regiment provided fire support.[2]

The first phase of Operation Windsor called for the concurrent capture of the village of Carpiquet and the hangars north and south of the airfield. This was to be accomplished by the North Shore

Regiment (New Brunswick) on the left and Le Régiment de la Chaudière on the right, each supported by a squadron of tanks reinforced by special armor, attacking the village from south of La Villeneuve, while the Royal Winnipeg Rifles simultaneously struck out for the south hangars from Marcelet. The Winnipeg attack was to be supported by the third tank squadron. A diversionary sally north to Vieux Cairon and Grouchy was also to be mounted from Villeneuve fifteen minutes later by a squadron of the Sherbrooke Fusiliers. In phase two, the Queen's Own Rifles were to pass through the secured village and seize the control tower and buildings at the east end of the airfield. Alerted by increased Canadian reconnaissance, however, the 12th SS Panzer Division confirmed 8th Brigade intentions by monitoring tank radio traffic and commenced to heavily mortar and shell Canadian attack positions from their time of occupation on 3 July.[3]

The 8th Canadian Brigade's attack commenced at 0500 hours on 4 July behind a creeping barrage fired by six field and two medium artillery regiments. Minutes after the opening of the covering barrage, the Germans also dropped a counterbarrage just behind it, which not only caused substantial casualties, but gave the impression that Canadian shells were falling short. The tanks and special armor nonetheless rolled relentlessly toward Carpiquet village, with bunker-busting engineer vehicles and flamethrowers reducing German forward outposts and strongpoints. Rubble in the built-up area reduced armored vehicle mobility and effectiveness, however, and a fierce house-to-house infantry struggle ensued. Finally, at 1400, Carpiquet village and the north hangars belonged to the Canadians. The intense artillery-support program had obviously not destroyed the essential framework of the well-dug-in and cleverly camouflaged defense established by the understrength 26th Panzergrenadier Regiment. The south hangars also still remained in German hands.[4]

Artillery support also failed to cover and shield the movement of the Winnipegs, whose axis from Marcelet took them somewhat south of barrage protective fire. Mortared incessantly by the enemy, the battalion was furthermore left to go it alone as the third tank squadron, earmarked for phase two, stayed back in reserve and only supported them with fire from the rear. Although opposed by the remnants of *Sturmbannführer* Bernhard Krause's 1st Battalion of the 26th Panzergrenadier Regiment, which had been badly battered in Operation Epsom, the Winnipegs appear to have encountered the stiffer opposition. An estimated seventeen tanks and self-propelled guns dug in to the east of the airfield subjected them to devastating fire. Yet in response to a personal appeal by the commanding officer, the battalion received only a reinforced troop of tanks for intimate support. When the two leading Winnipeg companies did finally reach the south hangars at 0900 hours, the intensity of enemy fire was so great that it was impossible to hold on. Ordered by brigade to withdraw around 1300 hours, they were compelled by the nature of the open ground to retire half-way back to their start line.[5]

Meanwhile, phase two had been set in train, with the Queen's Own Rifles committed to capture the airfield control buildings. Unfortunately, Carpiquet had not been entirely cleared of enemy, and the battalion took some time to reach the far end of the village. With the withdrawal of the Winnipegs from the south hangars, however, any thrust by the Queen's Own Rifles toward the control buildings risked exposing them to devastating flanking fire from that quarter. They were therefore ordered to wait, while the Winnipegs, their first attack shattered, were sent in again. At 1600 hours, the second attempt got underway with a supporting tank squadron trying to sweep through low ground around the Germans' left flank. Once again, the infantry reached the hangars, but the tanks, having lost contact, were stalled by antitank fire and threatened by counterattacking Panthers. At 2100 hours, Blackader ordered the battalion to return to its start line.

With phase two uncompleted, the Canadians now had to hold what was gained. A night counterattack by one of Frey's *Leibstandarte* battalions to recapture Carpiquet failed utterly, incurring 118 casualties largely inflicted by supporting German artillery fire. In all, the Canadians suffered 377 casualties in Operation Windsor. Tank losses were light, except for the squadron supporting the Winnipegs, which lost 6 out of 15. Krause's 1st SS Battalion took 155 casualties, compared to 132 each for the North Shores and Winnipegs.[6]

The decision to launch the Winnipeg Rifles over two kilometers of open ground without any accompanying tank support was most certainly a mistake. The decision to hurl them in again with the minimum tank support that they should have been provided in the first place could also be considered too little, too late. Whether or not disproportionate confidence in the capacity of massive artillery bombardment to overcome enemy resistance contributed to the neglect of suitable maneuver arrangements, it is difficult to fault the corps commander for attributing the limited success of Windsor to lack of control and leadership from the top. In Crocker's view, more divisional guidance should have been given and additional resources committed when things started to go wrong. Dempsey agreed that the operation was not well handled and observed that it proved conclusively that Keller was not fit to command a division. At a time when the situation demanded a clear-cut decision and firm control, he stressed, the divisional commander failed to take a grip. Montgomery concurred with Dempsey, adding that Keller was unfit to command a division since he proved unable to get the best out of his soldiers.[7]

The day after the attack on Carpiquet, Crocker's 1 Corps issued the order for Operation Charnwood, the direct capture of Caen by three infantry divisions supported by 350 tanks of two armored brigades. Planned for 8 July, Charnwood called for a concentric advance on Caen by the British 3rd Division on the left, the 59th (Staffordshire) Division in the center, and the 3rd Canadian Infantry Division on the right. The operation consisted of five phases: first, an assault by the British 3rd and 59th (Staffordshire) Divisions from the north to seize key points on a four-mile front; second, an attack by the 3rd Canadian Division from the northwest to secure the area as far south as Authie; third, a continued push by all divisions toward Caen and to the line Franqueville-Ardenne by the 3rd Canadian; fourth, the final reduction of Carpiquet and the mopping up of Caen to the River Orne and Caen Canal; and fifth, consolidation and

British divisional thrusts to obtain bridgeheads over the river. Support for the attack included special armor from the British 79th Division, the firepower of two artillery brigades, and naval gunfire from several Royal Navy warships, including the battleship *Rodney*, the cruisers *Belfast* and *Emerald*, and the monitor *Roberts*. Charnwood also saw heavy bombers of RAF Bomber Command employed for the first time in a close-support role on the battlefield.[8]

Dietrich's I SS Panzer Corps, Meyer's 12th SS Panzer Division *Hitlerjugend*, and Frey's attached *Leibstandarte* regiment stood in the path of Charnwood. On the *Hitlerjugend*'s right, the newly arrived 16th Luftwaffe Field Division, supported by a 21st Panzer Division tank battalion that had been left behind, held the front from roughly Epron to the Caen Canal. On the *Hitlerjugend*'s left, south and west of Verson, the II SS Panzer Corps had taken over. Within the *Hitlerjugend*'s sector, the 25th Panzergrenadier Regiment occupied a sector from La Bijude, north of Epron, through Buron to Franqueville. The 26th Panzergrenadier Regiment deployed with the 2nd Battalion in St. Germaine-la-Blanche-Herbe, the 3rd Battalion in reserve in northwest Caen, and the 1st Battalion resting south of the city with the divisional reconnaissance and artillery battalions. Frey's attached 1st SS Panzergrenadier Regiment defended a front from Franqueville through Les Jumeaux to the western part of Eterville. Four 88-millimeter batteries of the 12th SS Flak Battalion dotted the divisional area of responsibility, while the *Werfer*s of the division and 3rd Battalion, 83rd Regiment, occupied sites north and west of Caen. Of thirty-two Mark IVs and twenty-eight Panthers, nine Mark IVs had firing positions in Buron and Grouchy, five on the eastern edge of Carpiquet airfield, and eleven Panthers in the area between Bretteville and Eterville. Eighteen Mark IVs and seventeen Panthers remained in reserve near Ardenne in the outskirts of Caen.[9]

The British 1 Corps' attack on Caen commenced with an artillery and naval bombardment at 2000 hours on 7 July. Following this, 467 Halifax and Lancaster bombers dropped 2,562 tons of 500- and 1,000-pound bombs between 2150 and 2230 hours. After additional interdiction strikes by the 2nd Tactical Air Force, the artillery fired harassing salvos throughout the night. Because of a required 6,000-yard troop-safety distance, the rectangular target area chosen (4,000 yards long by 1,500 wide) lay well behind the Germans' forward ring of fortified villages and contained only a few enemy defensive positions. The well-dug-in 12th SS Panzer Division *Hitlerjugend* incurred relatively few losses, though the 16th Luftwaffe Field Division, recently arrived from Holland to relieve the 21st Panzer Division, suffered considerable shock, as well as the loss of a regimental headquarters, because it had only three days to prepare. Apart from a salutary effect upon Anglo-Canadian morale, however, the bombing produced far less than expected in the way of tactical advantage. That ground action did not commence until 0420 hours the following morning further degraded the bombing impact and served to alert the Germans of the imminence of an attack.[10]

In the wake of a shattering artillery barrage fired by 656 guns, the British 3rd and 59th (Staffordshire) Divisions advanced toward their respective objectives. The experienced 3rd badly mauled the severely shaken and comparatively low-grade 16th Luftwaffe Field Division, which came close to collapse, leaving the 12th SS's right flank dangerously exposed. Advancing through Lebisey by 0830, the 3rd reached the outskirts of Caen by evening and threatened to cut off 12th SS units still resisting the 59th Division. The 59th had attacked along the boundary between the 16th Luftwaffe and 12th SS Divisions, thrusting the 176th Infantry Brigade on La Bijude and Epron and the 197th Infantry Brigade on Galmanche, Malon, and St. Contest. The brigades were each supported by a regiment of tanks, but the 59th Division encountered heavy opposition from the 12th SS, which was fighting desperately from mutually supporting defensive positions in villages. Combat in La Bijude continued up to 1310 hours, and St. Contest held out until mid-afternoon. At 0630, perhaps on learning of good progress being made by the British 3rd Division, Crocker ordered the 3rd Canadian Division to commence phase two at 0730 hours.[11]

The 3rd Canadian Division's plan of attack specified three phases. Phase one, to be executed by Brig. Ben Cunningham's 9th Brigade and supported by the tanks of the Sherbrooke Fusiliers, called for the Stormont, Dundas, and Glengarry Highlanders to take Gruchy and the Highland Light Infantry of Canada to capture Buron. In phase two, the Stormont, Dundas, and Glengarry Highlanders were to secure the Château de St. Louet while the North Nova Scotia Highlanders took Authie and Franqueville. During phase three, Brig. Harry Foster's 7th Infantry Brigade, supported by the 1st Hussars, was to pass through the 9th Brigade to seize Cussy and the Ardenne Abbey. Following this, Blackader's 8th Brigade, supported by the Fort Carry Horse, was to capture the control buildings and southern hangars of Carpiquet airfield.

The 3rd Division's attack commenced at 0730 hours on 8 July, at which time the 59th Division moved against St. Contest, Malon, and Epron. The Canadian attack, supported by divisional artillery and guns from two artillery brigades, produced an unbelievably heavy volume of fire. Still, the *Hitlerjugend* fought on, responding with fixed-line machine-gun fire and, as the artillery lifted, more intense observed indirect and direct shots. Eventually, a charge by some fifteen Bren gun carriers of the 7th Reconnaissance Regiment (17th Duke of York's Royal Canadian Hussars) assisted the Stormont, Dundas, and Glengarry Highlanders in taking Gruchy by 0945 hours. Owing to communication problems, the Sherbrooke armored squadron had not been able to provide close support, though by day's end about a third of its tanks were knocked out. Significantly, the company of the 25th Panzergrenadier Regiment that had defended Gruchy was completely annihilated. It was not until 1430 hours, however, that the Stormont, Dundas, and Glengarry Highlanders pushed on to the Château de St. Louet.[12]

The advance of the Stormont, Dundas, and Glengarry Highlanders from Gruchy had been delayed by the Highland Light Infantry's battle for Buron. In its first major action, the battalion attacked Buron in set-piece fashion with two companies up and two back, the troops following an artillery barrage just like walking out in the rain, according to one participant. Outside of Buron, however, they encountered an antitank ditch twelve feet wide and fifteen feet deep covered by defensive fire from machine guns, mortars, and artillery. This halted their supporting tanks, which had in the meantime run into minefields and incurred casualties. The Highland Light Infantry was thus left to battle its way into the rubble of Buron and fight all day against 200 troops of the 3rd Battalion of the 25th SS Panzergrenadier Regiment. In this vicious and bloody struggle, mine-clearing tanks were used as they became available to flail Waffen SS fighting trenches until they fell in, exposing their occupants to sudden death by swinging chains. With the help of two troops of Royal Artillery 17-pounders and Sherbrooke tanks, the battalion was also able to knock out thirteen counterattacking panzers in one of the most successful antitank defensive actions of the campaign. The cost of success was high. With 262 casualties, the Highland Light Infantry suffered the greatest loss of any unit on 8 July. The Sherbrooke supporting tank squadron mustered only four out of fifteen Shermans.[13]

Following the reduction of Buron, the North Novas went on to secure Authie in a series of hotly contested actions that produced 25 SS prisoners at a cost of 262 casualties. At 1830 hours, with Authie secured, Foster's 7th Brigade commenced phase three of Charnwood, and by 2130 hours, in spite of German resistance from Bitot and Ardenne, Cussy fell to the Canadian Scottish supported by 1st Hussar tanks and two companies of Winnipegs. A Regina Rifle attack on the Ardenne Abbey failed in the face of German indirect fire and a counterattack by Panthers and Frey's panzergrenadiers, but as a result of Meyer's pleas to be granted permission to withdraw, the Germans abandoned the abbey that night.

Meyer had warned Dietrich that the collapse of the 16th Luftwaffe Division dangerously exposed his right flank, but on begging the latter for permission to retire rather than be overwhelmed, he had been refused on the grounds of Hitler's order to hold Caen at all costs. Eventually authorized by Dietrich's chief of staff to conduct a fighting withdrawal across the Orne, Meyer managed to extricate what was left of his division in a nightmarish operation. The new sector for his 25th Panzergrenadier Regiment ran from the eastern edge of Vaucelles to Fleury-sur-Orne, while Frey's 1st Panzergrenadier Regiment occupied a southern front from north of Louvigny to west of Eterville.[14]

In the meantime, the 8th Canadian Infantry Brigade occupied Carpiquet airfield just before noon on 9 July. As the 3rd Canadian and British 3rd Divisions advanced on Caen from the west and east, they unavoidably pinched out the 59th Division, which was closing in from the north. At 1335 hours, the Stormont, Dundas, and Glengarry Highlanders and Sherbrooke tanks reached the center of the city from the west, and the British linked up shortly thereafter. On 10 July, the 3rd Canadian Division held a ceremonial parade and raised the Dominion flag in the city center. Although the southern suburbs of Caen and the Falaise plain still lay in German hands, the Anglo-Canadians had scored a symbolic victory. As Hitler had decreed that Caen be defended unto death, the value of the city as a vital communications center and operational hinge had by this time almost been superseded by the city's importance as a symbol. For reasons of his own—not entirely related to purely military considerations—Montgomery had been equally determined to carry the city by storm. In the end, Caen was all but obliterated by air action and artillery fire in a struggle that degenerated into a brutal and primitive individual test of arms. As recounted by one former soldier of the 12th SS Panzer Division *Hitlerjugend*, the fighting around Caen was a "tough business" indeed.[15]

Underscoring this, during the German night counterattack of 5 July, Sgt. Leo Gariepy of the 1st Canadian Hussars reportedly witnessed a bloodbath unfold at first light. From the turret of his tank, he watched crazed troops of Le Régiment de la Chaudière slit the throats of both wounded and dead SS men. They were only stopped at pistol point by their own officers. According to Gariepy, whose story has neither been corroborated nor challenged, this was before the Waffen SS shot three Canadian scouts at St. Germain-la Blanche-Herbe. A special correspondent for the London *Daily Telegraph* wrote of this particular incident that it was no wonder German troops believed Nazi propaganda about Canadian soldiers being savages with scalping knives.

As far as is known, Gariepy's eyewitness report is one of two prominent war crimes commonly attributed to Anglo-Canadian forces by the Germans. The first apparently occurred on 8 June near Cristot, where a patrol of the British Inns of Court Regiment captured a nine-man *Panzer Lehr* reconnaissance party under Colonel Luxenburger. Allegedly, Luxenbuger, who had lost an arm in the Great War, was beaten unconscious and tied to an English scout car. Before returning to their lines, the patrol opened fire on the rest of the German group, killing all except for Capt. Count Clary-Aldrigen, who survived his wounds. The Germans shortly thereafter ambushed the British and mortally wounded Luxenburger with antitank fire that hit the scout car. The seriously wounded Clary-Aldrigen meanwhile managed to make his way to the command post of the 2nd Battalion of Mohnke's 26th SS Regiment at Le Mesnil-Patry. There, according to Hubert Meyer, three Canadian prisoners of war were shot in reprisal.[16]

Meyer further claimed that he had seen a dead Canadian captain's notebook that recorded no prisoners were to be taken. Although this would have been as illegal as a reprisal killing, Canadians were known to have issued a written order to bind or tie the hands of German prisoners captured in the raid on Dieppe on 19 August 1942. When this order fell into German hands, the Germans denounced such "Wild West" methods of controlling prisoners and, in retaliation, shackled numerous Commonwealth prisoners of war. The British response in kind ensured that the controversy raged well into 1943. This affair—coupled with an incident on the island of Sark, where a Commando raiding party shot a number of German soldiers with their hands tied behind their backs—led an incensed Hitler to secretly issue his Commando Order of 18 October 1942. Charging that Commonwealth troops were instructed not only to tie up prisoners, but also to kill unarmed captives thought to be an encumbrance to them, he ordered that all enemies on commando missions—in uniform or not—were to be slaughtered to the last man, even those trying to surrender.

The Nazis no doubt believed veteran British soldier Robert Graves when he wrote that Canadians in the Great War had the worst reputation for acts of violence against prisoners. But Graves also wondered how much they deserved this reputation and whether it simply reflected a tendency to brag. Announcing the shooting of a prisoner was a boast, not necessarily a confession. Specific evidence was always sparse, but rumors abounded. This seems also have been the case in the assertion that many British and American units routinely shot Waffen SS men, which, to Max Hastings, explained why so few of them ever surrendered. Surrendering was always an extremely dangerous act, of course, since it was too easy in the heat of battle to avenge a comrade who had just been killed. That this happened randomly is most likely, and both sides apparently shot snipers and flamethrower crews in anger. Jittery leading elements of the U.S. 90th Infantry Division moving forward from Utah Beach also opened fire on an approaching column of German prisoners. Aiming to make German troops fight harder, Nazi propaganda additionally attempted to demonize Anglo-Americans by citing instances of North American Indians scalping prisoners. Mere rumors of Germans bayoneting prisoners, however, were enough to convince the men of the 115th Regiment of the U.S. 29th Infantry Division to take no prisoners. Some Canadian war diary entries also hinted darkly of settling scores with the 12th SS.

From an operational perspective, killing prisoners made little sense as they were a valuable source of intelligence. Sowing terror through summary execution during and after surrender also had the counterproductive effect of making an enemy fight more desperately to the bitter end rather than surrender. On the other hand, a more chivalrous approach could actually lessen resistance by enticing a foe to give up and bring his comrades with him. The deliberate cold-blooded murder of unarmed prisoners of war by the Waffen SS thus flew in the face of military logic and stood in contrast to random acts of killing in the heat of battle. Determining responsibility turned out to be another matter, and of somewhat related significance, Maj. Gen. Chris Vokes may have commuted Kurt Meyer's death sentence in January 1946 because he did not want to set a precedent whereby a field commander could be held responsible for acts committed by his subordinates. Vokes had been the Canadian divisional commander who, in reprisal for alleged civilian attacks on Canadian soldiers in April 1945, leveled houses in the center of one German town and burned another almost completely to the ground.[17]

Despite the notorious cold-blooded murder of Canadian prisoners by the *Hitlerjugend*, not all Waffen SS men acted in this manner. To suggest that they were all sadists, criminals, or fanatics who wantonly committed atrocities would be as ludicrous as to accept the apologist view that the Waffen SS was not really part of Himmler's empire. Many joined for pragmatic reasons such as faster promotion, others simply because they were drafted and assigned to the Waffen SS rather than the army. Eberbach testified at the trial of Kurt Meyer that the Waffen SS could be divided into two categories, those who joined for idealistic reasons and those who were brawlers and bullies. In his view, as well as Geyr von Schweppenburg's, Kurt Meyer, Fritz Witt, and Max Wünsche belonged in the first category, Wilhelm Mohnke and Gerhard Bremer in the second. Wünsche, against whom no suggestion of war crimes ever seems to have been raised, epitomized the Nazi propagandist's model of a handsome, blue-eyed, blond Nordic knight.

On the other hand, documentary evidence shows that Theodor Eicke, Fritz Knochlein, Max Simon, and Heinz Lammerding—all with *Totenkopf* roots—were responsible for the unjustified killing of civilians and prisoners. In fact, most Waffen SS atrocities occurred during indiscriminate antipartisan pacification operations. There were other frontline Waffen SS leaders—former army officers like Paul Hausser, Theodor Wisch, Wilhelm Bittrich, and Georg Keppler or younger rising stars like Sylvester Stadler, Heinz Harmel, Walter Harzer, and Otto Weidinger—who were more of the professional, rather than ideological, type. Indeed, the longer the war went on, the more the Waffen SS identified with the frontline army and the more alike the two became. Bittrich would fight chivalrously at Arnhem, where he was heard to say that a man cannot lose all humanity even during bitter fighting.[18]

This would be tested in the battle for Hill 112, a bloody struggle reminiscent of World War I in which the Waffen SS again showed their tactical mettle. On 10 July, the British 8 Corps' 43rd (Wessex) Division under Maj. Gen. G. I. Thomas attacked at 0500 hours to seize the high ground in the area of Hill 112 and Maltot. For this operation, code-named Jupiter, Thomas had the additional support of the 4th Armoured Brigade, the 46th Highland Brigade, and two regiments of the 31st Tank Brigade. Two artillery brigades and the artilleries of two divisions provided indirect fire support with ground-attack aircraft available on call. Thomas assigned his own tank-supported infantry brigades to capture Hill 112 and Maltot with the aim of having the 4th Armoured Brigade exploit to the Orne.

Elements of three Waffen SS divisions stood between the British and the Orne, however. Late on 9 July, Meyer had ordered Wünsche, who now had fewer than thirty tanks, to occupy a position southeast of Maltot. That same evening, the remainder of the 1st SS Panzer Division *Leibstandarte* under *Brigadeführer* Theodor Wisch had begun to arrive in the Caen area. Two battalions of Rudolf Sandig's 2nd Panzergrenadier Regiment immediately took up right-flank and depth positions adjacent to Frey's regiment deployed with a battalion in Lovigny, another between Le Mesnil and Eterville, and a third west and southwest of Maltot. The *Leibstandarte*'s 1st Panzer Regiment under Jochen Peiper, with sixty Mark IVs, thirty Panthers, and forty-one tank destroyers of the divisional assault-gun battalion on strength, filtered in to a reserve position near Bully in the sector of the II SS Panzer Corps. Responsibility for the main ridge running south from Hill 112 to Hill 113 north of Evrecy rested with *Brigadeführer* Heinz Harmel's 10th SS Panzer Division *Frundsberg*.[19]

The 43rd (Wessex) Division attack kicked off at 0500 hours on 10 July with the 130th Infantry Brigade striking for Eterville and Maltot and the 129th Infantry Brigade advancing on Hill 112.

Churchill tanks supported both attacks, which resulted in the capture of Eterville and a successful advance to the slopes of Hill 112 by 0800 hours. This forced the withdrawal of a *Frundsberg* battalion and a *Leibstandarte* battalion from Eterville, but British attempts to get beyond Maltot after 0915 hours resulted in the loss of nine Churchills to German tank and antitank fire, including that from Tigers of both the 101st and 102nd Heavy Panzer Battalions. By 1400 hours, the Germans recaptured Maltot. At 1620, the British 130th Infantry Brigade launched another tank-infantry attack on Maltot that succeeded despite heavy losses, including those accidentally inflicted by RAF Typhoons. A German counterattack by panzergrenadiers and *Hitlerjugend* panzers around 1830 hours proved so strong, however, that the British brigade commander ordered withdrawal from Maltot.

Meanwhile, as the 129th Brigade had paid a high price in attempting to get beyond the crest of Hill 112, a Churchill-supported battalion of Thomas's reserve 214th Infantry Brigade made a final attempt to take Hill 112. After taking heavy casualties, the battalion managed to dig in near a small wood on the summit. A major counterattack the next morning by *Frundsberg* elements supported by Tiger tanks failed to dislodge the British, but German artillery fire became so intense that withdrawal eventually proved necessary, leaving Hill 112 a no-man's-land. During this period, Eterville changed hands several times, but by last light on 11 July, the British still held all but the eastern edge of the village.[20]

The struggle for Hill 112 precipitated a series of vicious clashes of such intensity that they produced a moonscape reminiscent of the Great War. Fought amongst dead bodies and burnt-out tanks in one of the most horrific engagements of the Normandy campaign, Operation Jupiter cost the British some 2,000 casualties. In the battle for Caen, Operation Charnwood, the Anglo-Canadians incurred 3,817 casualties—more than 1,000 in the 59th (Staffordshire) Division, somewhat less in the British 3rd Division, and 1,194 for the Canadians, more than they lost on D-Day. The Germans knocked out at least eighty tanks, losing ten of their own Panthers and twenty-two Mark

IVs on 8 July alone. Casualties on the German side are difficult to determine precisely, but the 12th SS Panzer Division lost an estimated 600 personnel and half its panzers in Charnwood and Jupiter. In fact, up to 11 July, the 12th SS suffered the heaviest loss of any panzer division in Panzer Group West. The infantry of the 16th Luftwaffe Field Division reportedly suffered 75 percent casualties, and the 10th SS Panzer Division *Frundsberg* incurred so many casualties in Jupiter that it had to be relieved in line.[21]

From the heady days of rejecting recruits for the smallest imperfections, the Waffen SS now sought to comb out the Reich Labor Service for reinforcements. To this point, German efforts to relieve their panzer divisions holding the line with replacement infantry formations in order to constitute a counterattack force had failed miserably. If Operation Epsom had forced all Waffen SS divisions to adopt only the defensive, Operations Charnwood and Jupiter confirmed their loss of any collective offensive capability at all beyond local counterattacks. Hitler's unshaken conviction that the main Allied invasion was still to be mounted east of the Seine exacerbated their plight since no additional infantry divisions could be released from the Fifteenth Army. In ordering a strictly defensive battle until more forces arrived in Normandy, Hitler conceded in early July the hopelessness of launching a multidivision attack along the Anglo-American boundary.

CHAPTER 6

Tank Charge to Conserve Infantry

While the Epsom and Charnwood offensives demonstrated that the British could mount multidivision corps attacks whereas the Germans could not, British manpower losses emanating from these operations gave rise to concern. The seriousness of the British casualty situation prompted the army adjutant-general to visit Normandy in early July to warn Montgomery and Dempsey that if infantry casualties continued at the rate they did, they could only be replaced by cannibalizing other army branches and breaking up some divisions to maintain the rest. Indeed, the 59th (Staffordshire) Infantry Division eventually disappeared in August and the 50th (Northumbrian) Infantry Division in November as a direct result of rising casualties. Other formations and units disbanded included the 27th Armoured Brigade, the 70th Brigade of the 49th Division (replaced by the independent 56th Infantry Brigade), two tank regiments in the 33rd Armoured Brigade, and a regiment each in the 8th and 34th Armoured Brigades. Dempsey took the adjutant-general's warning seriously, and having been greatly impressed by the shock effect of the bomber attack at Caen, he immediately set about devising an offensive plan with manpower conservation in mind.[1]

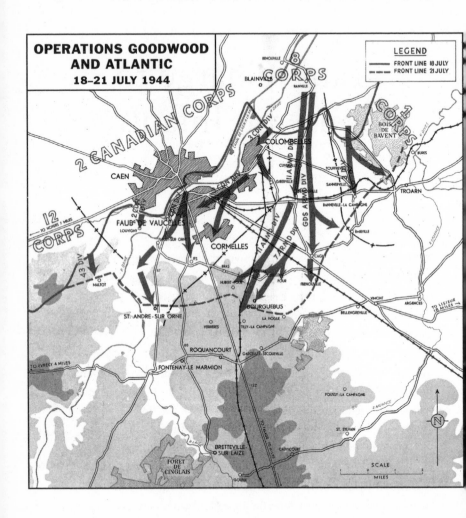

OPERATIONS GOODWOOD
AND ATLANTIC
18–21 JULY 1944

LEGEND
FRONT LINE 18 JULY
FRONT LINE 21 JULY

2 CANADIAN CORPS

8 CORPS

1 CORPS

BÉNOUVILLE
BLAINVILLE
RANVILLE
BOIS DE BAVENT
BURES

3 CDN DIV
COLOMBELLES
CAEN
CUVERVILLE
GIBERVILLE
TOUFFREVILLE
SANNERVILLE
TROARN
BANNEVILLE-LA-CAMPAGNE
GDS ARMD DIV

FAUB^G DE VAUCELLES
LOUVIGNY
IFS
CORMELLES
BRAS
HUBERT-FOLIE
FOUR
FRÉNOUVILLE
CAGNY
EMIÉVILLE

12 CORPS
TO NOYERS 7 MILES
43 DIV
MALTOT
ST. ANDRÉ-SUR-ORNE
BOURGUÉBUS
LA HOGUE
TILLY-LA-CAMPAGNE
VERRIÈRES
ROQUANCOURT
GARCELLES-SECQUEVILLE
FONTENAY-LE-MARMION
BELLENGREVILLE
VIMONT
ARGENCES
TO LISIEUX 18 MILES

TO EVRECY 4 MILES
POUSSY-LA-CAMPAGNE
TO FALAISE 18 MILES
ST. SYLVAIN
BRETTEVILLE-SUR-LAIZE
CINTHEAUX
FORÊT DE CINGLAIS
GRAINVILLE

N

SCALE
MILES

Dempsey had always been casualty conscious as a result of his experience in the Great War and now planned to use tanks to save infantry lives. Instead of continuing with infantry attacks in the British sector, he proposed using armored divisions to deliver a smashing blow to the Germans on the eastern flank. The operation, code-named Goodwood, aimed primarily at destroying the enemy by hitting him hard and wearing down his strength, causing him either to commit reserves or risk a breakthrough. Besides weakening enemy capacity to resist, other considerations included completing the capture of Caen and expanding the bridgehead to accommodate reinforcements, supplies, and airfields. Given that the British Second Army's tank strength was increasing all the time and that tank reinforcements were pouring into Normandy faster than the rate of tank casualties, Dempsey considered it desirable to plan an operation that utilized the surplus of tanks and economized on infantry. To compensate for a critical shortage in 25-pounder ammunition and difficulties in sustaining artillery support, he looked to employ heavy strategic bombers to blast a path for the armor. His ultimate aim was to seize all the crossings over the Orne from Caen to Argentan, thereby cutting off the enemy's main force that lay west of the Orne.[2]

Goodwood was therefore the brainchild of Dempsey. Hardly a fan of employing all-armored over combined-arms corps, Montgomery acceded to Dempsey's proposal because it offered the best chance of gaining a bridgehead opposite Caen without undue losses. As the 21st Army Group's commander, Montgomery was also primarily concerned with coordinating the efforts of Dempsey's Second Army and Gen. Omar Bradley's U.S. First Army to gain maximum effect. He originally slated Dempsey's Goodwood for 17 July to coincide with Bradley's Operation Cobra, which was planned for 19 July and later the twentieth, then the twenty-first. Goodwood ultimately went in on 18 July to prevent the enemy from concentrating an armored reserve, but bad flying weather delayed Cobra until 25 July.

Although three armored divisions spearheaded Goodwood and three infantry divisions Cobra—with one motorized and two armored divisions in reserve ready to exploit—both operations accorded with Montgomery's principal maxims of never losing the initiative and avoiding morale-sapping setbacks. While recognizing that certain ground features were vital to operational success, Montgomery regarded ground as something not to be fought *for*, but to be fought *over*, as did German panzer commanders. Certainly, he needed to expand the bridgehead for airfields, troop build-up, and maneuver room, but in dealing body blow after body blow alternately west and east of the Orne, he sought first and foremost to destroy the enemy's army. In this light, his final direction to Dempsey to engage German armor in battle and whittle it down to such an extent that it was of no further value to the Germans as a basis of the battle made eminently good sense.[3]

The original role of the British Second Army as stated early in 1944 was to protect the flank of the U.S. armies while they captured Cherbourg and the Brittany ports. No major advance was to be carried out until this was done, and on 10 June 1944, Montgomery confirmed his intention to draw German reserves onto the Second Army's front so that the U.S. First Army's front could extend and expand. After Epsom and Charnwood, however, Dempsey attempted to convert Montgomery to another theater strategy in which the main breakout role would be shifted away from the Americans to the British in Operation Goodwood. Although Montgomery refused to accept any fundamental alteration to his broad plan for Normandy, he saw that making the Germans think a British breakout was possible would draw in more of their armored reserves. He therefore acquiesced to launching Goodwood, but only after expressing doubts about the chances for an all-armored corps to break out.

Dempsey's widely distributed operation order of 13 July called for an advance to Falaise, but in a written note on 15 July, Montgomery deleted Falaise as an objective and inserted the much closer Bourguébus Ridge, which overlooked the Caen-Falaise plain. Supreme Headquarters Allied Expeditionary Forces (SHAEF) never received a copy of the amended order as issued by the Second Army on 17 July, however, and although O'Connor never recalled Dempsey ever mentioning exploitation, the Second Army's commander stood ready to seize any opportunity that offered a chance of a breakthrough. By deliberately inflating expectations for Goodwood in order to convince the bomber barons that using large numbers of strategic aircraft in a tactical role was vital and would yield worthwhile results, Montgomery gave the misleading impression that a breakthrough would be achieved. Thus, while Montgomery actually refused to commit himself beyond Bourguébus Ridge, Dempsey foresaw the chance of a complete breakthrough, and SHAEF expected big results.[4]

On 11 July, Dempsey commanded a total of five corps of more than fifteen divisions. The plan he devised called for the employment of four corps and a main attack by 800 tanks of the 8 Corps down a corridor blasted open by 1,600 heavy and 400 medium and fighter bombers. O'Connor's 8 Corps of three armored divisions was to assemble in the small bridgehead east of the Orne held by the 6th Airborne and 51st Highland Divisions and, after massive carpet-bombing intended to clear the way, strike south behind a creeping barrage to gain the heights of Bouguébus Ridge, from which further operations into the Caen-Falaise plain could be developed. Specifically, the 11th Armoured Division was to mask Cagny and seize the Bras-Bourguébus-Rocquancourt area, following which the Guards Armoured Division on the left was to clear Cagny, then strike east toward Vimont. Following behind, the 7th Armoured Division was to be prepared to support either forward division and occupy La Hogue and Secqueville-la-Campagne.

To mislead the enemy about the main effort, Crocker's 1 Corps was to launch a simultaneous supporting attack with infantry and tanks on the left flank toward Troarn and Emieville, while Guy Simonds's 2 Canadian Corps on the right attacked the Caen suburbs of Colombelles and Vaucelles in Operation Atlantic. A diversionary attack was also to be launched from the Odon sector on 15 July by Neil Ritchie's newly arrived 12 Corps, with a view to gaining Evrecy as a firm base for a subsequent advance toward Aunay-sur-Odon or

Thury-Harcourt. Farther west, the 30 Corps was to take Noyers and draw enemy reserves into the thick country on its front. Both Dempsey and Montgomery considered the preliminary aerial bombardment to be critical as there was insufficient space in the bridgehead to deploy enough artillery, which was also short on 25-pounder ammunition, for the delivery of sustained fire.[5]

East of the Caen-Falaise road, the German LXXXVI Corps under Gen. Hans von Obstfelder stood directly in the path of the Goodwood offensive. The remnant of the badly mauled 16th Luftwaffe Field Division screened the sector from Touffreville to Colombelles, while the 346th Infantry Division held the front from Touffreville to Cabourg on the coast. The 192nd Panzergrenadier Regiment of the 21st Panzer Division occupied another screening position between Colombelles and the Orne bridge in southern Caen. Just south of Cagny, the 125th Panzergrenadier Regiment under Lt. Col. Hans von Luck formed the nucleus of a battle group that included his own 1st and 2nd Battalions and the 200th Sturmgeschütz (Assault Gun) Battalion under Maj. Alfred Becker. Becker's battalion fielded thirty self-propelled 75-millimeter tank destroyer assault guns and twenty self-propelled 105-millimeter howitzers in five batteries in or around the villages of Giberville, Demouville, Grentheville, Le Mesnil-Fre-mentel, and Le Poirier. A Nebelwerfer battalion was also sited near Grentheville, with four 88-millimeter guns of the 16th Luftwaffe Flak Battalion near Cagny. Farther to the east, between Sannerville and Emieville, the 1st Panzer Battalion (twenty-two Mark IV tanks) and the 503rd Heavy Panzer Battalion (thirty-six Tigers, including a company of Tiger IIs) formed Feuchtinger's divisional reserve. The three divisional artilleries of the LXXXVI Corps and seventy-eight 88-millimeter guns occupied firing positions south of Bourguébus.[6]

Early on 11 July, within Dietrich's I SS Panzer Corps sector, Wisch's 1st SS Panzer Division *Leibstandarte* assumed responsibility for the 12th SS Panzer Division *Hitlerjugend*'s front, which ran east from the boundary with the II SS Panzer Corps between Hill 112 and Mal-tot to the Caen-Falaise road marking the boundary with the LXXXVI

Corps. The *Hitlerjugend*, having lost half of its panzers and suffered more casualties than any other panzer division in Panzer Group West, went into rest and refit around the Garcelles-Potigny area south of Caen. The situation remained so critical, however, that the 12th SS artillery regiment, along with one panzergrenadier battalion, remained behind under the *Leibstandarte*'s command. Originally, the 272nd Infantry Division was to have relieved the 12th SS Division, but it did not arrive until 13 July, whereupon it replaced the 1st SS Panzer Division in line, assuming a sector from the Orne bridge in Caen to Eterville. This enabled Dietrich to deploy Wisch's 1st SS Panzer Division in reserve between Ifs and Cintheaux while leaving his 2nd SS Panzer Battalion (fifty-nine Mark IVs), 1st SS Sturmgeschütz Battalion (thirty-five tank destroyer assault guns), a panzergrenadier battalion, and the self-propelled 1st SS Artillery Battalion west of the Orne as an additional corps reserve. Dietrich also had seventeen Tigers of the 101st SS Heavy Panzer Battalion posted around Grainville-Langannerie, and Wisch's 1st SS Panzer Regiment under *Obersturmbannführer* Jochen Peiper fielded forty-six Panthers in his 1st Panzer Battalion. All told, the I SS Panzer and LXXXVI Corps disposed 194 artillery pieces, 272 Nebelwerfers with 1,632 barrels, and 200 tanks, tank destroyers, and assault guns in a layered defense in depth.[7]

The 2,000-bomber attack that preceded Goodwood was the heaviest and most concentrated aerial onslaught in support of ground troops ever attempted. Yet while it destroyed forward German positions and inflicted substantial damage on panzer reserves in the Sannerville-Emieville area, many antitank guns and tanks located around Cagny and Bourguébus survived. All of Becker's assault-gun batteries except the one in Demouville remained operational, as did most of Luck's battle group and German artillery behind Bourguébus Ridge. In expectation of the attack, Panzer Group West had disposed the I SS Panzer and LXXXVI Corps in a twelve-mile-deep defense of five zones based on a grid of interlocking fortified villages and well-dug-in gun positions, backed up by immediate panzer reserves, antitank and flak gun lines, and even stronger mobile armored reserves farther in depth.

Although there is evidence that O'Connor achieved tactical surprise in spite of problems associated with movement into a constricted bridgehead, the 8 Corps' attack foundered largely because he insisted that the spearhead 11th Armoured Division clear the villages of Cuverville and Demouville. The 11th Armoured Division's commander, Maj. Gen. Pip Roberts, pointed out to O'Connor that this would tie up his 159th Infantry Brigade when its most important role was to support the rapid advance of his 29th Armoured Brigade before the Germans could recover from the shock of bombing. O'Connor refused to accept Roberts's suggestion to reallocate the task to the 51st Highland Division on the eastern flank of the 2 Canadian Corps, thus leaving the 29th Armoured Brigade to carry on with only the support of its integral motor infantry battalion. With insufficient infantry to deal speedily with unexpected effective fire emanating from the fortified hamlet of Cagny, which contained 88-millimeter guns and was rapidly reinforced by the Germans, Roberts masked and bypassed what became a key center of resistance that held up and stalled the subsequent advance of the Guards Armoured Division on Vimont. The accordion-like traffic congestion that developed also held up the 7th Armoured Division, earmarked to advance on the left of the 11th Armoured to capture Bourguébus heights and St. Aignan de Cramesnil.[8]

Shortly after the barrage covering the advance ended at 0900 hours, the leading tank regiments of the 29th Brigade came under devastating fire from Becker's assault-gun batteries in Le Mesnil-Frementel and Le Poirier. Eighteen Shermans went up in flames before the German batteries skillfully withdrew to take up blocking positions around Four, Soliers, and Hubert Folie. The 159th Infantry Brigade, which could have dealt with these guns, remained committed to clearing Cuverville and Denouville.

Just after 1000 hours, leading Guards Armoured elements advancing on Cagny also came under fire from four 88-millimeter Luftwaffe flak guns, most famously as a result of Luck's personal orders—at pistol point—that their antiaircraft-orientated commander engage British tanks. Ironically, by knocking out two Tigers in error, they also helped turn back a German counterattack by ten Tigers and nine Mark IVs. A much stonger *Leibstandarte* counterattack ordered that morning by Eberbach, however, had been set in train by Dietrich. Just as leading elements of the 29th Brigade pushed on between Four and Soliers, they encountered Peiper's 1st SS Panzer Regiment, which within minutes knocked out twenty-nine British tanks. Roberts had earlier requested the 8 Corps for assistance from the 7th Armoured Division, but owing to congestion, this was not forthcoming.

When the 29th Brigade's reserve tank regiment resumed the advance at 1430 hours, it came under heavy fire from Becker's assault guns in Soliers and Le Poirier, Luck's panzers in Frenouville, and *Leibstandarte* armor on Bourguébus Ridge. In attempting to withdraw, the regiment lost an entire squadron. The Guards Armoured Division nonetheless pushed on to take Le Poirier at 1630 hours, though the advance on Vimont stalled. Roberts made one final effort to take Bras by committing his reserve, the 11th Armoured Division Reconnaissance Regiment equipped with Cromwells, but the *Leibstandarte*'s defense proved too strong and cost another sixteen tanks destroyed. Meanwhile, the Guards Armoured cleared Cagny by 2000 hours.[9]

O'Connor had hoped to bring the 7th Armoured Division forward to help the sorely pressed 29th Armoured Brigade, but its movement was so slow that its 22nd Armoured Brigade finally assembled for a thrust on La Hogue only around 1800. In any case, early on 19 July, Rudolf Sandig's 2nd SS Panzergrenadier Regiment recaptured Le Poirier and assumed responsibility for the larger area, including Four and La Hogue. Frey's 1st SS Panzergrenadier Regiment meanwhile took over the Bras, Hubert-Folie, Soliers, and Bourguébus sector. The 1st SS Panzer (Panther) Battalion occupied a position behind the ridge east of Bourguébus. In response to Eberbach's request reflecting his concern over the strength of the British attack, the rest and refit of the 12th SS Panzer Division *Hitlerjugend* had also been cut short in order to have it relieve the 21st Panzer Division in the Emieville-Frenouville sector as soon as possible. Leading elements started arriving around 0530 hours on 19 July, and by the afternoon, a battle group under Waldmuller occupied a defensive position in Frenouville with Wünsche's panzers positioned in depth as an armored reserve.

Against these dispositions, O'Connor resumed the 8 Corps' attack by ordering the 11th Armoured Division to capture Bras and Hubert Folie at 1600 hours, with the 7th Armoured Division taking Bourguébus at 1700 hours and exploiting to Tilly-la-Campagne and Verrières. The Guards Armoured Division was at the same time to recapture Le Poirier and advance to Vimont. O'Connor's request for the further saturation bombing of Bourguébus was denied, most likely because all such air assets had been diverted to support Cobra, then planned for 20 July.[10]

The 11th Armoured's attack commenced at 1600 hours on 19 July when the Northamptonshire Yeomanry once again advanced on Bras with the expectation that the 3rd Royal Tank Regiment would pass through to capture Hubert-Folie. Within twenty minutes, the attack failed, but a second attack mounted by the Royal Tanks breached the village by 1710 hours, leaving it to be mopped up by the motorized battalion of the 29th Armoured Brigade. An hour later, the Yeomanry attacked Hubert-Folie, but assault-gun fire and Peiper's panzers shooting from hull-down positions on a ridge to the south took such a toll that the unit was reduced to but a squadron of tanks. By the time the 2nd Fife and Forfar Yeomanry launched another attack at 2000 hours, the *Leibstandarte* defenders had withdrawn to a more defensible line near Verrières.

A similar situation greeted the attack by the 7th Armoured Division on Bourguébus, where the 22nd Armoured Brigade initially encountered resistance in Four and Soliers from the 2nd SS Panzergrenadier Regiment before it withdrew to the Bourguébus–La Hogue ridge line. When the 5th Royal Tanks attempted to push around Bourguébus, however, they lost eight Shermans to Peiper's panzers. Meanwhile, the Guards Armoured Division easily recaptured Le Poirier at 1900 hours as the defenders withdrew under orders to Four. Further attempts to advance on Frenouville failed against the 12th SS, now newly equipped with the latest Jagdpanzers. When

Meyer withdrew from Emieville and Frenouville to a shorter, more defensible line on 20 July, the Guards Armoured seized both villages.[11]

Although Goodwood failed to achieve the tactical objectives set by Dempsey, it hurt the Germans more than the Allies realized at the time. Eberbach had been forced to commit all of his panzers, leaving few to respond to Cobra. The loss of 250 British tanks, many recoverable along with crews, was more affordable than casualties in men, which Dempsey claimed to be relatively light. In fact, despite the shocking number of tank casualties in the 8 Corps—126 in the 11th Armoured Division on 18 July alone, plus 60 more in the Guards Armoured Division—O'Connor's total personnel losses of 521 on the day were surprisingly few. The 11th Armoured Division suffered only 81 killed in its four tank regiments and 20 casualties in its four infantry battalions. Of course, the 8 Corps incurred another 499 casualties on 19 July, but even these compare favorably with losses of 651 on 18 July and 541 on 19 July by the reinforced British 3rd Infantry Division attacking on the 1 Corps' front to take Touffreville and Sannerville. In short, the advance of O'Connor's 8 Corps explosively expanded the Orne bridgehead from a tiny foothold to one five miles wide by twelve long with less loss of life than an infantry assault would have cost. Had more infantry been thrown into the fray, the British might likely have prevailed. Statistically, ample infantry was available as there were three battalions in each of the three infantry brigades in the 8 Corps, one per armored division, in addition to one motorized infantry battalion in each of three armored brigades. Yet of twelve infantry battalions available to O'Connor, five saw no action on 18 July.[12]

On a higher plane, Goodwood's symbiotic connection with Cobra was largely forgotten, most especially the fact that both operations were to have taken place concurrently for maximum effect. Had Cobra been launched on 19 or 20 July, Dempsey could legitimately have claimed to having tied down four corps of panzers and infantry. If the Germans had moved any of their main forces away to deal with Cobra, moreover, Goodwood would probably have succeeded as Dempsey had originally envisioned. In any case, he was certainly correct in asserting that Goodwood was a strategic success. For one thing, the enlargement of the bridgehead virtually eliminated any further German counteroffensive threat to the eastern flank. With all of Caen and the Odon and Orne Rivers now at its back, the Second Army posed a grave threat to the entire German right flank, which is why the 2nd and 116th Panzer Divisions, earmarked for St. Lô, were diverted to Caen. Given the battering they had taken during Goodwood, the Germans also lacked the strength to take back what they had lost. The fighting capacity and manpower of German forces had been stretched to the breaking point, and the new strategic reality rendered their position in the West next to hopeless. Even though the British had suffered heavier casualties than the Germans, who lost only seventy-five tanks and assault guns, the latter were now spread so thinly that it was clear to German field commanders that their forces simply could not continue to absorb punishment of this magnitude. Perhaps equally important, Goodwood forced the German logistical system to concentrate against the British, with the result that fewer supplies reached the U.S. sector in the crucial days before Cobra, causing serious shortages that facilitated the breakout.[13]

On the afternoon of 19 July, Dempsey ordered Simonds's 2 Canadian Corps to take over Bras and Hubert-Folie in order to relieve the severely mauled 8 Corps, which again brought Canadians into contact with the Waffen SS. The 2 Canadian Corps had been activated on 11 July on roughly 8,000 yards of frontage along the River Orne through Caen. It had under its command the recently arrived 2nd Canadian Infantry Division and a corps artillery brigade, as well as Keller's 3rd Division and Brig. R. A. Wyman's 2nd Canadian Armoured Brigade. The immediate task given to the 2 Corps was to hold the sector and prepare to establish a bridgehead over the Orne south of Caen in Operation Atlantic, the Canadian portion of Operation Goodwood. Atlantic called for the 3rd Canadian Infantry Division to clear the east bank of the Orne, thereby protecting the 8 Corps' right flank, from Ste. Honorine into Fauberge de Vaucelles. Specifically, Blackader's 8th Brigade was to lead the advance east of the river, capturing

Colombelles, Giberville, and Mondeville. Cunningham's 9th was then to pass through and clear Vaucelles, while Foster's 7th Brigade, in reserve west of the Orne in Caen, remained ready to cross over. Maj. Gen. Charles Foulkes's 2nd Division was to advance southward from Caen to seize, in succession, the high ground north of St. Andre-sur-Orne and the village of Verrières, which commanded the road to Falaise. To effect this, Brig. Sherwood Lett's 4th Brigade was to capture Louvigny on the Orne and, if practicable, cross over to seize the high ground north of St. Andre. Brig. Bill Megill's 5th Brigade was to cross at Caen and take the latter feature if it had not been secured by the 4th. Subsequent advance southward was to be undertaken by Lett's 4th or Brig. Hugh Young's 6th Brigade as circumstances dictated.[14]

Atlantic opened at 0745 hours on 18 July with the leading elements of Blackader's 8th Brigade crossing the start line on a two-battalion front behind one the heaviest barrages yet planned. The Queen's Own Rifles—advancing on Giberville, held by elements of the 16th Luftwaffe and 21st Panzer Divisions—watched helplessly as their barrage rolled away when they were forced to ground by German machine-gun fire from Colombelles. They now had to fight their way to their objective, which took from noon until 2230 hours to secure.

The Chaudière advance on the right had in the interim slowed from 1040 hours because of heavy resistance encountered from the area of a chateau north of the Colombelles steel works. Lack of maneuver room, exacerbated by road cratering, produced a telescoping of forces at this point. As the reserve battalion, the North Shore Regiment, and units of Cunningham's 9th Brigade closed up on the same axis, severe congestion resulted. When the artillery barrage ran away to the south, Blackader called on Typhoons to destroy the chateau at 1330. When this failed, the fire of all available divisional artillery was brought down upon the place, some shells unfortunately landing among the Stormont, Dundas, and Glengarry Highlanders, which worsened an already confusing situation. Eventually, the Chaudières, assisted by the Glengarrians, began to make inroads, and the North Shores were directed to clear the steel works. At 1635 hours, as a result of new orders from Keller, Cunningham's 9th Brigade now bypassed Blockader's 8th, with the North Novas moving on Vaucelles and the Glengarrians against Mondeville, formerly an objective of 8th Brigade.

When it first became apparent that Cunningham's 9th Brigade would be delayed in getting into Vaucelles, Simonds had directed Foster's 7th Brigade to prepare to cross over into the suburb. Evening consequently found the Regina Rifle Regiment established there before the North Novas and Highland Light Infantry from the 9th Brigade arrived. By noon on 19 July, the 9th Brigade had cleared the Germans from Vaucelles. Foster's 7th Brigade had in the meantime been ordered to capture Cormelles, an industrial suburb east of the main road to Falaise, which now constituted the boundary between the 3rd and 2nd Canadian Divisions. Reports that Cormelles was lightly held but might not remain so saw the preemptory dispatch of the Highland Light Infantry to that location, which led to additional confusion between brigades and further complaints of troops being shelled by friendly artillery. As it turned out, the Highland Light Infantry got two companies into Cormelles by late afternoon. They were relieved by the Canadian Scottish and Winnipegs that evening. The entire operation cost the 3rd Canadian Infantry Division 386 casualties.[15]

While Keller's 3rd Division captured Giberville and Colombelles, Foulkes's 2nd Canadian Infantry Division engaged in its first major action since Dieppe. At 1800 hours on 18 July, Lett's 4th Infantry Brigade sent a reinforced battalion, the Royal Regiment of Canada, supported by a squadron of Fort Garry Horse tanks, under cover of a barrage to capture Louvigny. Defended by the German 272nd Infantry Division, Louvigny fell to the Royals at a cost of 111 casualties by the following morning. In the meantime, the Black Watch (Royal Highland Regiment of Canada) from Megill's 5th Brigade, like the Reginas from Foster's 7th Brigade, had crossed the Orne into Vaucelles.

Around 1400 hours on 19 July, the Régiment de Maisonneuve passed through the Black Watch's bridgehead to spearhead the third-phase 5th Brigade attack south from Vaucelles. Despite two forward companies being caught beyond their start line on the opening line of

Recruiting poster for the Leibstandarte.

Left to right: SS-Gruppenführer *Walter Krüger,* Reichsführer der SS *Heinrich Himmler, and* SS–Oberstgruppenführer *Paul Hausser conduct an inspection of Heavy Panzer Battalion 502 near Kharkov on the Eastern Front, April 1943.*

Sepp Dietrich, January 1945. The soldier next to him wears a good example of the Waffen SS's camouflage uniform.

Theodor Eicke and men of the Totenkopf *Division on the Eastern Front, September 1941.*

In front of their camouflaged tank, panzer soldiers of the Waffen SS share a lighter moment with what might be a bottle of wine, June 1944.

British prisoners of war under guard by a gendarme of the Waffen SS, 21 June 1944.

French civilians make way for a Waffen SS soldier and his British prisoner, June 1944.

From left to right: SS-Obersturmbannführer *Max Wünsche,* SS-Brigadeführer *Fritz Witt, and* SS-Standartenführer *Kurt "Panzer" Meyer meet on the invasion front in France, 1944.*

Two soldiers of the Waffen SS pose next to the barrel of their tank near Caen.

A young member of the Hitlerjugend *Division in France, June 1944.*

A soldier of the Hitlerjugend *carrying an MG42 machine gun near Caen.*

Young men of the Waffen SS after receiving the Iron Cross, Second Class, in France, 1944.

Two panzergrenadiers of the Waffen SS in a foxhole in France, July 1944. Low-flying Allied aircraft were an almost constant threat.

A Panther knocked out by the Regina Rifles using PIATs and grenades in Bretteville on the night of 8 June. NATIONAL ARCHIVES CANADA / PA 130149 / DUBERVILL

A destroyed Tiger I in Villers-Bocage.
BUNDESARCHIV, BILD 101I-494-3376-14A / ZWIRNER / CC-BY-SA

German tank ace Michael Wittmann sits atop his Tiger in northern France, May 1944.
BUNDESARCHIV, BILD 101I-299-1802-08 / SCHECK / CC-BY-SA

The wreck of a Panzer IV in Normandy. NATIONAL ARCHIVES

American GIs inspect wrecked German armored vehicles of the 2nd SS Panzer Division Das Reich *near St. Denis-le-Gast, 31 July 1944.* NATIONAL ARCHIVES

Two U.S. soldiers examine a captured Nebelwerfer 41 rocket launcher. NATIONAL ARCHIVES

A group of Waffen SS soldiers captured in Normandy. NATIONAL ARCHIVES

A dead SS trooper lies in the street in Falaise, 17–18 August 1944. The soldiers of the I SS Panzer Corps were the only Germans allowed to wear the words "Adolf Hitler" on their sleeves. NATIONAL ARCHIVES CANADA / PA 161965 / DEAN

The grave of a member of the 17th SS Panzergrenadier Division Götz von Berlichingen, *July 1944. Note the "SS" and Nazi swastika in the fence.*
NATIONAL ARCHIVES

A Canadian soldier of the Highland Light Infantry advances toward Caen, 9 July 1944. NATIONAL ARCHIVES CANADA / PA 131401 / DEAN

Canadian engineers sweep a road for mines near Vaucelles, France, July 1944. NATIONAL ARCHIVES CANADA / PA 131385 / BELL

Near Caen, a Canadian infantryman waits for an artillery barrage to clear before moving forward, July 1944. NATIONAL ARCHIVES CANADA / PA 163403 / BELL

Sgt. Ben Landriault of the Toronto Scottish Carrier Platoon at Tilly-la-Campagne, 8 August 1944. NATIONAL ARCHIVES CANADA / PA 141857 / DEAN

Members of the Royal Hamilton Light Infantry at the graves of soldiers killed at Dieppe, September 1944. NATIONAL ARCHIVES CANADA / PA 176696

American GIs fighting in the hedgerows. NATIONAL ARCHIVES

A French village in bocage *country.* NATIONAL ARCHIVES

An American reconnaissance patrol near Chambois. NATIONAL ARCHIVES

Soldiers from the U.S. 4th Infantry Division wade through flooded marshes. NATIONAL ARCHIVES

A British Cromwell tank, July 1944. NATIONAL ARCHIVES CANADA

A Sherman tank of the Sherbrooke Fusiliers leads Canadian infantrymen down the Rue des Ursulines, 17 August 1944. NATIONAL ARCHIVES CANADA

Sherman Firefly 17-pounder. NATIONAL ARCHIVES CANADA / PA 131391 / BELL

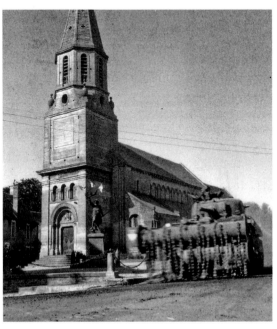

A flail tank passes by a church in Creully.
NATIONAL ARCHIVES
CANADA

A soldier of the Argyll and Sutherland Highlanders walks near a burning tank in St. Lambert sur Dives, 19 August 1944. NATIONAL ARCHIVES CANADA

Shermans in Normandy. NATIONAL ARCHIVES

An American GI crosses a road near a Sherman tank. NATIONAL ARCHIVES

Accused war criminals stand trial at Dachau in 1946 for the Malmedy massacre. Among them are Sepp Dietrich (11), Fritz Kraemer (45), Hermann Preiss (45), and Joachim Peiper (42).
NATIONAL ARCHIVES

Kurt "Panzer" Meyer on trial for war crimes in Aurich, Germany, in December 1945. The charges against him included the killing of prisoners of war at Buron, Authie, and the Abbaye Ardenne. His death sentence was commuted to life imprisonment, and he was released in 1954.
NATIONAL ARCHIVES CANADA /
PA 141890 / GLOSTER

barrage fire, their two rearward sister companies followed the barrage to capture Fleury-sur-Orne, the Maisonneuve objective, by 1425 hours. Later that afternoon, the Calgary Highlanders penetrated to Point 67 overlooking St. Andre-sur-Orne from the north. The Black Watch in turn took the village of Ifs, northwest of Bras, by dusk and successfully held it against a counterattack by the German 272nd Division.

To this point, the Canadians had done well, at a cost of relatively few casualties for what was accomplished. Flushed with such success, both Foulkes and Simonds now decided that the overall favorable situation was ripe for further exploitation rather than consolidation as originally planned. As an anticipatory measure, the Queen's Own Rifles and Sherbrooke Fusiliers were warned for a possible night attack, which the Germans actually dreaded. Hasty plans were also hatched during the evening of 19 July to send Young's hitherto uncommitted 6th Brigade, reinforced by the Essex Scottish Regiment from the 4th Brigade and supported by the Sherbrooke tanks, to attack Verrières Ridge at 1200 hours the next day. The effect of Goodwood, however, had been to draw substantially greater German strength into the area of Bourguébus Ridge. Here the Canadians faced more than the elements of the 16th Luftwaffe Field Division that defended Giberville and even the German 272nd Division, which was experiencing its first action.[16]

In response to Dempsey's direction of 19 July to take over Bras and Hubert-Folie from the 8 Corps, Simonds ordered the 3rd Canadian Infantry Division to relieve the battered 11th Armoured. Directed by Dempsey to complete the capture of Bourguébus, the 7th Armoured Division found the village abandoned but was stopped cold from advancing on Verrières by fire from the *Leibstandarte* and 101st Heavy Panzer (Tiger) Battalion. Some 7th Armoured tanks advancing from the east had traversed as far as Beauvoir farm, north of the ridge, which the 6th Brigade was preparing to attack. While they momentarily considered taking Verrières but chose not to for reasons of suspected enemy strength, their presence may have reinforced the presumption by Simonds that opposition was not great and that quick offensive action should readily break through the enemy screen. In any case, the 7th's tanks eventually withdrew and Young's 6th Brigade attack on a three-battalion 4,000-meter front went in at 1500 hours on 20 July, supported by heavy artillery fire and rocket-firing Typhoon strikes. Two tanks squadrons of the Sherbrookes assigned to Young did not accompany the infantry, but rather remained behind in a questionable counterattack role.[17]

On the right, the Queen's Own Cameron Highlanders of Canada, with a Sherbrooke tank squadron available for counterattack in support, advanced with two companies up through a field of wheat behind a barrage to take St. Andre-sur-Orne from the 272nd Division. On the left, intimately accompanied by five tanks, Les Fusiliers Mont-Royal attacked behind a barrage toward Beauvoir and Troteval farms on their way to their objective, Verrières village. Ominously, in the vicinity of Beauvoir and Troteval farms, where British tanks had previously roamed freely, enemy resistance began to grow. In attempting to press on after certain obvious locations had been cleared, leading Fusilier elements were attacked from the rear by German infantry issuing from farm cellars. At the same time, enemy antitank guns and panzers came into action. With its artillery forward observer dead, its forward company cut off, and its antitank support not yet having come up, the battalion hung on grimly throughout the night, unable to move either ahead or back.[18]

A greater disaster occurred in the center, where the South Saskatchewan Regiment, protected by a troop of tanks on each flank, assaulted under barrage cover through three kilometers of waist-high grain fields to the crest of Verrières Ridge. Tragically, on reaching its objective area after 1700 hours, the battalion consolidated on an open slope dominated by a higher feature held by Germans. The exposed Canadians, under direct observation and subjected to murderous indirect artillery and mortar fire, were now attacked by panzers from the left rear flank. Initially believing that the two flanking tank troops were sufficient to deal with roving panzers of the 1st SS and 2nd

Panzer Divisions, the Sherbrookes were slow to dispatch their reserve squadron forward. Meanwhile, panzers working back and forth along defiladed approaches under overcast skies wreaked havoc upon the demoralized troops of the South Saskatchewan Regiment. Easily picking off a troop of supporting 17-pounders as they raced to rescue the besieged Canadian infantry, the powerful panzers also managed to hold Canadian tanks at bay. Around 1800 hours, the 6th Brigade lost communication with the South Saskatchewans. Information received two hours later revealed that the acting commanding officer had been killed and that the battalion was withdrawing. On learning this around 2100 hours, Young instructed the South Saskatchewans to reorganize immediately behind the Essex, which had been ordered forward at 1730 hours to establish a firm base between Beauvoir farm and St. Andre.[19]

On reaching this position, which was also exposed to enemy observation, the Essex encountered the retreating South Saskatchewan. In their wake came counterattacking German panzers and infantry supported by mortars and artillery delivering a devastating weight of fire. Unable to consolidate, taking casualties, and out of touch with battalion headquarters, the two forward Essex company commanders, after joint consultation, decided to withdraw their subunits, at least one of which got out of control. Around midnight, by which time they had been rounded up, Young personally addressed these companies and arranged with division the resupply of rifles, Bren guns, hand-held antitank weapons, and associated stores, which arrived at 0400. While the Essex were dispatched back to their lines, the South Saskatchewans remained scattered to the wind.

Instead of meeting light opposition, the Canadians had run into elements of the 2nd Panzer Division and Peiper's 1st SS Panzer Regiment of the *Leibstandarte*. On 21 July, the Germans counterattacked, by which time Wyman's 2nd Canadian Armoured Brigade had been placed under the command of Foulkes's 2nd Division. Young's 6th Brigade, already given the Black Watch, now also received the 1st Hussars, which, with the Sherbrookes, were placed in close support of infantry to repel counterattack. Pressure on the front of the depleted Essex began to tell around 0900 hours, however, when the 1st Hussars reported that troops were moving to the rear. When this was shortly confirmed by a liaison officer, orders were given and patrols established to prevent any further rearward movement by the Essex Scottish.

As German infantry and tank infiltration of the Essex position increased, the Black Watch received orders to counterattack at 1600 hours in order to restore the situation. So that the artillery could complete the necessary arrangements, the attack was delayed until 1800 hours, at which time it was successfully carried out under cover of a creeping barrage. The line thus stabilized along the road running between St. Andre and Hubert-Folie. Beauvoir and Troteval farms were lost at the same time, as were most men of the forward Fusilier companies. Foulkes's 2nd Division suffered 1,149 casualties in Operation Atlantic, a much higher figure than the 386 sustained by Keller's 3rd, though more than half resulted from fighting on the second day in pursuit of a perceived opportunity. Total 2 Canadian Corps casualties of 1,614 were close to 90 percent or more of the 1,818 suffered by the 8 Corps between 18 and 22 July.[20]

Simonds's 2 Canadian Corps paid a high price for reaching too far against the Waffen SS. The attack on 20 July was by any measure a complete disaster and humiliation of Canadian arms. Canadian troops had fled in the face of the enemy, but the South Saskatchewans could hardly be blamed for having been placed in such a tactically untenable position. Unquestionably, they should have been more intimately supported by tanks. The doctrine that tanks were not supposed to lead attacks against prepared enemy antitank defenses played a part here. Yet as relative casualty rates averaging 76 percent for infantry and 7 percent for armor indicated, most crews from shot-up tanks got away to fight another day. Goodwood showed why tanks alone should not attack prepared positions, but the tail end of Atlantic showed that attacking with infantry alone could be equally unwise, especially in respect of casualties. That said, Canadian troops regardless of their experience, did all—and more—that their higher commanders could possibly have expected of them in the attack on Verrières Ridge.

CHAPTER 7

Cobra Spring

From Operation Epsom up to the U.S. First Army breakout in Operation Cobra on 25 July, between 520 and 725 panzers continuously deployed against the British sector, whereas during this same period the Americans rarely faced more than 190. Four of the seven divisions opposing the Anglo-Canadians were also Waffen SS, as were two Tiger battalions attached to the I and II SS Panzer Corps. The Germans correctly expected Goodwood to be followed by another massive attack, which is why they ordered the entire 2nd Panzer Division to the Caen area on 22 July. On the eve of Cobra, Demspey's divisions pinned down fourteen German divisions backed up by some 600 tanks while Bradley's fifteen divisions faced nine German divisions with roughly 110 panzers. Bradley disposed four corps from left to right: Maj. Gen. Leonard Gerow's V Corps west of Caumont, Maj. Gen. Charles Corlett's XIX Corps centered on and holding St. Lô, Maj. Gen. J. Lawton "Lightning Joe" Collins's VII Corps west of the Vire River, and Maj. Gen. Troy Middleton's VIII Corps from Collins's right to the Gulf of St. Malo.[1]

Hausser's Seventh Army opposed Bradley's First Army, with the German LXXXIV Corps covering the sector between the coast and the Vire River and the II Parachute Corps defending the front

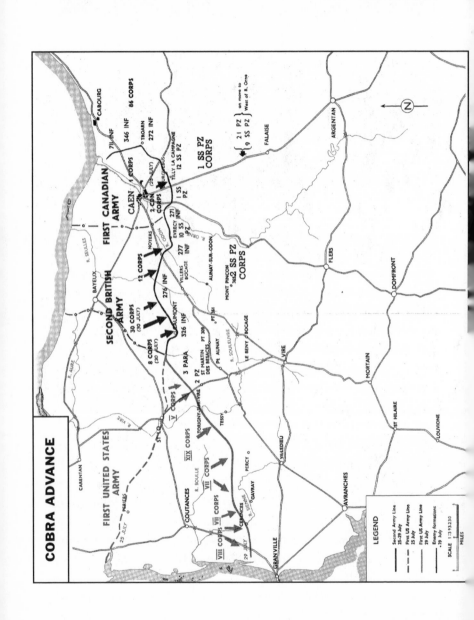

COBRA ADVANCE

FIRST UNITED STATES ARMY

CARENTAN

PERIERS
25 July

R. VIRE

ST-LO

COUTANCES

R. SOULLE

XIX CORPS

VII CORPS

VII CORPS

VIII CORPS

CERENCES
29 July

GAVRAY

PERCY

VILLEDIEU

GRANVILLE

AVRANCHES

ST HILAIRE

LOUVIGNE

R. SIENNE

TORIGNY-SUR-VIRE

TESSY

V CORPS

3 PARA

2 PZ

ST MARTIN
DES BESACES

PT 309

PL AUNAY

R. SOULEUVRE

LE RENY / BOCAGE

PT 361

MONT PINCON
365

2 SS PZ
CORPS

ALNAY-SUR-ODON

VILLERS
BOCAGE

277
INF

BEAUMONT

526 INF

276 INF

8 CORPS
(30 JULY)

30 CORPS
(30 JULY)

12 CORPS

SECOND BRITISH ARMY

BAYEUX

R. SEULLES

R. AURE

EVRECY 271

10 SS
PZ

NOYERS

R. ORNE

ODON

1 SS
PZ

FIRST CANADIAN ARMY

CAEN

2 CDN
CORPS

BOURGUEBUS

TILLY LA CAMPAGNE
12 SS PZ

1 SS PZ
CORPS

FALAISE

ARGENTAN

FLERS

DOMFRONT

MORTAIN

VIRE

$\left.\begin{array}{c} 21\ PZ \\ 9\ SS\ PZ \end{array}\right\}$ on move to
West of R. Orne

CABOURG

71 INF

346 INF

86 CORPS

o TROARN

272 INF

N →

LEGEND

— Second Army Line
  25-29 July
-- First US Army Line
  25 July
— First US Army Line
  29 July
— Enemy formations
  +29 July

SCALE 1:3 93,230

MILES

between the Vire and the Drome River just west of Caumont. Within the II Parachute Corps' sector, the highly rated 3rd Parachute Division (reinforced by a regiment of the newly arrived and experienced 5th Parachute Division) roughly faced the V Corps, while the remnants of the 352nd Infantry Division, a battle group of the 266th Division, and elements of the 275th, 343rd, and 353rd Divisions faced the XIX Corps. In the LXXXIV Corps' sector, the remnants of the *Panzer Lehr* Division—with a regiment of the 5th Parachute Division, a battle group of the 275th Division, and elements of the 2nd SS Panzer Division *Das Reich*—faced the VII Corps, with a third regiment of the 5th Parachute Division on their left. Behind them in army reserve stood the main body of the 275th Infantry Division. Roughly facing the U.S. VIII Corps from east to west were the remnants of the 17th SS Panzergrenadier Division *Götz von Berlichingen*; the main body of the 2nd SS Panzer Division *Das Reich*, with the remnants of the 6th Parachute Regiment; the remnants of the 91st Infantry Division, with a battle group of the 265th Division and elements of the 77th Division; and the remnants of the 243rd Infantry Division.[2]

Up to Cobra, the progress of Bradley's First Army had been costly and slow. After the firm link-up of Utah Beach forces with those of less fortunate Omaha on 13 June, the Americans faced the difficult task of battling through the bogs and watery flats around Carentan and innumerable hamlets of stout stone buildings in the Norman *bocage*. A patchwork of small fields bounded by sunken roads and six-foot-high earthen embankments crowned with virtually impenetrable thickets, the *bocage* hid troop movement and restricted the mobility and main gun range of tanks, which heaved up while climbing banks, exposing their soft undersides to deadly hand-held Panzerfaust fire. In time, the Americans would develop Rhino tanks affixed with pronged blades to cut through the *bocage*.

By 10 June, troops of the 101st Airborne Division were advancing on Carentan, the gateway to the Cotentin Peninsula and the much-desired port of Cherbourg. In two days of fierce fighting, the Americans forced the German 6th Parachute Regiment out of the town, but only into the swampy bush-covered flats where they regrouped and waited to retake this strategically located center with the object of splitting the American beachhead. To accomplish this task, *Brigade-führer* Werner Ostendorff's 17th SS Panzergrenadier Division *Götz von Berlichingen* took the 6th Parachute Regiment under its command and assumed responsibility for preparing an attack to be launched at dawn on 13 June. Leading elements of the 17th SS had started arriving in the LXXXIV Corps' Carentan sector during the night of 10 June after a 200-mile march from the Thouars area between Tours and Nantes, south of the Loire River.[3]

Although the *Götz von Berlichingen* had worked up in the West from October 1943 like the 9th SS *Hohenstaufen*, 10th SS *Frundsberg*, and 12th SS *Hitlerjugend* Panzer Divisions, it was a poor sister to all three. Composed of the 37th and 38th Panzergrenadier Regiments— each with three motorized battalions backed up by an artillery regiment and the 17th Sturmgeschütz Battalion and its thirty-seven self-propelled assault guns—the division had no tanks on its authorized panzer battalion establishment. Reportedly, the division was so poorly outfitted that four of its six panzergrenadier battalions had only improvised transport, some French and Italian in origin, while two battalions in each regiment were mounted on bicycles. Some of the bicycle-borne troops took so long to reach the combat zone that they remained effectively out of battle until the second half of the month. On paper, the personnel strength of the division as of 1 June 1944 was 17,321 all ranks, more than half under age twenty, but many troops were not fully trained, and the division, below strength in noncommissioned officers, lacked two out of five officers. Although deficient in weapons and equipment, the gravity of the Normandy invasion was such that the 17th SS was considered ready to undertake operations.[4]

After release from high-command reserve, the 17th SS Panzergrenadier Division eventually came under the command of the LXXXIV Corps in the St. Lô sector. The divisional reconnaissance battalion reached the Tessy area due south of St. Lô on 8 June and, two days later, took up a position on the right of the 352nd Division near Berigny on the St. Lô–Bayeux road. In the Trevieres-Littry area, one of its patrols clashed with elements of the British 7th Armoured Division, which triggered Allied fears of a counterattack by the entire 17th SS Division. Because of fuel shortages, however, the main body of the division remained stranded around Vers, with the result that only advance parties reached the designated divisional assembly area southwest of Carentan by 11 June. Fuel supplies rushed to the division enabled the advance to be continued to north of Periers, where the German 6th Parachute Infantry Regiment continued to hold the line.

On 11 June, Ostendorff went forward to contact the regimental commander, Col. Friedrich August Baron von der Heydte, while the battle for Carentan raged. Although Ostendorff was reputed to have been an effective commander of boundless energy, it is significant to note that the veteran soldier Heydte formed a low opinion of the 17th SS, whose divisional motto was "Kiss my ass." He not only resented the divisional chief of staff's dismissal of demands for closer liaison with the remark, "We don't do things that way," but also observed how SS officers gave conflicting orders. For their part, the senior commanders of the 17th SS later tried vainly to have Heydte court-martialed for giving up Carentan.[5]

On 13 June, the Germans counterattacked with the expectation of promised Luftwaffe support. Following a meager fifteen-minute barrage that opened at 0545 hours, the 17th SS Panzergrenadier Division assaulted with Sturmgeschütz support and the 6th Parachute Regiment under its command. According to one German paratrooper, the SS men displayed enormous confidence and enthusiasm in looking forward to their first action, but he ventured that they were in for a shock. The ground across which the German troops advanced was swamp covered with bushes, and the whole area was defended tenaciously by Maj. Gen. Maxwell Taylor's U.S. 101st Airborne Division. The attack nonetheless progressed well for almost four hours, with the Germans pouring over the American lines into the southern outskirts of Carentan, but then the Americans delivered a counterpunch. Alerted by Ultra intercepts, Bradley had earlier without explanation ordered

Gerow to send a combat command of the 2nd Armored Division to support Taylor's paratroopers. The cancellation of the promised Luftwaffe support without warning, which left the LXXXIV Corps' chief of staff furious, allowed the German panzergrenadiers and paratroopers to be hurled back by tanks from the 2nd Armored Division.

Yet more than lack of Luftwaffe support determined the outcome. Quite clearly, German forces lacked the means to mount a concerted attack to recapture Carentan, for as late as 12 June, the 17th SS Division paraded only two-thirds of its effectives. The attack, mainly carried out by the 37th Panzergrenadier Regiment with paratroopers, also suffered from a serious shortage of ammunition for the heavy weapons whose fire was needed to support the action. By the end of the day, Carentan remained firmly in American hands. Fighting continued for weeks, with few advances made by the panzergrenadiers, who were forced onto the defensive. On 16 June, Ostendorff was badly wounded and replaced by *Standartenführer* Otto Baum, who led the division from 16 June to 30 July. On 18 June, the 353rd Division relieved the 17th SS in the Periers-Neumesnil sector. By July, divisional strength had fallen to 8,500.[6]

Hard evidence later revealed that around the time of the battle for Carentan, the 17th SS Panzergrenadier Division committed atrocities. In the airborne assault of Normandy, the U.S. 507th Parachute Infantry Regiment of the 82nd Airborne Division accidentally dropped farther east than planned, with many paratroopers scattered to the wind. A number of these paratroopers linked up six miles south of Carentan in the village of Graignes, where they were warmly greeted by the inhabitants. With an eventual strength approaching 182 paratroopers, this force beat off an uncoordinated 17th SS Panzergrenadier attack on 11 June. In the face of another attack of regimental size launched at 1900 hours, however, the paratroopers melted away. The Germans then swarmed into the village, where an American medical captain still tended to the wounded in an aid station established in the church. On discovering the Americans, the Germans ordered them outside and divided them into one group of nine and another of five. They then marched the first group south and the group of five to the area of a local pond. There they bayoneted the wounded prisoners and threw them into the pond, one on top of another. They also killed three more prisoners in the church and two in a nearby field.

When the other group of nine arrived four kilometers north of Le Mesnil-Angot, the *Götz von Berlichingen* men ordered them to dig a pit. They then shot each prisoner in the back of the head and threw their bodies into the hole. Back in the village, they also rounded up forty-four inhabitants whom they accused of being collaborators. They subsequently shot two priests and two women, one of whom was eighty years old. The German troops then ransacked the houses and poured gasoline over the bodies of the murdered priests and women. After setting these on fire, they went on to burn the entire village, destroying 66 homes and damaging another 159 buildings. In all, they murdered nineteen airborne prisoners and twenty-eight villagers.[7]

The second Waffen SS division to fight on the American front rolled out of Montauban, north of Toulouse in southern France, on 8 June. With 15,000 men and 209 panzers and self-propelled assault guns, the 2nd SS Panzer Division *Das Reich*, under *Brigadeführer* Heinz Lammerding, commenced a 450-mile march that ended more than two weeks later in Normandy. To a man, the largely conscript division looked forward to participating in a counterattack that would throw the Allies back into the sea.[8] For French resistance fighters, however, news of the D-Day landing spurred them into open insurrection. From pockets of the countryside never really controlled by German garrison troops, various groups of the fragmented and quarrelsome French *maquis* resistance immediately began to mount bolder operations aimed at sabotaging and subverting German efforts. In this, they were substantially aided and abetted by the British Special Operations Executive, which arranged the sabotage of railway flat cars, forcing the *Das Reich*'s heavy armor to drive rather than go by rail to save gas. The SOE, along with the special operations arm of the U.S. Office of

Strategic Services, also attempted to foment guerrilla warfare in the German rear.

On 7 June, the day Lammerding received a warning order to move, an emboldened group of communist *franc-tireurs et patisans* overwhelmed most of the German garrison in the town of Tulle along the *Das Reich*'s route. In keeping with the policy of Army Group G to use fighting formations against the resistance, the *Das Reich*'s reconnaissance battalion, under *Sturmbannführer* Heinrich Wulf, received orders to restore the situation in Tulle. Irritated by the loss of forty-five division casualties to resistance fighters between Montauban and Tulle, Wulf's troops secured the town within twenty minutes at a cost of 3 dead and 9 wounded. On discovering the bodies of 139 German garrison soldiers killed by resistance fighters—40 allegedly mutilated and likely executed—all French males in the area were also rounded up the next day.[9]

From all indications, Lammerding now ordered reprisal hangings. Lammerding had been Eicke's operations officer in the 3rd SS Division *Totenkopf* and subsequently selected by Himmler to be chief of staff to the ruthless *Obergruppenführer* Erich von dem Bach-Zelewski, chief of armed SS antipartisan operations in Russia. In this capacity, Lammerding had planned and oversaw a series of extensive cleansing operations in the Pripet Marshes that claimed the lives of 15,000 Soviet partisans and resulted in the indiscriminate shooting of an undetermined number of Russian civilians. For success with Bach-Zelewski, Himmler rewarded Lammerding with command of the *Das Reich* in December 1943.[10]

On 5 June, Lammerding had written a memorandum urging a more aggressive "blood and ashes" campaign against the terrorist threat in the Cahors-Aurillac-Tulle area. With the object of convincing the population that the miseries of repression resulted from the actions of terrorists, he recommended deporting 5,000 males to Germany on 15 June and publicly hanging—not shooting—three terrorists for every German soldier wounded and ten for every German soldier killed by terrorist action. Lammerding's memorandum, forwarded to Army

Group G though not necessarily endorsed by General Blaskowitz, resulted in the placement of the *Das Reich* under the temporary command of the LXVI Reserve Corps for antiterrorist operations in the Tulle-Limoges area. In Blaskowitz's view, French civilians had a responsibility to distinguish themselves from terrorists in a visible way and take an active stand against them to the point of turning them in. His control over the *Das Reich* was limited, however.[11]

In a proclamation to the citizens of Tulle on 9 June, the Germans announced that for the 40 soldiers murdered in a most abominable way by communist gangs, 120 *maquis* or their accomplices would be hanged and their bodies thrown into the river. The proclamation further warned that in the future, Lammerding's originally recommended ratio of three hangings for every wounded German soldier and ten for every one killed would apply. Of the 3,000 males rounded up and screened at Tulle for their connections with the French resistance, 400 suspects between the ages of seventeen and forty-two remained, most of whom were not active resistance fighters. The hangings from lamp posts and first-floor balconies commenced one by one at 1600 and continued until 1900 hours, when the Germans apparently ran out of rope. In all, 99 men were hanged before the executions ceased. For hygiene reasons, the bodies were not thrown into the river, but tossed into the town garbage dump. Given the urgency to get to Normandy, plans to deal with other French resistance pockets farther east were cancelled the next day by a high command order placing the *Das Reich* under the tactical control of Army Group B in Normandy. Panzers and tracked vehicles that that had been forced to burn scarce gas by road for lack of flat car availability caused by sabotage and Allied air strikes were now ordered to move by train—panzers from the Perigueux railhead and half-tracks from Limoges.[12]

By this point, the *Das Reich* was strung out over 300 kilometers of unfavorable terrain and short of fuel, with 60 percent of panzers and 30 percent of half-tracks unserviceable. The Figeac-Clermont-Ferrand-Limoges triangle, according to Lammerding, was also entirely in the hands of terrorists who hounded the *Das Reich*, besieged timid

German garrisons, and completely paralyzed Vichy government forces. As he reported, the task of eliminating this danger called for ruthless and determined action on the part of local forces rather than panzer divisions. Yet on moving toward the Perigueux railhead, his division continued to encounter incessant pinprick resistance and road blockages from *franc-tireurs et patisans*.

On the evening of 9 June, north of Limoges, the *franc-tireurs* also captured the popular commanding officer of the 3rd Battalion of the *Der Führer* Regiment, *Sturmbannführer* Helmut Kampfe, which triggered a vigorous search to find him. The search yielded an SOE agent, Viloet Szabo, who was later shot, but never Kampfe. The next day, his close friend, *Sturmbannführer* Otto Diekmann, acting on a tip, instituted a sweep of the small town of Oradour-sur-Glane with 150 men of the 1st Battalion of the *Der Führer* Regiment. In short order, Diekmann's troops herded 650 inhabitants into the town common, ordering the men into three rows and about 400 women and children into the confines of the church a block away. Just before 1530 hours, the men were separated into groups of 40 to 50 and marched into nearby barns and garages. The Germans then opened fire on them and set their execution chambers ablaze. At the same time, SS men ignited an incendiary device in the church and began hurling grenades and emptying magazines into the female throng inside. After setting the entire town on fire and shooting down those still moving, they departed the following morning. Only a few French survived.[13]

The German war diary entry for the day recorded simply that surrounding Oradour-sur-Glane produced 548 enemy dead and 2 friendly casualties. In fact, 648 French citizens perished, with only 52 identifiable. This appears to have been good enough for Lammerding, but not for the *Der Führer*'s regimental commander, *Standartenführer* Sylvester Stadler, who wanted Diekmann court-martialed. Vichy officials, army headquarters, and the local German commander also thought that the *Das Reich* had overreached itself at Oradour. Requests for inquiries and the court-martial of Diekmann followed, but as he was killed in Normandy on 30 June, nothing ever came of them during the war. By Eastern Front measures familiar to Diekmann, who served there, Oradour-sur-Glane may have been a modest reprisal, but a consensus developed among many local *maquis* commanders that no armed action was worth such a terrible price. Had reprisals like this have been sustained, it is also probable that the resistance would have come under enormous pressure to desist absolutely from making any attacks on Germans. For this reason, as well as unfavorable terrain, the *Das Reich* battle with resistance fighters effectively ended north of Limoges at Bellac on the road to Poitiers. In the north, the *maquis* did not attempt to attack such a formidable force as the *Das Reich*.

On 13 June, the division crossed the Loire at Saumur and Tours and, owing to the Allied air threat, began moving only by night. Two days later, their panzers followed from Perigueux, and between 15 and 30 June, the division, having lost only thirty-five killed on the long march, trickled into the rear areas of the Normandy front. As elements arrived, they were committed in driblets to plug gaps in the sagging German line. Weidinger's *Der Führer* battle group deployed to the British sector on 28 June. Only on 10 July, after having suffered heavy losses, were they united under Lammerding, who was wounded sixteen days later.[14]

By the time the 2nd SS Panzer Division *Das Reich* reached Normandy, the Allied beachhead had solidified, and on 18 June, Collins's U.S.VII Corps plunged through the neck of the Cotentin Peninsula to the western coast at Barneville-Carteret. This movement sliced the German Seventh Army in half and doomed Cherbourg, which Hitler declared a fortress to be defended to the last round. Hitler's hopes and German morale had been raised by the commencement of the V-1 rocket offensive against London from Pas de Calais bases on 13 June. Hitler thought that this would oblige the Allies to land there to deal with the rocket bases and offer a better chance of defeating them as the Germans were best prepared in that area. He further expected that winning here would lead to the abandonment of the secondary Normandy feint. Such thinking meant that the Germans in Normandy had to stand fast. In fact, divisions were not released from the Pas de Calais until the end of June, by which time Cherbourg had fallen to Collins and Dollmann had committed suicide. The unfortunate Hausser, who thereafter assumed command of the Seventh Army, almost immediately began to experience the enormous difficulties involved in the logistical supply and reinforcement of German forces far to the west of Caen. Serious fuel and ammunition shortages would continue to plague German forces in the distant west of Normandy.[15]

The top priority given to the capture of Cherbourg by Bradley's First Army allowed the Germans a two-week window in which to strengthen their defenses of the southern Cotentin. On 3 July, Middleton's VIII Corps attacked to gain the Coutances–St. Lô ridge line with three divisions abreast—the 79th Infantry on the right, the 82nd Airborne in the center, and the 90th Infantry on the left. In five days of battle west of the town of La Haye-du-Puits, the 79th Division, for an advance of six kilometers, incurred 2,000 casualties, many inflicted by a battle group of the *Das Reich* hastily dispatched to that sector to shore up the sagging German line. Only the 82nd Airborne attained its objective, the Poterie Hills north of the town, but by the time of their capture, the division paraded half the strength it brought to Normandy. Advancing on Mont Castre, the 90th Infantry Division suffered roughly the same number of casualties as the 79th and also failed to take its objective.

On 4 July, the 83rd Infantry Division of Collins's VII Corps attacked from south of Carentan toward Sainteny, halfway to Périers, but failed to advance more than a few hundred meters down the Carentan-Périers road at a cost of almost 1,400 casualties. For a total gain of about one and a half kilometers the next day, another 750 casualties resulted. On 6 July, Collins committed the 4th Infantry Division on the right, but by evening, both divisions were not quite two-thirds of the way toward Sainteny. Significantly, the 17th SS Panzergrenadier Division and the rest of the 2nd SS Panzer Division held the line against the VII Corps.[16]

The commitment of the *Das Reich* forward of Sainteny to hold back the VII Corps ensured that the Germans had no reserves at hand when Corlett's XIX Corps launched an attack on St. Lô. As a preliminary step, the 30th Infantry Division crossed the weakly defended Vire-Taute Canal on 7 July and established a small bridgehead near St. Jean-de-Daye. At this juncture, on learning that elements of the dispersed 2nd SS Panzer were on their way from the west, Bradley assigned the 3rd Armored Division to Corlett. In order to take advantage of this initial success, Corlett planned to pass the 3rd Armored through the 30th Infantry and have it seize a ridge west of St. Lô for later operations against the crossroads in town. The hasty introduction of the 3rd Armored into the bridgehead created considerable congestion, however, buying valuable time for the *Panzer Lehr* Division, which was rushing to restore the situation. Eventually, on 9 July, the 3rd Armored advanced to take Hauts-Vents by evening.

Meanwhile, another leading company of 3rd Armored tanks took a wrong turn and collided with an American tank destroyer battalion that, mistaking them for the 2nd SS, knocked out two Shermans. On the same day, elements of the 17th SS Panzergrenadier and the 2nd SS Panzer Divisions, having lost contact with the LXXXIV Corps, attacked only to return to their departure positions. The already depleted and exhausted *Panzer Lehr* delayed attacking until the night of 11 July, when four assault groups ran headlong into the recently transferred U.S. 9th Infantry Division, which was preparing to attack southward. The hastily mounted attack over unfamiliar ground with no time for reconnaissance only momentarily surprised the Americans, who handily prevented the Germans from attaining their objectives. The *Panzer Lehr* lost eighteen panzers and more than 700 men—one quarter of its effective combat strength—but it had momentarily saved St. Lô.[17]

By 15 July, after twelve days of fighting, Middleton's VIII Corps had cleared La Haye-du-Puits, captured Mont Castre, and reached the Ay Estuary–Seves River line. The cost of fighting through eleven kilometers of *bocage*, which still left the VIII Corps only one third of the way to its original objective of the Coutances–St. Lô ridge, amounted to 10,000 casualties. The VII Corps' attack of 4 July cost another 4,800 dead, wounded, and missing in gaining fifteen square kilometers of ground. The XIX Corps' attack on St. Lô continued after the defeat of the *Panzer Lehr*'s counterattack, with the U.S. 29th Infantry Division leading the way. Through 11 and 12 July, the division incurred 1,000 casualties for scant progress. Following the commitment of the newly arrived 35th Infantry Division two days later, more fierce fighting against the tough but increasingly enervated German 352nd Infantry Division occurred, but on 18 July, the 29th liberated the town of St. Lô. This cut the lateral east-to-west movement of the fuel- and ammunition-starved Germans. Again the casualties were heavy—3,000 lost in the 29th and another 2,000 in the 35th. All told, from 7 July to the capture of St. Lô, Corlett's XIX Corps suffered 10,077 casualties. In fighting during the month of July from the Carentan plain to the seizure of the St. Lô–Périers road, the U.S. First Army's casualties totalled 40,000.[18]

A desperate Bradley now began to look for better ways of cracking German defenses than continuing to fight a costly battle of attrition. For the first time, he decided to attack on a narrow front with Collins's VII Corps delivering the main effort in a southwestern thrust aimed at capturing Coutances and cutting off the western flank of the German LXXXIV Corps. Bounded on the east by the Vire River, the VII Corps was to attack across the St. Lô–Périers road through a parallel rectangular "carpet" previously plastered by saturation bombing. As planned, Operation Cobra called for an initial breach by three infantry divisions: the 30th on the left to secure the eastern shoulder, the 4th in the center to cut the St. Lô–Coutances road, and the 9th on the right to secure the western shoulder. Once the breach was made, the motorized 1st Infantry Division, supported by a combat command of the 3rd Armored Division, was to drive on Marigny and thence to the high ground north of Coutances. At the same time, the remainder of the 3rd Armored was to advance south, protecting the left flank of the 1st Infantry Division. Concurrently, the 2nd Armored Division, which like the 3rd had six rather than the normal three tanks battalions, was to strike from the eastern half of the breakthrough and sweep deep into enemy territory, establishing blocking positions from Tessy-sur-Vire to Cérences near the coast. Overall, the object was to have the VII Corps turn west and encircle the enemy in front of Middleton's VIII Corps, which would be advancing from north to south. During this phase, the V and XIX Corps were to intensify attacks in the east to hold German attention.[19]

No military operation ever goes exactly according to plan, and Cobra was no exception. Originally planned for 21 July, the operation had to be put off until 1300 hours on 24 July because of unfavorable weather. Persistent overcast and low-hanging clouds on that date produced a further postponement, however, and the last-minute cancellation of the bombing. Unfortunately, not all of the aircraft were recalled, and several bombers continued with their runs, killing 25 and wounding another 131 soldiers in the 30th Infantry Division. While this contretemps lured some Germans into thinking it was a failed attack, Collins feared that they might now prepare for the worst.

More favorable weather predictions encouraged American commanders to try again the next day. With the arrival of the predicted good weather, 350 fighter-bombers began striking with bombs and napalm at 0938 hours on 25 July. They were followed by 1,500 Eighth Air Force heavy bombers and about 400 medium bombers of the Ninth Air Force, which in several instances dropped their bomb loads short. Total VII Corps losses amounted to 108 dead and 472 injured, mostly in the three assaulting divisions. Despite this devastating shock, the 9th, 4th, and 30th Infantry Divisions managed to rally and hesitantly cross the start line around 1100 hours, supported by more than 1,000 artillery pieces. The Germans suffered greatly, but some had infiltrated the safety zone and survived along with others in well-dug-in positions. The reserve 275th Division and Flak battalion of the 17th SS were wiped out, but the German artillery escaped intact. By the evening of the first day, stiffer resistance than expected denied the three American divisions their objectives and held their advance to two miles.[20]

The American attack, which caught Hausser off guard as he expected the main blow to land in the Caen area, nonetheless penetrated the fragmented German line. Collins therefore daringly decided on the afternoon of 25 July to risk unleashing two of his mobile exploitation formations to attain the first day's objectives. On the morning of 26 July, the 1st Infantry Division, supported by Combat Command B* of the 3rd Armored Division, struck out toward Marigny. On the way, it ran into German reinforcements, including two panzer companies of the 2nd SS Division *Das Reich*, which prevented it from reaching more than the outskirts of Marigny by dark.

Meanwhile, on the VII Corps' left flank, the 2nd Armored Division passed through the 30th Infantry Division, reaching the crossroads town of St. Gilles by midafternoon and Canisy, far behind the *Panzer Lehr*'s lines, by dusk. South of Canisy, the division pushed on through the night to the area of Le Mesnil-Herman, northwest of Tessy-sur-Vire, at 0300 hours. The German defense had been broken through. Driving through the night, the 4th Infantry Division in the center experienced the same melting away of German forces. By dawn, the division was eleven kilometers south of the St. Lô–Périers road.

On the morning of 27 July, Marigny fell to the 1st Division, and Collins ordered the 3rd Armored Division to drive between Marigny and St. Gilles to complete the envelopment of the Germans. Middleton's VIII Corps meanwhile began to push south, triggering panic among the usually reliable Waffen SS. Men of the 17th SS Panzergrenadier Division *Götz von Berlichingen*, defending near Périers, broke under the VIII Corps' onslaught and streamed to the rear. The LXXXIV Corps was disintegrating. As the Germans withdrew, the VIII Corps' pace rapidly increased; it captured Coutances on 28 July and established contact with the VII Corps, which was closing in from the east. Two days later, Middleton's troops entered Avranches.[21]

---

* In action, the American armored division usually divided into three combat commands—CCA, CCB, and CCR (reserve)—each a tailored mix of tank, infantry, and artillery, with reconnaissance, engineer, tank destroyer, antiaircraft, and supporting services.

The American breakthrough aimed at envelopment, but it became a breakout and pursuit instead. On the evening of 27 July, a shocked Hausser realized that his LXXXIV Corps was in grave danger of being cut off and annihilated. He therefore ordered the corps to withdraw southward and take up a strong north-south defensive line cutting the road to Coutances. In the small corridor, he concentrated elements of four divisions, but the withdrawal of the rest of his corps into the face of Collins's VII Corps turned into a disorderly rout. In the chaos, *Obersturmbannführer* Christian Tychsen, who had replaced the wounded Lammerding in command of the 2nd SS Panzer Division *Das Reich*, tried vainly to rally his men. He died on 28 July in an air attack after only two days in command. Significantly, of Hausser's two panzer divisions, the *Panzer Lehr*, with only 2,200 men and forty-five tanks, had splintered under the full brunt of the Cobra assault, and the weakly led *Das Reich* remained dispersed in battle groups. This, too, is significant since most of the 150 to 180 panzers and 30,000 German fighting men in the area north of Coutances between the Vire River and the ocean on 25 July belonged to the *Das Reich*.

By 28 July, what was left of the 2nd SS Panzer Division occupied the high ground at Montpinchon and Cerisy-la-Salle, east of Coutances. Here they were joined by the weakened 17th SS Panzergrenadier Division, commanded by the senior officer remaining, *Standartenführer* Otto Baum, one of Eicke's favorites apparently unsullied by criminality, who took charge of the leaderless *Das Reich* and remnants of the 6th Parachute Regiment and prepared to execute a southern withdrawal guarding the flank of the LXXXIV Corps. When leading elements of the U.S. 3rd Armored Division bumped into Baum's force on the same day, they found the going extremely tough. Late that evening, the commander of the LXXXIV Corps ordered Baum to counterattack the American penetration, a decision supported by Hausser, who feared that pulling back straight south would split the Seventh Army in two. Kluge, who had personally taken command of Army Group B after Rommel was wounded on 17 July, objected violently. Preferring to counterattack in the east to plug the gap between the collapsing LXXXIV Corps and the II Parachute Corps, he cancelled the order for a counterattack in the west.[22]

The redoubtable commander of the 6th Parachute Regiment, Heydte, did not receive the cancellation when ordered at 0300 hours on 29 July to attack from the area of Roncey toward Percy. Grimly but gamely, he cobbled together some *Das Reich* panzers and a few 17th SS assault guns, and around 0800 hours, he launched his paratroops against leading elements of the U.S. 2nd Armored Division at Notre Dame-de-Cenilly. By midmorning, his hasty attack foundered, not surprisingly perhaps, because the *Das Reich* tank commander, although only a major, refused to take orders from Heydte. In the end, having lost half his force, Heydte and the panzer major withdrew independently southward toward St. Denis-le-Gast.

In the confusion of this war without fronts, similar German actions became commonplace. Just north of St. Denis around 0100 hours on 30 July, 1,200 men and ninety tanks, assault guns, and other armored vehicles of the 2nd and 17th SS Divisions smashed through the command posts of both the 3rd Battalion, 67th Armored Regiment, and the 2nd Battalion, 41st Armored Infantry, the reserve regiment of the 2nd Armored Division. The German drive also struck the 78th Armored Field Artillery Battalion, positioned between St. Denis and Lengronne. About the same time, another 2,500 men of the 2nd SS Panzer Division and other formations hit other elements of the 67th Armored and 41st Infantry Regiments near Camry, north of Lengronne. The confusing engagement, fought desperately in the light of burning vehicles, lasted until dawn. The 2nd Armored Division survived the night shaken, but only slightly bruised as the Germans fought only to escape, not to exploit their penetration by rolling up the American line to the left and right.[23]

At the end of July, Kluge launched his eastern counterstroke to plug the six-mile gap between the LXXXIV Corps and the II Parachute Corps. Conducted by the XXXXVII Panzer Corps with the British-mauled 2nd Panzer and 116th Panzer Divisions (the latter released from the Fifteenth Army), the counterattack plan called for the

352nd Infantry Division to secure the assembly area along the Vire River and for remnants from the *Panzer Lehr* to hold the Americans off at Percy. As the 2nd Panzer moved on Tessy-sur-Vire, however, Corlett's XIX Corps sent the newly assigned 30th Infantry Division and a tank command from the 2nd Armored Division to take the town and push on toward Percy. He also pushed the 28th and 29th Infantry Divisions up the west side of the Vire. This resulted in a fierce clash with the 2nd Panzer Division on 28 July, which broke the momentum of the XXXXVII Panzer Corps' counterattack before it developed.

By the time the 116th Division was ready to attack, it received new orders not to attack westward into the American flank, but to go to the rescue of the 2nd Panzer Division, which was locked in battle in Tessy-sur-Vire. On the morning of 30 July, the 116th Division attacked east of Percy over ground far less favorable than that which it would have travelled in a thrust due west. As in Operation Epsom, massed panzer attack in daylight proved folly because of Allied air superiority. In the afternoon, the 116th's commander called a halt to the attack and gave orders to hold on until the weary 2nd Panzer Division withdrew east across the Vire. The last hope of halting the American breakout thus died.[24]

Once again, the Waffen SS played the "fireman" role as they had on the Eastern Front, always fighting and perhaps even fanning the flames, but never coming close to putting out the fire. An important difference, of course, was that on the Eastern Front, they enjoyed Stuka support within the fair-weather *blitzkrieg* combination that proved stronger than the sum of its parts—wide-open spaces, good weather, and air superiority. Loss of the air part, however, doomed the combination and condemned the Germans in Normandy to fight offensively only by night in less favorable conditions.

At the same time, they became primarily a battle group force, unable to mount and coordinate operations at divisional and corps levels. The 2nd SS Panzer Division *Das Reich*, with half the manpower and the bulk of the panzers, failed to play any decisive role as, from the beginning, it trickled in piecemeal to plug gaps and help shore up sagging German lines. Ad hoc battle groups under Weidinger deployed first to the British sector during Epsom, then to the 353rd Infantry Division around La Haye-du-Puits on 5 July. Another battle group, under *Obersturmbannführer* Gunther-Eberhardt Wislency, commander of the *Deutschland* Regiment, served with the *Panzer Lehr* until 18 July, enduring sixty-four American attacks in eleven days, fifty-six without panzer support. The 17th SS Panzergrenadier Division, with no tanks on establishment, also had to be buttressed by the *Das Reich*'s panzers. Long dependence on Stuka support had further contributed to the German neglect of artillery, which proved hard to coordinate in any case to support widely dispersed battle groups fighting independently of each other. Battery for battery, the Germans matched the Allies, but they could not mass artillery fire with great effect. The direct fire of panzers was no substitute for the concentrated indirect fire of artillery in offensive operations, and German officers like Helmut Ritgen recognized this. German artillery was too weak.

That said, 2nd SS Panzer companies were among the few—including the pulverized *Panzer Lehr*, 3rd Parachute, and 353rd Divisions—to put up effective resistance after 25 July. Although restricted to less advantageous short ranges, the superior panzers of the *Das Reich* scored ninety-eight tank kills in one eight-day period alone. Panther aces like *Unterscharführer* Ernst Barkmann also chalked up individual tallies of twenty-five kills, but such personal successes were more reminiscent of mythical Norse heroes battling for personal glory or Valhalla than the modern profession of arms—and certainly not enough to reverse American operational ascendancy.[25]

Had the 2nd SS Panzer Division *Das Reich* arrived in Normandy sooner, the Germans would have stood a better chance. Better yet, had Kluge accepted the advice of Maj. Gen. Hans Speidel, Army Group B's chief of staff, and transferred the 1st SS Panzer Division *Leibstandarte* to the American front before the fall of St. Lô, the German position would have been greatly strengthened. Kluge refused because his eyes remained firmly fixed on the Caen sector, where he still planned to use both the I and II Panzer Corps in a major spoiling attack against Anglo-Canadian forces. Goodwood put an abrupt end to his attack plans, but not his fears of a breakthrough in that area. Revealingly, on the day of Cobra, Kluge chose to go to the Caen area, where Operation Spring opened, as he continued to believe that a renewal of a British offensive in the Caen area would have far more serious consequences than an American breakthrough in the *bocage*. In fact, Montgomery planned to follow Spring with a 12 Corps attack west of the Orne on 28 July and a subsequent push by the 8 Corps east of the Orne toward Falaise on 30 July. All three operations were to be preliminary to another Goodwood-style offensive. The Operation Spring attack launched by Simonds's 2 Canadian Corps on the Caen front on 25 July reinforced Kluge's fatal conviction during the first critical hours of Cobra that the American main attack farther west was diversionary.[26]

The 2 Canadian Corps' operation had three phases, the first of which called for simultaneous night attacks by the 2nd and 3rd Canadian Infantry Divisions to capture by first light, respectively, May-sur-Orne/Verrières hamlet and Tilly-la-Campagne. In phase two, the 2nd Division was to take Fontenay-le-Marmion and Rocquancourt, while the 7th Armoured Division seized the high ground at Cramesnil-la-Bruyère, prepared to exploit forward to the area of Cintheaux. Once the 7th Armoured reached its objective, the 3rd Division, less one brigade, was to secure Garcelles-Secqueville. During the last phases, which were tentative only, the Guards Armoured Division was to pass through the 7th Armoured and, with the remaining brigade of the 3rd Division, capture La Hogue woods. The 7th Armoured was then to push on to the high ground north of Cintheaux, considered to be the key to the Germans' main defense system south of Caen. While considerable air support was allocated to Spring, the operation was not deemed dependent upon it. A total of nine field, nine medium, and two heavy regiments actually fired in support of Spring.[27]

The Canadians faced elements of five Waffen SS panzer divisions, three army divisions, and one Jagdpanther and three Tiger battalions. The 1st SS Panzer Division *Leibstandarte* held the front from Verrières

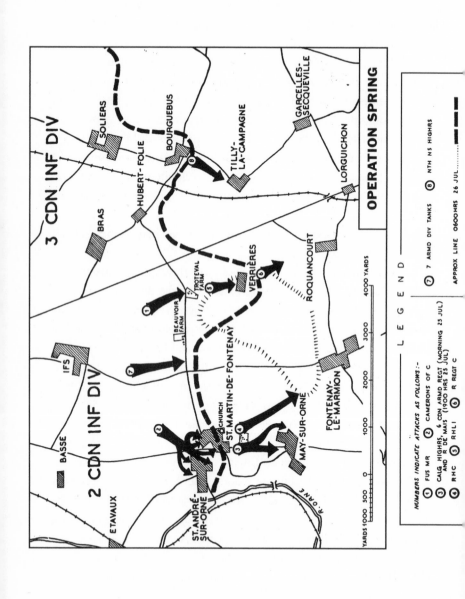

OPERATION SPRING

3 CDN INF DIV

2 CDN INF DIV

SOLIERS

BOURGUEBUS

HUBERT-FOLIE

BRAS

GARCELLES-
SECQUEVILLE

TILLY-
LA-CAMPAGNE

LORGUICHON

BASSE

IFS

TROTEVAL
FARM

BEAUVOIR
FARM

VERRIÈRES

ROQUANCOURT

ETAVAUX

ST. ANDRÉ-
SUR-ORNE

CHURCH

ST.MARTIN-DE-FONTENAY

MAY-SUR-ORNE

FONTENAY-
LE-MARMION

R.ORNE

YARDS 1000   500   0   1000   2000   3000   4000 YARDS

L E G E N D

NUMBERS INDICATE ATTACKS AS FOLLOWS :-

① FUS MR   ② CAMERONS OF C
③ CALG HIGHRS, 6 CDN ARMD REGT (MORNING 25 JUL)
   AND R DE MAIS (1900 HRS 25 JUL)
④ RHC   ⑤ RHLI   ⑥ R REGT C

⑦ 7 ARMD DIV TANKS   ⑧ NTH NS HIGHRS

APPROX LINE 0600 HRS 26 JUL ....

eastward and the 272nd Infantry Division the area between the village and the Orne. The 101st SS Heavy Panzer Battalion lay north of Rocquancourt and the 503rd Heavy Panzer Battalion south of Tilly. The 654th Heavy Jagdpanther Battalion, the only one in the west, was but minutes away. The 12th SS *Hitlerjugend* lay northeast of Tilly. As a result of Goodwood and Atlantic, the 272nd Division had been reinforced with a 2nd Panzer Division battle group consisting of about a dozen Panthers, a depleted panzergrenadier battalion, and a tank destroyer platoon of 75-millimeter Jagdpanzers. Behind this divisional reserve placed within thirty minutes of May-sur-Orne, Dietrich retained his own corps reserve of two battle groups from the 9th SS Panzer Division *Hohenstaufen*. These two battle groups, one commanded by *Obersturmbannführer* Otto Meyer and the other by *Obersturmbannführer* Emil Zollhofer, constituted the only Waffen SS reserve in France. The remaining operational reserve in the theater was the 116th Panzer Division, deployed astride the Laison River about forty-five minutes from Verrières.

The Canadians had good intelligence about what they faced, which is why Simonds reasoned that the built-up areas of St. Andre-sur-Orne and May-sur-Orne to the west offered the best cover for an attack in which even a partial success might gain Verrières Ridge. It also appeared clear that the attack would have to be conducted in darkness and the crest of Verrières Ridge gained before daylight exposure to devastating long-range panzer and assault-gun fire.[28]

As the road between St. Andre-sur-Orne and Hubert-Folie had been selected as the start line, the 2nd Division's attack plan included a preliminary operation by the 6th Brigade to secure St. Martin-de-Fontenay and the area of Troteval farm. This action commenced on the evening of 24 July with the Fusiliers de Mont-Royal capturing Troteval farm and the Queen's Own Cameron Highlanders of Canada, supported by Sherbrooke Fusilier tanks, clearing through St. Andre toward St. Martin. The divisional plan from this juncture called for the 4th and 5th Brigades to pass, respectively, through the Fusiliers de Mont-Royal and Camerons, taking each under its command and thus creating a gap through which elements of the 7th Armoured Division could exploit forward. Within the 4th Brigade, the Royal Hamilton Light Infantry was ordered to attack Verrières hamlet, after which the Royal Regiment of Canada was to advance to take Rocquancourt. In the 5th Brigade, the Calgary Highlanders were directed to capture the eastern outskirts of May-sur-Orne, from which, at 0530 hours, the Black Watch, supported by a squadron of 1st Hussar tanks and a troop of 17-pounders, would advance to seize Fontenay-le-Marmion. During this phase, the 22nd Armoured Brigade of the 7th Armoured Division was also to move up from Ifs, prepared to counter possible panzer counterattacks and exploit forward as opportunities presented themselves. Those battalions not involved in the attack—the South Saskatchewans from the 6th Brigade, the Essex from the 4th Brigade, and the Maisonneuves from the 5th Brigade— were curiously grouped as a reserve under the 6th Brigade.[29]

The main attack opened at 0330 hours on 25 July and, on the 2nd Division's front, yielded an early spectacular success by the 4th Brigade. Despite having to clear an insecure start line before attacking, the Royal Hamilton Light Infantry under Lt. Col. John Rockingham managed under cover of darkness to rush into Verrières hamlet. There-after, supported by 17-pounder fire from Troteval farm and on-call concentrations by field and medium guns, he wrested control of the hamlet from the Germans in a fierce close-quarter struggle that forced well-dug-in armored and infantry elements of the 1st SS Regiment to withdraw by 0800 hours. As the hamlet lay in a depression just below the crest of Verrières Ridge, they also managed to consolidate. The violent counterattack that followed was, in turn, repelled by 6- and 17-pounder fire and hand-held antitank weapons. Rockingham's remarkable success, accomplished despite a low ratio of attackers to defenders, caused enough of a stir in Panzer Group West headquarters for Kluge to drive to Dietrich's headquarters and authorize the use of the 9th SS Division *Hohenstaufen* to counterattack.[30]

Once the Royal Hamilton Light Infantry reported that they firmly held Verrières, the Royal Regiment commenced phase two.

The battalion moved out toward Rocquancourt at 0600 hours, supported by a tank squadron of the 1st Hussars. Elements of the British 1st Royal Tank Regiment paralleled to the west from Beauvoir farm, while the 5th Royal Tanks closer to Troteval farm traded shots with German armor near Tilly. With fighting still in progress in Verrières, the Royal Regiment's commanding officer chose to skirt the hamlet and push on, unfortunately without artillery barrage support. Even this may not have helped, however, as the Royals faced two well-entrenched panzergrenadier battalions supported by Jagdpanzers of the 1st SS Sturmgeschütz Battalion and Mark IVs of the 2nd SS Panzer Battalion. The Royal Tank Regiment reported about thirty German panzers hull-down on the ridge between Rocquancourt and Fontenay. Once over the ridge, both units found themselves in the killing zone of an elaborate and cleverly camouflaged German reverse-slope defense that produced an avalanche of fire from antitank guns, panzers, machine guns, tank destroyers, mortars, artillery, and infantry. Enfiladed from the dominant Tilly-la-Campagne feature and similarly exposed to fire from the right, the 4th Brigade's advance was abruptly and savagely halted.[31]

Meanwhile, to the west, where the Germans straddled both sides of the river, the 5th Brigade's attack had also run into serious snags from the beginning. The task of clearing the enemy from the built-up area of St. Martin proved simply beyond the capacity of the depleted Camerons, who had been under constant pressure in St. Andre since 20 July. The one-kilometer open stretch between St. Martin and May-sur-Orne also afforded the Germans covered approaches that enabled them to infiltrate into the Canadian rear. Even as the Calgary Highlanders crossed their start line, the last company at 0347 hours, the Camerons were struggling in the darkness to secure it. A grim battle ensued almost immediately, forcing the Calgaries to clear position after position, but each time they assumed the enemy had been blasted away, more Germans seemed to trickle in behind them. Poor communications and casualties among key personnel aggravated this increasingly nasty and confused situation. When one company reportedly did manage to enter May-sur-Orne shortly before 0600 hours, it was forced by heavy mortar and artillery fire to retire 200 yards to the north. A second company was likewise summarily ejected midmorning. At 0630 hours, the reserve company reported that unable to progress, it was digging in only 300 yards beyond the start line.[32]

At 0715 hours, the Black Watch, originally slated to attack Fontenay-le-Marmion at 0530 hours, was now told to go ahead. As the battalion commander had been mortally wounded earlier that morning, a company commander took charge and recoordinated artillery and tank support on the mistaken assumption that May-sur-Orne appeared to be lightly held. In fact, it was held by a well-entrenched battalion of the German 272nd Division. At 0910, the Black Watch attacked on foot from the factory area south of St. Martin up the open slope toward Fontenay-le-Marmion and almost immediately came under effective fire from May. The 1st Hussars tank squadron that was assigned for support at the same time became embroiled in desperate battle with enemy antitank guns and panzers.

Around 1030, the commander of the 272nd Division ordered his 2nd Panzer reserve to restore the situation by striking against St. Martin. Led by about a dozen Panthers, the reserve battle group reached the crest of the ridge at the same time as the Black Watch, which was all but annihilated. Of 300 officers and men committed to this action, not more than 15 made it back, the acting commander falling with the mass of his soldiers. The Panthers then tore into May, but stalled south of St. Martin in the face of concentrated artillery fire. Another attack on May by the Maisonneuve battalion ran into the 9th SS and failed utterly. Because of a misunderstanding, the Calgaries also pulled back to St. Andre-sur-Orne rather than the prescribed factory area south of St. Martin[33]

On Keller's 3rd Division's front, Cunningham's strongly supported 9th Brigade launched the North Novas against Tilly-la-Campagne while holding the Highland Light Infantry ready to pass through to secure Garcelles-Secqueville. The North Novas advanced across a kilometer of open fields from Bourguébus with three companies up, initially in darkness because the artificial moonlight of searchlight batteries shining their beams on low cloud failed to come on. When they did eventually light up, the reported effect was that the troops were silhouetted so that they were good targets for the enemy. On reaching the environs of Tilly, the North Novas discovered that the artillery had not subdued the soldiers of the *Leibstandarte*, who reportedly shot, shouted, and threw grenades like wild men. In the darkness, the fighting became terribly confused, but dawn broke with all companies bloodily repulsed. Tilly had in fact been turned into a strongpoint defended by the 3rd SS Panzergrenadier Battalion supported by panzers and pioneers of the 2nd SS Panzergrenadier Regiment.

When a tank squadron of the Fort Garry Horse moved up to assist the Canadian infantry, counterattacking panzers and concealed antitank guns forced it to withdraw to the west of the village. After losing eleven of its sixteen tanks in the fighting, the squadron received permission to fall back to Bourguébus. The infantry in the meantime had been ordered to dig in and hold where they were. Later that afternoon, they were told to make their way back under cover of darkness. With the failure of this one battalion to take Tilly, the 3rd Division's attack ended. Keller tried to have Cunningham throw in another battalion, but cancelled his order at 1600 hours after heated objections from Cunningham and two of his battalion commanders.[34]

At 1500 hours, Simonds ordered the 2nd Canadian Division, with the corps artillery in support, to capture Rocquancourt at 1830 hours, attack May-sur-Orne again at 2100 hours, and take Fontenay-le-Marmion the next morning. He also erroneously expected Cunningham's 9th Brigade to consolidate Tilly during the night. Around 1800 hours, however, Dietrich launched the 9th SS Panzer Division's counterattack, with Zollhofer's battle group driving on St. Martin and Meyer's striking to recover the center of Verrières Ridge. Zollhofer commanded a panzergrenadier regiment, a flak troop, and some Jagdpanzers, while Meyer's group consisted of the 9th SS's Panther and Mark IV panzer battalions, the assault gun battalion, and a flak troop with accompanying engineers and infantry. On reaching the crest, Meyer's group encountered such an intense hail of fire from 17-pounder antitank guns and tanks of the 22nd Armoured Brigade that he likened it to a Russian *pakfront*. Supported by a squadron of the 1st Royal Tanks and rocket-firing Typhoons, the Royal Hamilton Light Infantry could not be dislodged from Verrières. Reporting that anyone who crossed the ridge would be a dead man, Meyer turned instead to reinforcing the success of Zollhofer in recapturing St. Martin and pushing north from there.[35]

By any measurement, Spring was a tactical debacle, although the capture of Verrières showed what could be accomplished by well-led and well-handled Canadian troops. Against the strongest concentration of panzers in the West and the largest number of Waffen SS formations on either the Eastern or Western Fronts, Canadian divisional attacks had been delivered only by battalions. The clearance of St. Andre and St. Martin should have been tackled by the entire 6th Brigade. A properly coordinated attack by the 5th Brigade supported by armor may also have secured May-sur-Orne and possibly, given the lay of the land, turned Fontenay-le-Marmion from behind. The same can be said for the 3rd Division's attack on Tilly, which was too much for one battalion.

In short, it is difficult to escape the conclusion that Canadian commanders could have done more to ensure that their troops were adequately concentrated to attain success in battle. The lot of 2nd Division units might have been made easier, of course, had the 2 Corps taken greater pains in coordinating with the British 12 Corps the masking or suppression of German observation and daylight activity across the Orne in the area of Hill 112.

Operation Spring ended on the evening of 25 July, which, except for Dieppe, was the bloodiest day of the war for Canadian arms.[36] It also constituted the highwater mark of Waffen SS success in the Normandy campaign.

CHAPTER 8

A Murder of Panzers

Waffen SS formations in Normandy reached the peak of their collective performance in defending against Operation Spring. When Eberbach proposed following this highly successful defense with a major counterattack to destroy Allied forces south of the Orne, however, Kluge rejected the idea and ordered the 9th SS Panzer Division *Hohenstaufen* to relieve the battered 272nd Infantry Division in line. The 272nd, in turn, replaced the 12th SS. With his eyes fixed firmly on Cobra, he now sent the 2nd and 116th Panzer Divisions west to shore up Hausser's collapsing Seventh Army, but notably not Waffen SS formations.

Just as Cobra showed signs of success, Montgomery followed suit, cancelling the 12 and 8 Corps' operations planned to follow Spring and ordering Dempsey on 27 July to throw caution to the wind and immediately attack with six divisions from Caumont toward Vire to strike Hausser's flank. The object of this operation, code-named Blue-coat, was to prevent the Germans from redeploying reinforcements against Cobra. Reflecting his approach that it was more important to kill Germans rather than take ground, Montgomery specified that there would be no geographical objective for Bluecoat. Dempsey accordingly prepared a two-corps attack with Bucknall's 30 Corps

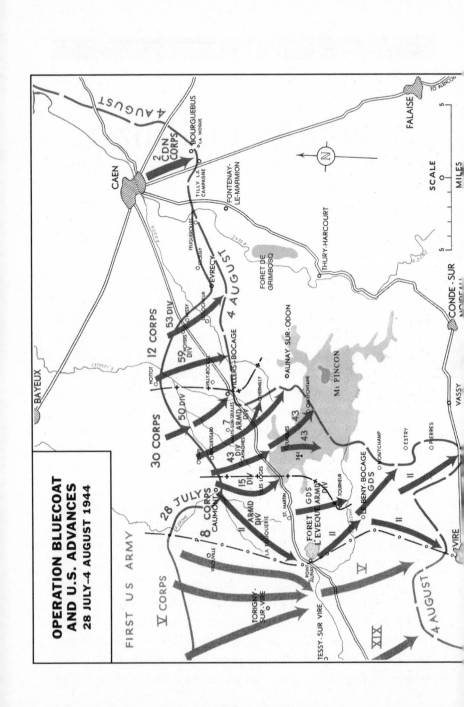

OPERATION BLUECOAT
AND U.S. ADVANCES
28 JULY–4 AUGUST 1944

directed on Le Bény-Bocage with the aim of seizing high ground in that vicinity and the area southwest of Villers-Bocage. O'Connor's 8 Corps was to seize the high ground east of St. Martin-des-Besaces with a view to protecting the right flank of the 30 Corps and subsequently exploiting to Petit Aunay north of the junction of the rivers Souleuvre and Vire and northwest of Le Bény-Bocage.[1]

After an impressive regrouping of fighting elements was accomplished within forty-eight hours, Bluecoat kicked off on the 30 Corps' front at 0600 hours on 30 July, supported by corps and divisional fire plans and 700 heavy bombers. Bucknall directed the 50th Division on the left to secure the high ground west and northwest of Villers-Bocage and the 43rd (Wessex) Division to take Point 361, west of Aunay-sur-Odon. The 7th Armoured Division remained in reserve ready to exploit. The attack by the 8 Corps opened an hour later on a two-division front with the support of 866 medium-bomber strikes. The 11th Armoured on the right protected the flank of the 15th (Scottish) Division, supported by the 6th Guards Tank Brigade as they struck out toward Point 309, east of St. Martin-des-Besaces. The 8 Corps made better progress than the 30 Corps as the battle unfolded, which reflected poorly on Bucknall's leadership.

Meanwhile, the 11th Armoured had taken Petit Aunay, seized a bridgehead over the Souleuvre River near Le Bény-Bocage by morning 31 July, and linked up with Gerow's U.S. V Corps. This action threw the Germans into a crisis as it penetrated the boundary separating Panzer Group West from the Seventh Army. Had the British exploited this breakthrough by taking Vire on 2 August, they could possibly have turned the Seventh Army's withdrawal into a rout. As Vire lay within the XIX Corps' sector and American and British troops were already becoming entangled, however, Dempsey directed the 8 Corps to press on toward Flers.[2]

The German commitment of Bittrich's II SS Panzer Corps to check Bluecoat on 1 August nonetheless conformed to what Montgomery desired. The British attack not only drew in the 9th SS Panzer Division *Hohenstaufen* and the 10th SS Panzer Division *Frundsberg*, but had sucked in the 21st Panzer Division from east of the Orne and the 503rd Heavy Panzer Battalion as well. The 12th SS Panzer Division *Hitlerjugend* also sent a fast group of thirteen Panthers, a panzergrenadier company, six 105-millimeter Wasp self-propelled guns, and six armored cars under *Sturmbannführer* Erich Olboeter, which remained under the command of the II SS Panzer Corps from 2 to 8 August.

The flagging progress on the 30 Corps' front continued to test Dempsey's patience. When the 7th Armoured, committed to take Aunay-sur-Odon, recoiled on 2 August to the position it had occupied forty-eight hours before, he sacked first Bucknall and his artillery commander, then both Erskine and Hinde. On 4 August, Lt. Gen. Brian Horrocks replaced Bucknall, and two days later, his 43rd (Wessex) Division captured Mont Pincon in a remarkable feat of arms. Although Dempsey had failed to effect a breakthrough in the *bocage*, he had pushed forward twelve to twenty miles on a twelve-mile front, forcing the Germans to commit substantial reserves and fixing at least two of their better panzer divisions in place so they could not be used against the Americans.[3]

Meanwhile, in keeping with Montgomery's direction that the First Canadian and Second British Armies continue to attack the Germans in the east to keep them from transferring forces to the western flank, the 2 Canadian Corps once again turned its attention to the capture of Tilly-la-Campagne, which was defended by the 2nd Panzergrenadier Regiment of the *Leibstandarte*. On the night of 29 July, a reinforced company of the Essex Regiment (4th Brigade, 2nd Canadian Infantry Division), supported by artillery and the direct fire of a tank troop, captured an enemy-held orchard midway between Verrières and Tilly in a vicious, costly action. From this position, the Calgary Highlanders of the 5th Brigade attacked Tilly in the early hours of 1 August, while a company of the Lincoln and Welland Regiment (10th Infantry Brigade, 4th Canadian Armoured Division) launched a diversionary feint from Bourguébus. Despite barrage and associated support from both divisional artilleries and an artillery brigade, the Calgary attack stalled in the face of withering German machine-gun and counterbar-rage fire that was perceived as Canadian shells falling short.

A second daylight assault supported by a tank troop of the Royal Scots Greys enabled some Canadians to get into Tilly, but unable to consolidate, they retired to the area of their original start line. Pushed forward to assist in piecemeal fashion, a company of the 4th Brigade's Royal Regiment met the Calgary Highlanders coming back. At this juncture, the 5th Brigade's commander, Brig. Bill Megill, ordered the shattered Calgaries to attack again at 1430 hours, supported by a squadron of the 2nd Armoured Brigade's Fort Carry Horse. This effort, with its aura of the reinforcement of failure, was similarly repulsed short of Tilly by concentrated *Leibstandarte* fire.[4]

Following Montgomery's personal appeal to Crerar to keep up the pressure on the 2 Canadian Corps' front, the entire Lincoln battal-ion executed a silent night attack against Tilly on 1 August. The plan called for two companies to strike south from Bourguébus and occupy blocking positions between Tilly and La Hogue in order to forestall an anticipated panzer counterattack from the latter village. The two other companies were then to advance directly on Tilly, the first seizing an intermediate position through which the second would assault the village. This actually amounted to a one-company attack, albeit supported from first light by the fire of a reinforced Sherman squadron of the 29th Reconnaissance Regiment (The South Alberta Regiment), a troop of 17-pounder antitank guns, and the divisional and corps artillery. In the event, the intermediate posi-tion was secured, but the blocking companies were forced back to Bourguébus in some confusion.

Despite this reverse, the commander of the 10th Canadian Infantry Brigade, Brig. Jim Jefferson, ordered the last company to assault Tilly. The *Leibstandarte* defenders, not surprisingly, stopped it cold. Two days later, Jefferson informed the Lincoln officers that insufficient determi-nation had been shown in attacking what should have been a two-company objective. A further attempt to capture Tilly on August 5 by the Argyll and Sutherland Highlanders of Canada, backed by a South

Alberta squadron, also failed. The strongly fortified village finally fell to the 51st Highland Division on 8 August, but only after having been cut off and following a protracted struggle by two Seaforth battalions of the 152nd Brigade supported by armor.[5] Clearly, Tilly was never a two-company objective and should never have been attacked by small units piecemeal. In fact, the most productive attacks on the Western Front were not even delivered by single divisions, but rather by corps of several divisions. Corps attacks won the war in the West.

On the same day that the British seized Mont Pincon, Corlett's U.S. XIX Corps captured Vire. This breached two important places in the defensive line that Eberbach had shortened to allow his Fifth Panzer Army (as Panzer Group West was redesignated on 5 August) to hold fast from Bourguébus Ridge to Thury-Harcourt, thence to Mont Pincon and Vire. On 6 August, the British 12 Corps also established a small bridgehead over the Orne near Thury-Harcourt, with the 176th Infantry Brigade of the 59th (Staffordshire) Division supported by tanks of the 107th Regiment, Royal Armoured Corps. At 0800 the following day, they erected a small bridge and beat off two attacks by the German 271st Infantry Division, which defended the front between Thury-Harcourt and St. Martin-de-Fontenay.

During the day, the bridgehead was also enlarged with the introduction of more troops. This alarmed the I SS Panzer Corps enough for Dietrich to order a counterattack on 7 August. His only reserve at hand was the 12th SS Panzer Division *Hitlerjugend*, which had been broken down into three battle groups—one under Wünsche, another under Meyer, and Fast Group Olboeter. Dietrich ordered Wünsche to restore the situation. At the time, Wünsche commanded one Panther and one Mark IV company, each with seventeen panzers, between five and ten Tigers of the 101st Heavy Panzer Battalion, two panzergrenadier battalions from Mohnke's 26th Regiment, an artillery battalion, and a flak platoon. After one panzer grenadier battalion cleared the Forêt de Grimbosq, Wünsche launched a combined panzer and panzergrenadier attack supported by artillery at 1830 hours. Although Wünsche's force destroyed twenty-eight British tanks, his attack foundered under Typhoon strikes and the artillery fire of seven regiments corrected by forward observers located in excellent observation sites on heights across the Orne. The bridgehead survived, and Wünsche lost nine Panthers and 122 men before being hastily recalled to deal with Operation Totalize.[6]

On the American front, meanwhile, the 12th Army Group under Bradley took direct control of the U.S. First and Third Armies on 1 August. Lt. Gen. Courtney Hodges replaced Bradley as commander of the First Army, and on the same day, the Third Army, under Lt. Gen. George Patton, took control of Middleton's VIII Corps just as its leading 4th Armored Division approached Rennes in Brittany. The mistaken notion nonetheless arose that Patton's Third Army made the breakthrough when, in fact, it was achieved by Bradley and Collins. At this juncture, the First Army (three corps totaling nine divisions) occupied a sector between the VIII Corps, which was driving south from Avranches, and Dempsey's Second British Army, which was advancing on Caumont. Hodges immediately faced the challenge of wheeling the VII Corps from a southwest orientation toward the east and the River Seine. As a first step, he ordered Collins's VII Corps to seize Mortain, twenty miles east of Avranches, while the VIII Corps under Middleton struck westward into Brittany to secure vitally needed ports. Through the gap that developed between these two formations, Patton deployed Maj. Gen. Wade Haislip's XV Corps with orders, from 2 August, to be prepared to exploit east toward Le Mans.[7]

On 2 August, Hitler also ordered Kluge to launch a strong counterattack through Mortain and Avranches with the object of cutting the American forces in two and denying them resupply. Thunderstruck by this direction, Kluge expressed serious misgivings, pointing out that panzers remained the backbone of the German defense and that where they were withdrawn, the front was likely to give way. He went on to warn that if the plan did not succeed—as he expected it would not—catastrophe would inevitably result. Given the American capture of Mortain and the British interception of the II SS Panzer Corps, Kluge did not think there was a chance of closing the Avranches gap.

Hausser entertained similar doubts as Kluge, who proposed instead forming a group of mobile divisions to cover Hausser's exposed southern flank while the Seventh Army withdrew to a defensible line anchored on the Caen sector. Hitler insisted, however, that the thirty-kilometer-wide bottleneck at Avranches offered German arms a unique target and opportunity for a complete reversal of the situation. On the other hand, what appeared brilliant in theory looked impractical given geographical challenges to logistics, especially ammunition and fuel supply.

German successes in Normandy had also been mainly defensive as Tigers and Panthers enjoyed a huge advantage in firing at long range from hull-down positions. They were not, however, well suited to distant or sustained offensive operations that called for extended movement. Despite a highly efficient armor repair-and-recovery system carried out as far forward as possible, the Germans experienced difficulty in keeping their Tigers and Panthers running. Unlike the sturdy Mark IV panzer, these tanks required expert care. Most Tigers broke down because of mechanical failure emanating from such issues as suspension and gear box defects. The more often the Panther moved, the more its mechanical problems increased. In fact, mechanical breakdown constituted the greatest single cause of German panzer losses, slightly edging out gunfire. Maneuver was the kiss of death for German panzers in the summer of 1944.[8]

On 4 August, Hitler categorically ordered Kluge to execute the detailed plans for Operation *Lüttich* that he had personally drawn up for him. These called for the commitment of a minimum of four panzer divisions and 1,000 Luftwaffe fighter aircraft to support the operation. Hitler further demanded that the attack not be launched until every tank, gun, and plane had been assembled. Both Kluge and Hausser realized that this was impossible given the rapidly deteriorating situation and agreed to strike on the night of 6 August. By adjusting the German front on the arrival of two infantry divisions from the Fifteenth Army, Kluge earmarked an offensive group that included the 1st SS Panzer Division *Leibstandarte*, the 2nd SS Panzer Division *Das Reich*, the 2nd Panzer Division, the 116th Panzer Division, and a battle group from the 17th SS Panzergrenadier Division *Götz von Berlichingen*.

Originally, the *Leibstandarte*, equipped with 100 new Panthers, was to be the main striking force, but as a large element remained west of the Orne in Army Group B reserve, Hausser slated the main body to serve as a second wave in the attack on Juvigny. The XXXXVII Panzer Corps, under Gen. Hans *Freiherr* von Funck, charged with conducting the attack between the See River in the north and the Selune in the south, called for the main thrust to be delivered through St. Barthelemy and Juvigny, initially by the depleted 2nd Panzer Division (built up to 100 tanks with panzer battalions from the *Leibstandarte* and the 116th Panzer Division). Funck anticipated that by the time the 2nd Panzer broke through, the rest of the *Leibstandarte* would have arrived to strike through to Avranches. The remainder of the 116th Panzer Division with about 25 tanks was to protect the northern flank by advancing from the Sourdeval area. The *Das Reich*, still commanded by Baum, with a 17th SS Panzergrenadier battle group and about thirty tanks, was to capture Mortain by encirclement, then advance southwest to St. Hilaire, while *Panzer Lehr* reconnaissance elements guarded the southern flank. The Luftwaffe's promise of 1,000 fighters had been reduced to 300.[9]

The fighters never arrived, and at 1630 hours on 6 August, the *Leibstandarte* reported that its panzers required refuelling. Even though it had been allocated absolute route priority, the division was still at Tinchebray, twenty kilometers from its attack position, at 2200 hours largely because of vehicle march congestion for lack of trained general staff officers. The 2nd Panzer Division thus had no chance of receiving the assigned *Leibstandarte* Panthers. Neither had the 116th Panzer Division produced its assigned panzer battalion for the 2nd Panzer Division, which launched a surprise attack at midnight on 6 August with only about thirty Mark IVs and assault guns. As a result, it cleared only the northern part of St. Barthelemy.

Only at 0200 hours did forty-three Panthers of the 1st SS Panzer Battalion and several Mark IVs of the 2nd SS Panzer Battalion, plus a motorized panzergrenadier battalion and the *Leibstandarte* reconnaissance battalion, join the 2nd Panzer Division's attack, which was already in progress. While the reconnaissance battalion advanced with the right wing toward Le Mesnil-Tove, the rest of the *Leibstandarte* formed a major part of the left-flank thrust on Juvigny.

In the meantime, on the northern flank, the 116th Panzer Division had been unable to concentrate to attack at midnight and did not attempt to advance until 1630 hours. It got nowhere, and four hours later, the commander was fired. To the south, the 2nd SS Panzer Division did better, fighting its way block by block into Mortain, establishing defensive positions there, and advancing two kilometers southwest to Romagny. The 17th SS Panzergrenadier battle group failed to take Hill 314 east of Mortain as ordered, however, because the American 2nd Battalion and a company of the 3rd Battalion, 120th Infantry Regiment, 30th Infantry Division, stubbornly defended the commanding height from which American artillery fire could be observed and corrected. Despite a reputation for killing prisoners that made an enemy fight on, a Waffen SS officer bearing a white flag vainly called upon Americans defending Hill 282 to surrender. Similarly, the U.S. 823rd Tank Destroyer Battalion's defense of L'Abbaye Blanche withstood the *Das Reich*'s assault, even though their towed guns revealed their locations by firing. In early afternoon, Baum ordered the attack halted because of Allied air strikes and American artillery fire. The division went over to the defensive that night.[10]

The strongest thrust of the day occurred on the front where the 2nd Panzer Division led off. The *Leibstandarte* reconnaissance battalion joined the right-wing advance on Le Mesnil-Tove, while the rest of the *Leibstandarte*, under the 1st SS Panzer Battalion, formed a major part of the left-wing assault on Juvigny. For some reason, the main body of the 2nd SS Panzer (Mark IV) Battalion passed 6 and 7 August resting in woods near Bretteville-sur-Laize. The right-wing attack made reasonable progress, driving through Le Mesnil-Tove up to the outskirts of Le Mesnil-Adelée by 0800 hours. Here the Germans ran into a company roadblock of the 119th Infantry Regiment and, faced with punishing artillery fire and air strikes, ground to a halt twenty-five kilometers from Avranches.

At 1310 hours, elements of the U.S. 3rd Armored Division's Combat Command B attached to the 30th Infantry Division tried to retake Le Mesnil-Tove in an attempt to cut off the German 2nd Panzer spearhead. The American counterattack failed to break through, but the Germans had to fight hard to retain the village.

Meanwhile, on the left wing, the reinforced 2nd Panzer Division attacked at 0550 hours to seize St. Barthelemy, which was defended by Lt. Col. Robert Frankland's 1st Battalion, 117th Infantry Regiment, and elements of the 823rd Tank Destroyer Battalion. Following an ineffective forty-five-minute artillery barrage, *Leibstandarte* panzers and grenadiers struck from the east and southeast, aiming ultimately for Juvigny, while 2nd Panzer Mark IVs and assault guns attacked from the north and northeast. In the fog and *bocage*, the Germans lost the long-range advantage of their powerful panzer and assault guns in chaotic close-quarter fighting. Frankland also gave orders to let panzers pass through and strip them of their infantry, which cost the *Leibstandarte*'s 3rd Panzergrenadier Battalion (which earlier defended Tilly) many casualties. The battle ultimately cost Frankland 334 casualties out of 828 men—more than the 300 lost by the 2nd Battalion, 120th Infantry Regiment, at Hill 314, but the St. Bathelemy struggle delayed the Germans for six critical hours.[11]

Leading *Leibstandarte* elements were still three kilometers from Juvigny when the fog burned off and the first rocket-firing *Jabos*—Allied fighter-bombers—roared overhead shortly after 1230 hours. As earlier agreed, the Typhoons of the 83 and 84 Groups of the British Second Tactical Air Force concentrated exclusively on attacking enemy panzer columns, while American fighters and fighter-bombers of the IX Tactical Air Command of the U.S. Ninth Air Force operated farther afield interdicting enemy air and ground forces to isolate the battle area. Up to 2040 hours, Typhoons swarmed over the Mortain battlefield, attacking German armor nonstop. Of a total of 458 individual sorties flown on 7 August, 271 struck German forces in the

Mortain sector. Although the inaccurate rocket fire of the Typhoons produced fewer tank kills than claimed, the overall effect, when coupled with the stubborn resistance of the 30th Infantry Division and its attached 823rd Tank Destroyer Battalion, was enough to force the Germans onto the defensive.

Neither Kluge nor Hausser saw any point in continuing to attack at Mortain, but that evening, Hitler ordered Kluge to renew the attack using the II SS Panzer Corps and the 12th SS Division *Hitlerjugend* from the Fifth Panzer Army. The Operation Totalize attack by the 2 Canadian Corps down the Falaise road on the night of 7 August put an end to the *Hitlerjugend*'s involvement, but Hitler persisted, replacing Funck with Heinrich Eberbach, a staunch Nazi, to lead a second attack on Avranches with Panzer Group Eberbach on 11 August. Over Hausser's protestations, he also ordered the 9th Panzer Division north to participate, even though it was then the only panzer division standing in the way of Haislip's U.S. XV Corps, which captured Le Mans on 8 August. When the XV Corps turned north on the evening of 10 August, threatening the double envelopment of the Seventh and Fifth Panzer Armies, Hitler reluctantly agreed to postpone the renewed offensive against Avranches. In the event, the attack never materialized, and Panzer Group Eberbach turned instead to deal with Haislip.[12]

One of the more interesting aspects of the German Mortain attack was the clumsy, fumbling deployment of the *Leibstandarte*, which was originally slated to deliver the main thrust. As things turned out, the division never fought as a single entity, but rather participated as a number of dispersed battle groups. One battle group under the 1st SS Panzergrenadier Regiment, consisting of a panzergrenadier battalion, an artillery battalion, a Nebelwerfer battery, and four or five assault guns, never even took part in the Mortain attack. Hausser instead subordinated the battle group to the 84th Infantry Division to help stem the Allied attack south of Vire. From 7 August to the night of the tenth, it fought under the command of the 84th. Some elements of the 2nd SS Panzer (Mark IV) Regiment did not begin to move west from the area of Bretteville-sur-Laize until the night of 7 August and then took three days to reach the Domfront area. The balance of the *Leibstandarte*—the 1st and 2nd Battalions of the 2nd SS Panzergrenadier Regiment, about twenty assault guns of the 1st SS Sturmgeschütz Battalion, and the pioneer battalion—was still moving west toward Mortain, and when the attack commenced at midnight, these elements were still more than five kilometers east of the town. That night, they arrived in the Barthelemy area, and at dawn, the two panzergrenadier battalions, supported by panzers, advanced in the fog toward Bellefontaine and Juvigny. On encountering counterattacking elements of the U.S. 4th Infantry Division, they began to take heavy casualties, many from Allied air activity and artillery fire. With the rest of the German forces on the Mortain front, they now adopted the defensive.[13]

For the Americans, the battle for Mortain ended on 12 August with the relief of Hill 314 by the 35th Infantry Division. By this time, the Germans had commenced their withdrawal to the east to avoid being trapped by American and British pincers that relentlessly proceeded to close. The German panzers had simply been massacred by superior artillery and Allied airpower, as evidenced by the nearly 100 armored vehicles they left abandoned in the immediate vicinity. Indeed, the Germans appeared to be incapable of turning the skillful defensive prowess exhibited in Operation Spring into equally effective offensive action on a large scale.

When Funck's XXXXVII Panzer Corps slammed into and flowed around the 30th Infantry Division on Hill 314, Hodges reacted by reinforcing Collins's VII Corps to seven divisions and increasing its artillery allocation. His staff coincidentally coordinated with the IX Tactical Air Command the provision of Allied close air support and airdrop resupply for the beleaguered division, which suffered 1,000 casualties a day. American success hinged on the stalwart defence of the 30th Infantry Division as Hill 314 offered a commanding view of the German axis of attack. Almost immediately, the VII Corps organized counterattacks against both flanks of the enemy penetration.

The 2 Canadian Corps' attack toward Falaise, launched the same day that the Germans struck at Mortain, also broke open the northern flank of the base of the German salient by 0800 hours on 8 August. This compelled enemy logistical units to withdraw southward, which deprived Hausser's Seventh Army of its rear installations and necessitated that resupply be provided by the Fifth Panzer Army. Observing that a breakthrough had occurred near Caen the like of which he had never seen, Kluge knew that his head was in a noose. The Canadian advance threatened to catch the Seventh Army in full stride as it struck west, tearing into its right rear flank.

In order to take advantage of a similar opportunity in the south, Bradley ordered Patton to turn Haislip's XV Corps north from Le Mans toward Alençon and Argentan on 10 August to effect a short encirclement at Falaise. On 16 August, the day the Canadians entered Falaise, Bradley also decided to send Patton's Third Army racing toward the Seine to effect a longer envelopment, leaving the First Army to help reduce the Falaise pocket.[14]

CHAPTER 9

Surrender
Invites Death

On 4 August, Montgomery directed the First Canadian Army to launch a heavy attack from the Caen sector toward Falaise no later than 8 August and a day earlier if possible. The main purpose of this operation, code-named Totalize, was to cut off enemy forces facing the British Second Army, which was advancing from the west. The historic nature of the date was not lost on Crerar, who envisioned emulating the decisive attack delivered by the Canadian Corps at Amiens in 1918. In a 5 August address to senior officers, he ventured that the decisive period of the war had been reached and that the First Canadian Army was well placed to inflict a crushing blow on the Germans that would convince even Waffen SS troops that a quick termination of the war would follow. With the bulk of the German Seventh Army still fighting in the west, Crerar saw a golden opportunity for the First Canadian Army to cut into its rear and trap the main body. Such a movement successfully executed on 8 August would have bagged the entire German force that attacked toward Mortain on 6 August. Crerar thus entertained high hopes that 8 August 1944, the anniversary of the Battle of Amiens, would be an even blacker day for the German armies than *Der Schwarze Tag* of the same date twenty-six years before.

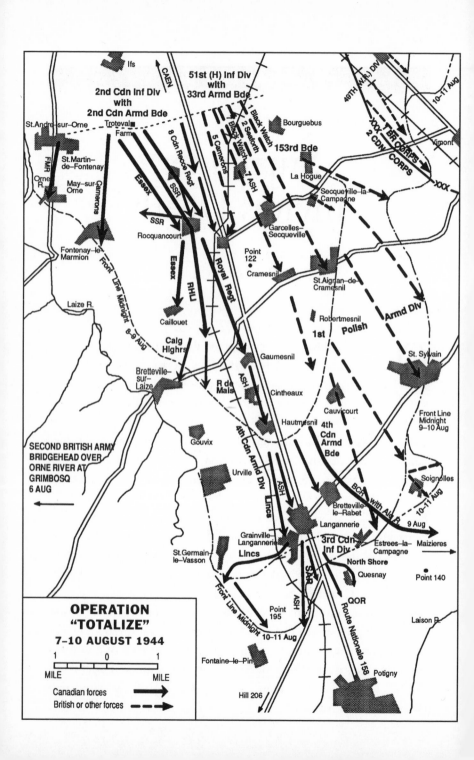

Ifs

CAEN

51st (H) Inf Div
with
33rd Armd Bde

49TH (W.R.) DIV

10–11 Aug

2nd Cdn Inf Div
with
2nd Cdn Armd Bde

Troteval
Farm

St.Andre–sur–Orne

8 Cdn Recce Regt

1 Black Watch

2 Seaforth

Bourguebus

Vimont

St.Martin–
de–Fontenay

FMR

Orne
R.

May–sur–
Orne

Camerons

Essex

SSR

5 Camerons

Black Watch

7 ASH

La Hogue

153rd Bde

Secqueville–la–
Campagne

I BR CORPS

2 CDN CORPS

XXX

SSR

Rocquancourt

Essex

Fontenay–le–
Marmion

Garcelles–
Secqueville

Point
122
Cramesnil

St.Aigran–de–
Cramesnil

Laize R.

RHLI

Caillouet

Calg
Highrs

Bretteville–
sur–
Laize

R de Mais

ASH

Robertmesnil

1st   Polish   Armd Div

St. Sylvain

Gaumesnil

Cintheaux

4th Cdn Armd Div

ASH

Hautmesnil

Cauvicourt

4th
Cdn
Armd
Bde

Front Line
Midnight
9–10 Aug

Gouvix

Urville

ASH

Lincs

Soignolles

BCR with Alg R

10–11 Aug

SECOND BRITISH ARMY
BRIDGEHEAD OVER
ORNE RIVER AT
GRIMBOSQ
6 AUG

Bretteville–
le–Rabet

9 Aug

St.Germain–
le–Vasson

Grainville
Langannerie

Lincs

Langannerie

3rd Cdn
Inf Div

Estrees–la–
Campagne

Maizieres

North Shore

Quesnay

Point 140

SAR

Front Line Midnight
10–11 Aug

ASH

Point
195

QOR

Route Nationale 158

Laison R.

**OPERATION
"TOTALIZE"**

7–10 AUGUST 1944

Fontaine–le–Pin

Potigny

1   0   1
MILE   MILE

Hill 206

Canadian forces

British or other forces

The fearsome reputation of the Waffen SS would be enough in itself, however, to reinforce a fatal flaw in the Totalize plan. Canadians knew that they would be fighting the Waffen SS in Operation Totalize and had learned of the murder of Canadian prisoners by the 12th SS Panzer Division *Hitlerjugend*, which created something of a stir in Allied headquarters. At Crerar's instigation, an Anglo-Canadian Court of Inquiry had been convened to look into the matter, and leaflets promising to bring the perpetrators to justice had been air-dropped behind German lines. Crerar followed these actions with a guidance to be read out to all troops stating that revenge must not under any circumstances take the form of retaliation in kind. He urged instead that Canadian anger be converted into a steel-hard determination to destroy the enemy in battle. In his 5 August address, he also warned that to surrender to Waffen SS troops was to invite death and exhorted his infantry to use their own weapons to get forward, as opposed to relying on a colossal scale of artillery and air support. In addition to this, he stressed the importance of keeping the initiative and the need to maintain momentum in the attack. While condemning the tendency to consider objectives on the ground an end rather than as a means of killing the enemy, he cautioned that on reaching an objective, everyone must swiftly prepare for a quick, determined, small-scale counterattack by German panzers and infantry.[1]

In response to Crerar's direction, Simonds produced a plan for an attack in three phases opening with flanking strikes by strategic bombers during darkness, followed by an armored night assault using armored personnel carriers to transport infantry. A key concern to Simonds had been how to move infantry forward with tanks at tank speed during the attack. If the major threat to the tank was the long-range, hard-hitting 75-millimeter or 88-millimeter gun, the main danger to infantry came from concentrated artillery, mortar, small-arms, and machine-gun fire. As the 3rd Canadian Division artillery was in the process of reconverting to towed 25-pounders from 105-millimeter Priest self-propelled guns—with which they had been equipped since D-Day—Simonds hit upon the idea of stripping seventy-six available Priests of their guns and reconfiguring them as infantry carriers. The result was the Kangaroo, which could carry ten infantrymen and protect them against bullets and fragments.

Simonds recognized the impossibility of attaining tactical surprise in respect of objectives or attack direction, but he sought to achieve it in time and method. The challenge was how to get the armor through the enemy gun screen to sufficient depth to disrupt the German anti-tank gun and mortar defense in country highly suited to such weapons. Like Montgomery and Dempsey, Simonds seized on the employment of heavy bombers, but saw that using all available air support for a break-in would leave little for a breakthrough. Unless a pause were incorporated to move artillery and ammunition forward, there would also be diminished gun support. If, however, the initial break-in could be accomplished by infiltrating the screen in bad visibility with limited support from heavy night bombers, heavy and medium day bombers could support the breakthrough at the very moment artillery support was expected to slacken. Through this method, which involved transporting infantry in armored carriers closely behind leading tanks, Simonds hoped to avoid a slackening pause and maintain a high tempo to operations.[2]

Crerar's role dealt with intelligence, artillery, and logistical matters, but centered heavily on arranging air support since it was the one area in Totalize planning that remained the sole prerogative of the First Canadian Army. For the operation, two visual control posts coordinated close air support for the 2 Canadian Corps. As strategic bombing support had to be requested through the Second Tactical Air Force's 83 Group and the Allied Expeditionary Air Force, making the case for the tactical employment of strategic bombers required considerable effort. Many top airmen considered it a misuse of airpower, and Crerar's chief of staff spent two days in England presenting convincing arguments.

Heavy bomber strikes in darkness also raised concerns about troop safety, and the commander in chief of Bomber Command, Air Chief Marshal Sir Arthur Harris, remained cool to the idea. He would agree to carrying out the task only if master bombers were satisfied that red- and green-colored concentrations fired by 25-pounders could be clearly identified in the dark. It took a trial on the night of 6 August to confirm this and pave the way for the opening of the first phase of Totalize at 2300 hours on 7 August with heavy protective bombing of both flanks of the 2 Corps' armored thrusts.

Air support for the second phase, estimated to start at 1400 hours on 8 August, was more comprehensive and, because of a last-minute change, became largely the responsibility of the U.S. Eighth Air Force, with coordination to be effected through 83 Group. The overall effect of entrenching air support timings meant, of course, that all land-force movement was contingent on bomber strikes. The location of the 1st SS Panzer Division *Leibstandarte* also reinforced the need for such bombing before launching phase two.[3]

The plan Simonds submitted to Crerar called for a corps attack by three infantry and two armored divisions, two armored brigades, and two artillery brigades. To this, he added the support of two additional artillery brigades, a searchlight battery for movement lighting in the event of low cloud cover, four squadrons of special armor with flail tanks, engineer assault vehicles, flame-throwing Crocodiles, and the whole of the available air effort. Simonds expected very heavy fighting on the front held by the 1st SS Panzer Division *Leibstandarte* on the right and the 9th SS Panzer Division *Hohenstaufen* on the left, each disposed with one infantry regiment back and one forward, with all panzers and assault guns in support. The presence of the 12th SS Panzer Division *Hitlerjugend* in close reserve also meant that a counter-attack was likely on the eastern flank.

Simonds thus envisioned three phases: first, a night penetration by the 2nd Canadian and 51st (Highland) Infantry Divisions through the foremost defensive zone based on May-sur-Orne, Fontenay-le-Marmion, Tilly-la-Campagne, and La Hogue; a second by the 4th Canadian Armoured and 3rd Canadian Infantry Divisions to pierce the partially prepared rearward position along the line of Hautmesnil and St. Sylvain; and a third by the 1st Polish Armored Division to seize the high ground north of Falaise while the 4th Armoured took the high ground west of Potigny. Given the open nature of the ground, which ideally suited the characteristics of German long-range antitank weaponry, Simonds reasoned that the defense would be most handicapped by bad visibility, smoke, fog, or darkness that minimized the advantage of long-range fire.[4]

New intelligence that the 9th SS had withdrawn and that the 1st SS had been relieved by the 89th Infantry Division and fallen back on Bretteville-sur-Laize along the second German defensive line prompted Simonds to reconsider his plan. Given the fearsome reputation of the *Leibstandarte* and its formidable display of defensive power in Atlantic and Spring, Simonds now expected the tougher fight to occur in phase two rather than phase one.

On 6 August, Simonds cancelled phase three and directed his two armored divisions to attack together in phase two and continue without pause onto their final objectives. Without firing a shot, the *Leibstandarte* had thus forced a change in Canadian plans that included placing much greater stress on the absolute need for a bomber strike before launching the phase-two ground attack. In fact, the *Hohenstaufen* had already left for the Caumont area on 1 August to counter the Bluecoat threat from the Second British Army. The *Leibstandarte* had retired to the area of Bretteville-sur-Laize and St. Sylvain, but was earmarked to participate with the 2nd, 116th, and 2nd SS *Das Reich* Panzer Divisions in the abortive Mortain offensive against Avranches. The previously mentioned delay in the departure of *Leibstandarte* elements from the area of Bretteville-sur-Laize clouded Simonds's intelligence picture.[5]

The 89th Division, believed to have left Norway on 12 June, had relieved the *Leibstandarte* in the line on the night of 5 August and taken over the entire front between the Orne and La Hogue previously held by both Waffen SS panzer divisions. With an established structure of two regiments of three battalions each, the division fielded roughly 3,000 frontline troops, many of whom were of non-German extraction. It nonetheless fielded seventy-eight mortars and was backed up by two heavy artillery battalions, numerous Nebelwerfer multibarrelled mortars, two self-propelled antitank units, and about sixty 88-millimeter guns. The 89th had never been in action before and was not thought to be capable of offering great resistance in the face of heavy bombardment or deep penetration. On the right flank of the 89th, the 272nd Infantry Division had relieved the *Hitlerjugend* east and south of Cagny on the night of 4 August. While deducing that the second breakthrough phase might meet stronger resistance than originally anticipated, Simonds expected counterattacks by the 89th and 272nd Divisions to be half-hearted efforts at best. He therefore urged his two infantry divisions attacking in the first phase to be handled more boldly than originally planned.[6]

With the departure of the *Leibstandarte*, the *Hitlerjugend* constituted Dietrich's only mobile reserve, and he had already ordered Wünsche's *Hitlerjugend* battle group to counterattack the British bridgehead at Grimbosq on 7 August. Meyer's 12th SS battle group possessed about 1,500 frontline troops, including *Sturmbannführer* Hans Waldmüller's 1st SS Panzergrenadier Battalion, the divisional artillery regiment (less Wasps with Fast Group Olboeter sent to the II SS Panzer Corps to deal with Bluecoat), the divisional flak battalion, and the *Hitlerjugend*'s 2nd SS Panzer Battalion with thirty-nine Mark IV panzers (twelve allegedly borrowed from the 9th SS Panzer Division), eight Tigers of the attached 101st Heavy Panzer Battalion, and twenty-seven Jadgpanzer IVs. Meyer moved his battle group to southeast of Bretteville-sur-Laize on 7 August so that it would be more centrally positioned within the I Panzer Corps and nearer to the British bridgehead north of Thury-Harcourt. At 2140 hours that evening, he received orders to deploy to the area northwest of Conde-sur-Noireau as soon as possible to help prevent a British breakthrough between Vire and Thury-Harcourt.[7]

The first phase of Totalize called for a night attack on the Fontenay-le-Marmion–La Hogue position by two infantry divisions employing armored personnel carriers, each supported by an armored brigade, under cover of a rolling barrage. The task of the 2nd Canadian

Infantry Division, committed west of the Caen-Falaise road with the 2nd Canadian Armoured Brigade under its command, was to secure the line Caillouet-Gaumesnil and ensure the mopping up of St. Andre, May-sur-Orne, Fontenay-le-Marmion, and Rocquancourt. East of the road, the 51st (Highland) Division, with the 33rd British Armoured Brigade under its command, was to capture the areas of Lourguichon Wood, Garcelles-Secqueville, Cramesnil, St. Aignan-de-Cramesnil, and Secqueville-la-Campagne. There was to be no preliminary artillery bombardment during the first phase, but commencing at 2300 hours on 7 August, RAF Lancaster bombers were to obliterate the areas of May-sur-Orne and Fontenay-le-Marmion on the right flank and La Hogue and Secqueville on the left.

The second phase, expected to begin after noon on 8 August with a massive air strike, called for the 2nd and 51st Divisions to push on boldly to secure the right and left flanks while Maj. Gen. George Kitching's 4th Canadian Armoured Division dashed southward along the Caen-Falaise road to seize Point 206 between Fontaine-le-Pin and Potigny. Simultaneously, Maj. Gen. Stefan Maczek's 1st Polish Armored Division was to pass through the 51st Highland Division and advance directly east of the Caen-Falaise road to take Point 159, which overlooked and dominated Falaise. Each armored division was to have one medium artillery regiment under its command and the support of medium and fighter-bombers on call to deal with possible threats from the 12th SS Panzer Division. To enable them to blast their way forward, two artillery brigades (five medium regiments each) were also made available, one to each division. This phase was to be heavily supported by fighter-bombers, medium bombers, and American B-17 heavy day bombers. While the 2nd Canadian Infantry and 51st (Highland) Divisions in phase two secured the right and left flanks around Bretteville-sur-Laize and Cavicourt, respectively, the 3rd Canadian Infantry Division was to remain in reserve near Caen, prepared to move on Simonds's order to take over the areas of Hautmesnil, Bretteville-le-Rabet, and Point 140 east of the Caen-Falaise road.[8]

On 7 August, the maneuver elements for Operation Totalize formed up. In both the 2nd and 51st Divisions, an armored and infantry brigade constituted the main assaulting force. In each case, they were organized in columns and given axes of advance. Within the 2nd Division, four columns were deployed with four vehicles abreast on a sixteen-yard frontage, which was roughly the width that could be cleared by four flail tanks. Every ten feet along the length of a column, there was another group of four vehicles. Each column was headed by two tank troops, followed by two mine-clearing flail troops and one lane-marking engineer petard troop. Marshalled behind these came an infantry battalion or, in one instance, a reconnaissance regiment mounted in Kangaroos or half-tracks. Farther back in each column travelled the remainder of a tank squadron, two antitank troops, a machine-gun platoon, and an engineer section. The rear of all four columns was covered by a fortress force of one armored regiment less a squadron. Columnar deployment within the 51st Division, though similar, was limited to a left and right split, each based on an armored regiment and infantry battalion, roughly 200 vehicles strong, and including specially designated navigating tanks.

All columns rolled closer to the start line after dark, and at 2300 hours, 1,020 Lancaster and Halifax bombers began dropping a total of 3,462 tons of bombs on flank targets identified by artillery red and green marker shells. At 2330, both divisions crossed the start line in their respective formations, picking up from 2345 hours a rolling barrage fired by 360 guns of nine field and nine medium regiments, advancing 100 yards a minute in 200-yard lifts to a depth of 6,000 yards. Altogether, 720 guns, each with up to 650 rounds, supported the attack. To assist the columns in keeping direction, a Bofors tracer barrage coordinated by corps was fired over divisional thrust lines. Artificial moonlight and wireless radio directional beams, two per divisional front, were also employed.

On the 2nd Division's front, the 2nd Canadian Armoured Brigade led off with the 4th Brigade mounted in armored personnel carriers and the 8th Reconnaissance Regiment (14th Canadian Hussars) under its command. In addition to flails and engineer armored vehicles, it was further bolstered by a company of medium machine guns, a platoon of heavy 4.2-inch mortars, a platoon of engineers, and two anti-tank batteries (one self-propelled and the other a towed 17-pounder). The 5th Brigade—with the Fort Garry Horse (less one squadron), a self-propelled antitank battery, a company of medium machine guns, and a platoon of heavy mortars—followed behind, prepared to restore momentum, if lost, by assaulting the 2nd Armoured Brigade's objectives. It was also to move on orders of the divisional commander to capture Bretteville-sur-Laize. The 6th Brigade—with a squadron of flamethrowing Crocodiles, two antitank batteries, three heavy mortar platoons, and a company of medium machine guns—was to commence mopping-up operations at H-Hour.

In spite of the slow rate of advance, a dense cloud of dust arose; thickened by ground mist and enemy smoke, it proved impenetrable to searchlights. After fifteen minutes, drivers could not see vehicles immediately ahead, forcing them to turn their tail lights on. In the ensuing confusion, heightened by German mortar and antitank fire, some tanks turned around and collided with oncoming carriers. Not surprisingly, it became progressively difficult to keep direction. The Royal Regiment passed east rather than west of Rocquancourt, the Royal Hamilton Light Infantry ran straight through it, and the Essex went wildly astray.

Yet while the movement of armored columns by night proved a harrowing experience despite all navigational aids, it nonetheless worked brilliantly, and within hours, chaos produced success. The rapid advance of the 51st (Highland) Division took it past Tilly to secure Lorguichon by 0445 hours, Garcelles-Secqueville by 0530, and Cramesnil by 0730. With the exception of Tilly, which, though bypassed, held out until 1200 hours, the division had seized all of its first-phase objectives, including St. Aignan-de-Cramesnil, and was ready for the 1st Polish Armored Division to pass through. Similar success attended the 2nd Division's attack, which rolled around Rocquancourt southward into the debussing area between Cramesnil and

Caillouet. By 0600 hours, leading elements of the 2nd and 51st Divisions were fighting in the vicinities of their first objectives and had nearly cleared them. While mopping–up operations against rearward enemy pockets continued, the first phase of Totalize was successfully completed for the relatively light total of 380 casualties. Though few realized it at the time, the German front had been smashed and the road to Falaise lay open.[9]

The first phase of Totalize had been a resounding success, but Simonds's decision to pause for six hours before launching the second phase produced the loss of momentum that Crerar had specifically sought to avoid. Driven by fear that the 1st SS Panzer Division *Leibstandarte* defended the second German defensive zone, Simonds insisted that the armored divisions await the support of heavy bombers. He apparently did not want a repeat of Atlantic, where he had received a bloody nose from counterattacking Waffen SS. Similarly vicious German reactions in Spring surely reinforced his decision to pause. The pause, however, invited the Germans to mount the very counterattacks that Simonds feared and had hoped to avert by striking deep into the German defensive depth in phase one. The commanders of the 4th Canadian and 1st Polish Armored Divisions had also warned him of the potential danger of such a long pause between phases. As Crerar so correctly pointed out, losing the momentum of the attack was something that should have been avoided at all costs. In this case, moreover, the loss was self-imposed rather than forced by the Germans, who really had little to do with limiting the success of the armored divisions on 8 August. Waiting for the second bomber strike guaranteed a loss of momentum. The limitation on forward reconnaissance imposed by the bomb line further highlighted the wisdom of Simonds's earlier admonition that there was nothing more dangerous than to sit down in front of the Boche and not know what he was up to.[10]

The best time to have launched a second–phase attack on the Germans was when they were reeling and disorganized, unable to immediately recover because of severe disruption. This opportunity presented itself on the morning of 8 August, when the shattered

German defense was in turmoil, but it was a fleeting moment that should have been seized upon by continuing to press the attack. The inescapable fact remains that the momentum of the first-phase attack, which exceeded expectations, could only have been maintained by keeping up the pressure in phase two. Every passing minute allowed the Germans time to catch their breath and regroup. That neither Simonds nor Crerar actually knew that the route to Falaise lay open was of less consequence than recognizing the historical reality that breakthroughs have not always been easily discernible.

Vague and imprecise information about the enemy should never preclude fighting for information or quick and aggressive action by reserves. In Operation Cobra, for instance, Collins ordered one division to pass through another despite the risk of congestion and less-than-positive reports of conditions generally being chaotic. His later decision to commit the 3rd Armored Division was even based on bad information. Yet his unleashing of exploiting forces before break-through elements had secured their immediate objectives turned out to be one of the vital decisions of the Cobra operation.[11] Maintaining similar momentum in Totalize would have necessitated either moving the bomb line and air strikes farther south (an almost impossible task given coordination and time constraints) or canceling the bombing attack altogether to enable the armored divisions to strike directly toward their assigned objectives.[12]

While Simonds waited, *Oberführer* Meyer acted. On hearing the bombing on the morning of 8 August, he rushed forward to Urville and met with Mohnke to assess the situation. He then drove to the area of Cintheaux, where he personally rallied fleeing 89th Division soldiers by standing in the middle of the road, calmly lighting a cigar, and asking them if they were going to leave him alone to face the Allied attack. Returning to Urville, he met Eberbach, who approved his plan of action, but later warned Kluge that if the Canadian attack continued the next day, he would not be able to stop it. For his part, Meyer quickly reinforced Waldmüller with the 2nd Panzer Battalion of thirty-nine Mark IVs and eight Tigers and ordered him to counterattack at 1230 hours to recapture St. Aignan, which had been taken by the British.

On meeting Waldmüller in Cintheaux just as a lone heavy bomber flying command post appeared to signal the start of a major Allied air strike, Meyer ordered him to attack immediately. This hugging action left panzers and German soldiers safely inside the bomb line, behind which heavy bombers were not to strike for fear of hitting Canadian troops. Although the German counterattack proved unsuccessful and cost tank ace *Hauptsturmführer* Michael Wittmann his life, it served to spoil the continued advance of the Polish division for most of the day. Simonds had ordered both armored divisions to feed forward after Fontenay-le-Marmion was reported clear at 1710 hours, but Waldmüller's counterattack appeared to convince him of the need to exercise caution and await the second air strike.[13]

The action of Wünsche in counterattacking the British bridgehead north of Thury-Harcourt further appears to have clouded the picture. In fact, plans to strengthen the German defense had already been set in motion with the hasty recall of Wünsche's battle group from the area of the Grimbosq bridgehead, where it had been fighting the British Second Army. Meyer had already directed *Obersturmbannführer* Bernard Krause and his 1st Panzergrenadier Battalion battle group from Mohnke's 26th Regiment to occupy the heights east of Potigny near Quilly-le-Tesson and defend the bottleneck between the natural tank obstacles of the Laison and Laize Rivers. Wünsche's battle group now joined him on the heights west and northwest of Potigny and, at 0300 hours, redeployed to Quesnay Wood. Wünsche still had thirty-nine Panthers and was to be reinforced by thirteen Tigers from the 102nd SS Heavy Panzer Battalion, which was released to Eberbach from the II Panzer Corps' reserve. Olboeter's fast group, also on release from the II Panzer Corps, was to occupy Point 195. Meyer later ordered Waldmüller to move his battle group to the area of Point 140 and the Mazieres-Rouvres-Assy ridge.[14]

The start line for Simonds's second phase was the lateral road between Bretteville-sur-Laize and St. Aignan. The bomb line running from the north edge of Robertmesnil along the north edge of Gaumesnil to the south edge of the quarry west of Gaumesnil was forward of it. According to the air plan, Bretteville-sur-Laize on the right and St. Sylvain on the left were to be bombed preliminary to the advance of the 4th and 1st Divisions at 1400 hours on 8 August. Once the dust settled, other non-cratering strikes were to be carried out astride the Falaise road from Gouvix through Hautmesnil to Cauvicourt. Fighter-bombers were to engage targets in the areas of Bretteville-le-Rabet, Quesnay Wood, and Estrées-la-Campagne. As it happened, weather forecasts on 7 August, which indicated that visual bombing by Flying Fortresses would have to take place earlier, required the air attack to be advanced to 1226 hours, ending at 1355, which became the final H-Hour for ground-force movement.

In the event, the bombing was hardly worth the wait as it proved largely ineffective and partly counterproductive. Owing to enemy antiaircraft fire and heavy clouds of dust and smoke, only 70 percent of the U.S. Eighth Air Force's bombers managed to attack, and only three of four targeted areas were adequately bombed. Two 12-plane groups of the 492 bombers that attacked also mistakenly bombed elements of the 2nd Canadian Armoured Brigade, 2 Canadian Army Group Royal Artillery, 9 Army Group Royal Artillery, and the 1st Polish and 3rd Canadian Divisions, killing 65 soldiers and wounding another 250, including Keller, who had to be evacuated. Although this fratricide did not prevent the 1st Polish and 4th Canadian Divisions from crossing the start line for the attack on time, the Eighth Air Force's bombing had not fatally crippled the now-recovered German defense. Obviously, the attack inflicted damage upon the enemy, but its incorporation within the second phase, more than any other factor, allowed the Germans to recover from foreordained defeat. Canceling the bombing would have been no more difficult earlier than it was around 1330 hours when Simonds personally called Crerar to stop all bombing since it was also falling on friendly forces.[15] Fear of the *Leibstandarte* drove Simonds to insist, however.

The 1st Polish Armored Division, shocked by Waldmüller's counterattack just before H-Hour, ran headlong into his Mark IVs and Jagdpanzer IVs, which were now defending the Gouvix–Hautmesnil–St. Sylvain line, which had meanwhile been better prepared by rearward German troops frantically digging in and coordinating defensive arcs of fire. Counterattacked again from the east, the Polish attack ground to a halt by 1600 hours, after a paltry gain of just over a mile and the loss of some forty tanks. On the right flank, little better headway was made by the 4th Canadian Armoured Division. As intended, the 4th Armoured Brigade was to bypass Cintheaux and Hautmesnil, capture Bretteville-le-Rabet, and push on to secure Points 195 and 206, respectively northeast and due west of Potigny. The 10th Brigade was to take Cintheaux and Hautmesnil and relieve and mop up after the 4th Brigade in Bretteville-le-Rabet. A battle group comprising the 22nd Canadian Armoured Regiment (The Canadian Grenadier Guards), The Lake Superior Regiment (Motor), an antitank battery, and a squadron of engineers led the 4th Brigade's advance.[16] Apparently in imitation of German practice, this assembly was called Halpenny Force after its commander, Lt. Col. Bill Halpenny.

The 4th Armoured Brigade's commander, Brig. Leslie Booth, had pushed the use of battle groups like Halpenny Force as he correctly reasoned that the tank had little chance of success against German battle groups of all arms. His superficial adoption of this concept, however, overlooked the fact that German groups at least possessed "infantry guns" of artillery caliber. The Anglo-Canadian artillery system, in contrast, had no infantry guns and stressed that low-level indirect artillery supporting fire was best coordinated at the brigade level, where the commanding officer of the gun regiment had the required staff and communications to do so. For lack of similar facilities, single battalions and tank regiments could not, from a planning standpoint, lay on and coordinate artillery fire as well as brigades. Halpenny Force could have used some artillery assistance from Booth's brigade headquarters, but none was forthcoming because Booth essentially abrogated his responsibilities in this area by just slapping together tanks and infantry in battle groups like Halpenny Force and telling them to get on with it. They thus went into battle without the artillery support and assistance that they could and should have gotten from Booth's headquarters. Not surprisingly, Kitching later found Booth two miles away from the battle fast asleep in his tank.[17]

Apart from one distinguished troop action, Halpenny Force made no faster progress on crossing the start line than it had in closing up to it. Instead of having the Lake Superiors deal smartly with the small hamlet of Gaumesnil, which lay south of the bomb line and was originally to have been taken by the 2nd Canadian Division, it waited until the Royal Regiment secured it at 1530 hours. Had Halpenny been more energetic and Booth more helpful, they could have quickly dealt with such pockets of resistance by bringing effective artillery fire to bear, which was the one missing ingredient denying their success and a sure means of suppressing long-range enemy gun fire. By 1800 hours, Halpenny Force had advanced only beyond Cintheaux, only a kilometer away, at which time two companies of Argyll and Sutherland Highlanders from the 10th Brigade seized the village, while another two pushed south to take Hautmesnil. Shortly after this, Halpenny decided, in armored doctrinal fashion, to laager two of his tank squadrons in a rear rally near Gaumesnil to refuel and refit, an action that was completed around 2000 hours.

The opening of the second phase of Totalize, while not a complete disaster, had clearly not gone well. At 1830 hours, a concerned Simonds attempted to regain the momentum lost during the pause by directing the 4th Armoured Division to press on through the night to secure Bretteville-le-Rabet and Point 195, the highest feature before Falaise. Kitching, in turn, ordered the 4th Armoured Brigade to capture both objectives; the 10th Infantry Brigade was to follow up the armor and, after the seizure of Bretteville, occupy the villages of Langannerie and Grainville astride the Falaise road. The task of taking Bretteville still fell to Halpenny Force, but was to be executed by two Grenadier tank squadrons and two infantry companies of the Lake

Superiors at first light on 9 August. The mission of capturing Point 195 was given to Worthington Force, after Lt. Col. Don Worthington, commander of the 28th Canadian Armoured Regiment (The British Columbia Regiment), which was accompanied by two infantry companies of the Algonquin Regiment.[18]

During the early hours of 9 August, both forces set out for their objectives, momentarily passing each other in the dark around Bretteville-le-Rebat, which Worthington Force sought to avoid by skirting to the east. Once beyond the village its axis led southwest across the Falaise road, northwest of Quesnay Wood, straight on to Point 195. Halpenny Force, in the meantime, prepared to attack Bretteville, which fell to the Lake Superiors and Grenadier tanks in a hard-fought action against 89th Division elements some time after 0600 hours. It was reported clear at 1400 hours, by which time 10th Brigade troops were fighting to secure Langannerie and Grainville. The two Grenadier tank squadrons returned to laager in a rear rally near Gaumesnil after the action and were only sent forward that evening to assume a mobile counterattack role.

Just before 0700 hours, Worthington Force reported that it was on its objective, and by 0800, the 2 Corps received word that the 4th Armoured Brigade was in possession of Bretteville-le-Rabet and Point 195. Within half an hour, however, Worthington Force requested artillery support as it was under severe panzer counterattack. When queried around 0900 hours about whether the support had been effective, it failed to reply. At 1030, the uncommitted 21st Canadian Armoured Regiment (The Governor General's Foot Guards) was ordered to proceed as quickly as possible to assist Worthington Force on Point 195. Supported by the last company and 3-inch mortars of the Algonquins, a troop of antitank guns, flails, and a platoon of medium machine guns, this battle group did not get underway until after 1500 hours. For some reason, artillery support was not immediately available, and the force was soon stopped by fire from the area of Quesnay Wood. Shortly before last light, having lost fourteen tanks, it laagered in Langannerie.

In the meantime, suspicions were being confirmed that Worthington Force was not, as it had mistakenly reported, on Point 195. In fact, it had continued southeast instead of southwest in the rush to gain its objective before daybreak. Tragically lost, it had ended up on open ground east of Estrées-la-Campagne in the area of Point 140 on the Polish front. It was six kilometers almost due east of its assigned objective. Worthington Force had nonetheless broken through and caused the Germans to panic momentarily as it threatened to turn Dietrich's flank. Two kilometers to the north, Soignolles still lay in German hands, while Waldmüller's battle group, on its way to occupy Point 140, shifted east. On discovering the presence of the Canadians, Meyer ordered Wünsche to attack from Quesnay Wood. In short order, Wünsche encircled Worthington Force and, in combination with Krause's battle group on Potigny Heights, annihilated it with Tiger and Panther fire supplemented by artillery and mortars.[19]

The Canadians only gradually learned of the immensity of this disaster in the late afternoon of 9 August. The Poles, whose tanks and artillery at one point fired upon Worthington Force until warned off by yellow recognition smoke, were unable to effect its rescue. Stalled at Estrées-la-Campagne from about noon, they managed only to capture Soignolles the next day, which proved the final limit of their advance despite the exhortations of Simonds. On the 4th Armoured Division's front, meanwhile, the connected hamlets of Langannerie and Grainville had fallen to the 10th Brigade, which after last light on 9 August had pushed on toward Point 195. That night, in what was probably the single most impressive action of Totalize, the Argyll and Sutherland Highlanders under Lt. Col. Dave Stewart seized Worthington Force's objective without a casualty.

Stewart, who later claimed that he always tried to protect his unit from two enemies, Germans and his own high command, led his Argylls silently and single-file in a daring, but well-reconnoitered approach march to capture Point 195. Without having unduly aroused the enemy, they dug in and reorganized by first light on 10 August. When the surprised Germans eventually realized what had happened, they reacted violently with a storm of shells and a series of strong counterattacks. The Grenadiers, who had been ordered to follow the Argylls and exploit forward to the area of Point 206, were stopped in their tracks by one such SS attack around noon. Shortly thereafter, the Foot Guards were ordered forward to assist in the fighting, which continued for the rest of the day. It was clear, however, that neither the Germans nor the Canadians were going anywhere. Significantly, Stewart and his Argylls received hardly an accolade for this action.[20]

To break the resulting impasse and restore lost momentum, Simonds at 1000 hours ordered the 3rd Division to fight its way across the Laison River east of Potigny to the ridge west of Epancy. With the 2nd Armoured Brigade under its command and supported by two artillery brigades as well as the Polish divisional artillery, the division attacked at 1600 hours. The temporary commander, Brigadier Blackader, assigned the task of clearing Quesnay Wood to his 8th Brigade under the acting command of Lt. Col. Jock Spragge. For various reasons—delays in artillery coordination among them—this infantry attack did not go in until 2000 hours. A fire plan of grouped concentrations on call was provided from seven medium regiments and divisional artilleries. The brigade attacked with two battalions up, the North Shores left, and the Queen's Own Rifles right, in a south-easterly direction that took the latter unit through Quesnay village.

At first, all went well, and the lead Queen's Own company crossed a 150-yard cleared space on the edge of the wood with little opposition. When two following companies crossed it, however, the *Hitlerjugend* opened fire with tanks, small arms, and mortars. The North Shores, though greeted similarly, were driven out of the woods mainly by friendly shell fire. In reporting on this disastrous attack, the acting brigade commander complained that there had not been enough time for reconnaissance or coordinating artillery tasks. Information on the enemy was also considered scanty and not sufficient to make a sound detailed plan, which meant that artillery fire should have been more intense. The 8th Brigade's attack, bloodily repulsed by battle groups under Wünsche and Krause, signalled the end of Totalize.[21]

Explanations have been offered for the underwhelming performance of Simonds's armored divisions during the second phase of Totalize. Inexperience has usually topped the list, though much has also been made of the road congestion and enemy fire from pockets of resistance that reputedly held up the forward deployment of divisional artilleries integral to attacking armored divisions. The realization that the attack was not to go in until around 1400 after heavy bombing strikes did not, however, induce any sense of urgency that may have goaded these divisional artilleries into more aggressive forward movement. That gunners wanted predesignated gun positions to be clear of all enemy mortar and machine-gun fire was unreasonable in the circumstances. Congested road movement could also have been greatly reduced by restricting the forward movement of the rear and administrative echelons of first-phase assault divisions and giving priority to the forward movement of the second-phase attacking armored divisions. Had the air strike been cancelled and high command attention turned to the staff problem of getting fighting troops and supporting artillery forward, the tempo could have been sustained. The roughly six-hour wait for the commencement of phase two, however, contributed to the tendency of the first-phase assault divisions to tidy up the battlefield and bring their rear echelons forward, increasing congestion.[22]

The armored divisions had been standing by on notice to move and, given the relatively short distances involved, should have been able to get their fighting echelons forward before the congestion increased. Again, all of this would have required a greater degree of urgency and staff attention that could have been ordered in the circumstances. Had the armored divisions attacked mid-morning rather than in the afternoon, they would have encountered far less coordinated resistance and beaten serious German counterattacks to the punch. When Simonds's armored divisions finally attacked at 1355 after bomber strikes between 1226 and 1355 hours—roughly the period of German counterattacks north of the bomb line—they got nowhere.

Worthington Force, on the other hand, actually demonstrated just what might have been accomplished by an aggressively handled armored force headed in the right direction. Setting out at 0200 hours, it drove deeply into the German defense to reach what it thought was its objective by 0700 hours. Had Worthington Force been unleashed in daylight at 1100 on 8 August, it might well have found its way and covered a similar distance to Point 195 by 1600 or even earlier.[23]

Arguably, Crerar should have directed Simonds to smash straight through immediately, but this would have necessitated cancelling the air strike on which so much staff effort had been expended that it was almost bureaucratically entrenched. After taking casualties from bombing errors, however, it was cancelled quickly and easily. Alternatively, the Germans could have been outflanked from the west via Clair Tizon, as was eventually done by the 2nd Division. According to former first operations officer of the 12th SS Panzer Division, Hubert Meyer, it may also have been wiser to send the reserve 3rd Division to outflank the Germans to the east. Meyer also said that contrary to popular belief, the bulk of roughly eighty 88-millimeter antitank guns, mostly belonging to three Luftwaffe flak regiments, were deployed south of Potigny; only the divisional batteries were forward. It was thus mainly the 12th SS's resourceful handling of panzers that stemmed the 2 Canadian Corps' attack.[24]

On the basis of the evidence as it relates to German countermoves and deployments, it is difficult to imagine that Canadian arms could have done any worse had they opted to cancel the bombing and attacked earlier. By maintaining the momentum of the attack, they would at least have stood a chance of forcing the situation to develop to their advantage, rather than waiting to let it develop to the advantage of the defending enemy. A flawed concept—reinforced largely by fear of the *Leibstandarte*, which ironically was not even there, and compounded by serious map-reading and other errors—prevented Canadian exploitation and allowed the 12th SS *Hitlerjugend* to triumph in defense.

CHAPTER 10

Intractable Enemy

After Operation Totalize, the bloodied but unbowed 12th SS Panzer Division *Hitlerjugend* went into reserve for rest and refitting. There is also some evidence that Meyer's men took on the role of battle police to stiffen the resolve of infantry divisions holding the front line. Whatever the case, they constituted the core of an intractable enemy standing between the Canadians and Falaise. From a less tactical perspective, however, they appeared vulnerable.

By 10 August, Patton had four divisions advancing eastward. That evening, Haislip's U.S. XV Corps turned north, thrusting an armored division on either side of Alençon toward Argentan, only twenty miles from Simonds's 2 Canadian Corps. Fully aware of the possibility of envelopment, Kluge appealed to Hitler to release Panzer Group Eberbach from Mortain to deal with the XV Corps' threat. Hitler gave his approval on 11 August, but insisted that the Mortain attack be resumed after Eberbach had dealt with the threat. He later authorized the withdrawal of the Seventh Army, already set in train by Hausser, as far east as Flers in order to release panzer forces from the line for the attack on Haislip.

On 12 August, the Americans captured Alençon and flowed round Argentan, compelling Eberbach to commit his group of the 1st SS,

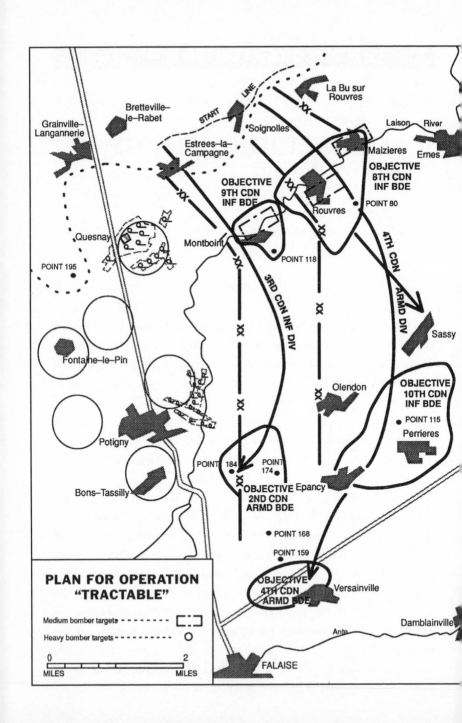

PLAN FOR OPERATION "TRACTABLE"

Grainville–Langannerie

Bretteville–le–Rabet

Estrees–la–Campagne

START LINE

Soignolles

La Bu sur Rouvres

Laison River

Ernes

Maizieres

OBJECTIVE 8TH CDN INF BDE

POINT 80

OBJECTIVE 9TH CDN INF BDE

Rouvres

Quesnay

Montboint

POINT 118

POINT 195

4TH CDN ARMD DIV

Sassy

3RD CDN INF DIV

Fontaine–le–Pin

Olendon

OBJECTIVE 10TH CDN INF BDE

POINT 115

Perrieres

Potigny

POINT 184

POINT 174

Epancy

OBJECTIVE 2ND CDN ARMD BDE

Bons–Tassilly

POINT 168

POINT 159

OBJECTIVE 4TH CDN ARMD BDE

Versainville

Damblainville

PLAN FOR OPERATION "TRACTABLE"

Medium bomber targets

Heavy bomber targets

0   2
MILES   MILES

Ante

FALAISE

2nd, and 116th Panzer Divisions to defend the area west of that town rather than attack and destroy Haislip's XV Corps. By midday on 14 August, Eberbach reported that he did not possess the strength to drive the Americans back from Argentan. To make matters worse, on the same day, Simonds's 2 Canadian Corps launched another major attack toward Falaise at noon.[1]

Following the failure of Totalize to reach its objectives, Montgomery on 11 August directed Crerar's First Canadian Army to capture Falaise as a first priority to be done quickly. To the south, Argentan was also to be secured with strong American armored and mobile forces. The object of these two moves was to close the gap between the 21st and 12th Army Groups, thereby trapping German forces in the west that were now dangerously overextended as a result of operations against the Americans in the Mortain area. This directive officially set in train the short envelopment, an idea hatched by Bradley, enthusiastically endorsed by Eisenhower, but only perfunctorily accepted by Montgomery. His preferred strategy remained to establish a bridgehead across the Seine in a longer envelopment. The problem was that classic encirclement operations not only called for a surrounding line of circumvallation, but also a line of contravallation to hold relief forces at bay. Against Germans versed in breakback operations into pockets, this made the short envelopment an extremely perilous prospect. With only three divisions west of Argentan, Haislip worried about Eberbach's three as they were receiving reinforcements. His XV Corps could hold the southern shoulder, but was not strong enough to plug the gap. Without a blocking force at Trun-Chambois or along the Seine, any force interposed at Falaise ran the risk of being sandwiched between enemy forces breaking out and those sent to their relief.[2]

Montgomery nonetheless quickly authorized Bradley to move north of the inter–army group boundary that was established on 5 August twelve miles south of Argentan. That Bradley developed a similar caution of early encirclement became evident on 12 August when he refused Patton permission to proceed north of Argentan to drive the British into the sea. As Bradley later explained, better a solid shoulder at Argentan than the possibility of a broken neck at Falaise. He later claimed that Patton had never to this point fought anything more than an enemy division and here ran the risk of encountering several, some Waffen SS. Bradley still went to his grave blaming Montgomery for the failure to close the trap by advancing from Falaise. Yet both Bradley and Montgomery appear to have believed at the time that the Canadians, only ten kilometers from the town, had to succeed in their second try. It was only subsequently that Bradley criticized Montgomery for not reinforcing the Canadians with what he described as more battle-seasoned troops of the British Second Army.[3]

Within the First Canadian Army, planning commenced on 11 August to launch another heavily supported attack toward Falaise, this time east of the road thrusting south from the general line of Estrées-la-Campagne and Soignolles. At 1000 hours the next day, Simonds held a conference with all three Canadian division commanders on the operation, curiously called Tallulah after Alabama actress Tallulah Bankhead. On 13 August, following Montgomery's practice and perhaps for reasons of security, he issued verbal orders for what was now more optimistically designated Operation Tractable. After his orders group, which included brigadiers, he went on to personally brief all armored commanders down to unit level. Making known his extreme displeasure with their Totalize performance in no uncertain terms, Simonds directed that armor was henceforth neither to balk at movement by night nor to expect infantry protection in harboring. He further warned that while there would probably continue to be instances of the misemployment of armor in future operations, this was to be no excuse for lack of success. Canadian tank units and formations were to be pushed to the very limits of their endurance.[4]

Tractable has been described as Totalize in smoke. The principal object of Tractable was to dominate the northern, eastern, and southern exits from Falaise so that no enemy could escape. Occupation of the town was to be completed by the British Second Army following the success of Tractable, as per Montgomery's direction of 13 August.

The First Canadian Army was then to exploit southeast to capture or dominate Trun. In Operation Tractable, which aimed to skirt east of Quesnay Wood and Potigny, the 2 Canadian Corps was to be assisted by the 2nd Tactical Air Force and Bomber Command. Two hours after the attack opened, heavy bombers were to strike these areas to protect the right flank. Again Simonds planned to use massed armor and infantry mounted in armored personnel carriers to break speedily through the German gun screen. Only this time, he chose to cloak their movement with smoke rather than darkness. Once more, preliminary bombardment was dispensed with in order to avoid identifying attack frontage, which enabled the Germans to bring heavy defensive fire to bear on rearward assaulting elements, thus reducing their capacity to penetrate in depth.

Simonds first aimed to secure the high ground northwest of Versainville and then push on toward Falaise. To accomplish the former, the corps was to attack with two roughly equal divisional groups: the 4th Canadian Armoured Division on the left with the 8th Brigade under its command and the remainder of the 3rd Canadian Infantry Division on the right with the 2nd Canadian Armoured Brigade (less the Sherbrooke tanks) under its command. Within the 4th Division, the 4th Armoured Brigade was to seize the Versainville high ground (Point 159) and exploit to Eraines and Damblainville, while the 10th Brigade formed a pivot at Epancy-Périers. On the 3rd Division's front, the 2nd Armoured Brigade was to capture Point 184 northwest of Epancy and Point 174 southwest of Olendon. The task of the 3rd Division proper was to clear the Laison River Valley between Montboint and Maizières and exploit to form a pivot at Sassy. Upon reaching the river, the 8th Brigade was to revert to the 3rd Division's command and capture Rouvres-Maizières while the 9th Brigade took the Montboint high ground, leaving the 7th Brigade to follow up. Simonds allotted one artillery brigade in immediate support of each division until the 2nd Armoured Brigade attained its objective, after which both artillery brigades, less one medium regiment, were to support the 4th Division. Meanwhile, flank protection was to be provided by the 2nd Canadian Infantry Division pushing on and beyond a bridgehead established at Clair Tizon on the evening of 13 August.[5]

As in Totalize, Simonds's 2 Corps assaulting elements were drawn up in tightly packed formation with armored brigades, including flails and special armor, in the van. Simonds appears to have listened to complaints about narrow frontages as he directed the armored brigades to attack on a wide front, if possible with three units up, though he stipulated fifteen-yard intervals between tanks on marshalling. The armored brigades were to push straight through to their objectives, advancing at a rate of twelve miles an hour, bearing in mind that the proper employment of armor meant taking positions that the enemy had to retain in order to regain his freedom of maneuver. A carrier-borne infantry brigade charged with dismounting and clearing the valley of the Laison River followed within each divisional column—the 8th Brigade in the 4th Division and the 9th Brigade in the 3rd Division column. Last in the order of march came the marching infantry brigades—the 10th with the 4th Division and the 7th with the 3rd Division—whose task it was to pass through and join the armor on objectives.

The ground attack was to be preceded at 1140 hours by medium bombers hitting the German 85th Infantry Division in Montboint, Rouvres, and Maizières. For fifteen minutes, enemy tank, gun, and mortar positions throughout the Laison Valley were to be struck. The forward movement of the columns was then, from 1155 hours, to be screened by artillery smoke—of impenetrable density on the flanks and of mist density on the front—controlled by artillery observers. The attack was to be postponed in the event of direct frontal winds. Over and above counterbombardment fire by all available medium artillery, concentrations on call were prearranged on known or suspected German 88-millimeter antitank gun positions. These were to be engaged during the advance whether they opened fire or not. Two hours after commencement, heavy bombers were to strike Quesnay Wood, Potigny, and German defenses astride the Falaise road for one and a half hours. The I SS Panzer Corps, now under *Brigadeführer* Fritz Kraemer since Dietrich became temporary Fifth Panzer Army commander on 9 August, bore the brunt of the Canadian attack, largely in the 85th Division's sector.[6]

The German position to be assaulted was not considered to be posted in any great depth. It was estimated to comprise a light infantry screen backed up by a large number of 88-millimeter guns along the general line of the Laison with Nebelwerfers behind reverse slopes. The newly arrived 85th Infantry Division, which had relieved the 12th SS Panzer Division *Hitlerjugend* by nightfall on 11 August, defended east of the Caen-Falaise road, the 89th Infantry Division west of the road, and the 271st Division on the left flank. The *Hitlerjugend*, which constituted the only I Panzer Corps reserve, deployed seventeen Mark IVs just west of Soulangy and a panzergrenadier battalion, backed up by seven to fifteen Panthers, ten Jagdpanzer IVs, and eleven Tigers of the 101st and 102nd Heavy Panzer Battalions around and south of Point 159. Krause's battle group occupied a position on the left flank at Villers-Canivet, while Olboeter's battle group went to contain the Canadian bridgehead at Clair Tizon. In fact, the division was but a shadow of its former self, mustering 1,000 men in six understrength rifle companies. Not surprisingly, both Simonds and Crerar were apparently satisfied that they had sufficient force to deal with the situation. The 1st Polish Division and the 33rd Armoured Brigade, for example, were each directed to form a firm base, the former near the start line at Estrées-la-Campagne.[7]

The Canadian attack launched just before 1200 hours on 14 August rekindled hope that Falaise would be secured the second time around. For the first time, the Canadians were also using a terrible new weapon, the Wasp flamethrower mounted on a modified universal carrier. Apart from some clear patches in the smoke screen, everything went well from the beginning, and leading elements were on the Laison within an hour. In the hot summer sun, however, the kilometer-wide tank phalanxes threw up huge dust clouds that, combined with high-explosive concentrations and smoke, plunged columns into incredible disorder. In Charge of the Light Brigade fashion, tanks, carriers, and half-tracks steering only by the sun all vied for the lead as control became virtually impossible to maintain. When they arrived on the river, most units were widely dispersed and in need of reorganization. As if this self-inflicted wound were not enough, the Laison was now found not to be fordable by tanks at almost all points.[8]

Ironically, a major observation made by Simonds during training in Britain was that a corps plan could not await engineer ground reconnaissance, for it would then be unable to keep up with operations. The best that could be done was to demand photographic reconnaissance of obstacles well in advance and, through a study of these and the map, prepare flexibly for the worst case. Given that corps planning had to look several days ahead, Simonds was essentially correct, but to have misjudged the Laison with its muddy bottom and steep banks was an error of major consequence. In an after-action report, the 2nd Armoured Brigade categorized the river as a definite tank obstacle and recommended that in the future, tank commanders rather than engineers determine whether an obstacle was a tank obstacle. Fortunately, engineer vehicles carrying fascines—bundles of poles for filling ditches and streams—were eventually able to bridge the Laison's six-foot breadth for tanks that had neither bogged nor crossed by improvised fords and demolition free bridges.[9]

On the 4th Division's front, the search for crossings forced the armor northeast along the river beyond Ernes, where tanks were lined up for two hours amid scenes of great confusion. Since this formation had the farthest to go to secure its final objective, delay here was critical. Although Foot Guard tanks were over the river by 1430 hours, they, like other units, required some reorganization before pushing onward. About this time, the brigade commander, Brig. Leslie Booth, was also mortally wounded and his entire tactical headquarters effectively put out of action. With no succession of command having been detailed within the brigade, it was not until after 1900 hours that the commanding officer of Foot Guards, Lt. Col. Murray Scott, received notification from Kitching to take over. Suffering from a broken ankle and considering it too late for armor to cover the remaining five kilometers to Versainville, he suspended operations for the day. Significantly, the Canadian smashing of the Laison defense did cause Kraemer's I SS Panzer Corps to ask to fall back along Sassy-Aubigny, but Dietrich's Fifth Panzer Army refused at 1530 hours, ordering the Ernes-Solangy line to be held at all costs.[10]

First light on 15 August found the 4th Armoured Brigade beyond Olendon, which had been secured by the 10th Brigade. On the 3rd Division's front, the 2nd Armoured and 7th Infantry Brigades were in possession of the greater part of the Point 184 objective northeast of Souligny. Farther east, the 8th Brigade held Sassy. By the time operations were resumed, however, Montgomery had directed the First Canadian Army to capture Falaise and close off its eastern exits. It was thus even more imperative that the 4th Armoured Division capture its final objective as soon as possible. The 4th Armoured Brigade under the wounded Scott, who was in some pain, accordingly renewed its advance toward Versainville, but not until 0930 hours because of a decision to refuel and replenish. Brigade tactical headquarters only resumed functioning in the early afternoon. Progress was also slowed initially by fierce German resistance from Epancy, which was eventually reduced mainly by the Algonquins of the 10th Brigade and partly by the Lake Superiors.

Not until mid-afternoon did the Grenadier Guards and the reconstituted British Columbia Regiment of the 4th Armoured Brigade, now grown cautious for lack of infantry and artillery support, approach the final objective of Point 159 above Versainville. Unfortunately, the more distant Foot Guards erroneously reported at 1650 hours that the two units had taken the height, a message that was happily and prematurely passed on to Simonds. Shortly thereafter, Kitching relieved the injured Scott at his own request, replacing him with Halpenny. It was only after dining with a jubilant Simonds at corps headquarters that Kitching learned that the objective had not been captured. In fact, the Canadian attack had been bloodily repulsed. He in turn informed Simonds, much to the latter's understandable disappointment and considerable annoyance. News from the 3rd Division was similarly disconcerting, for although the Canadian Scottish had wrested Point 168 from the *Hitlerjugend* in a costly but spectacular action, assaulting 7th Brigade troops were thrown out of Souligny before dark by Krause's battle group. As in Totalize, the Germans had managed to deny Canadian arms the planned goal they sought. From east to west, the now half-strength but resilient 272nd, 85th, 89th, and 271st Infantry Divisions still held a cohesive defensive line and the vital ground running from Périers through Epancy and Soulangy to Villers-Canivet.[11]

The ultimate failure of Tractable was largely obscured by a contretemps of considerable magnitude, though it had little impact on the battle. In a performance reminiscent of Totalize, seventy-seven bombers—forty-four of them from No. 6 (RCAF) Bomber Group—mistakenly unloaded short on Canadian rearward units, especially 2 Canadian Army Group Royal Artillery Brigade and elements of the 1st Polish Armored Division. Troop attempts to remedy this blunder by setting out yellow markers and letting off yellow flares and smoke, a procedure rehearsed just for such an eventuality, only brought more bombs as a similar target indicator color was employed by air force markers that day. Regrettably, Bomber Command had never been informed of a Supreme Headquarters Allied Expeditionary Force (SHAEF) directive that authorized the use of this color for indicating positions of forward ground troops. While, in a strict sense, SHAEF should have so advised Bomber Command, the fact that all communication with the latter went through Headquarters First Canadian Army suggests that it had a responsibility to ensure that all aspects of the operation, especially those related to the safety of troops, were thoroughly checked and coordinated. In any event, when all bombing was ordered stopped at 1520 hours, most of the 769 Lancasters and Halifaxes had delivered on target. With close to 400 Canadian and Polish casualties, however, the raid had a devastating effect on ground-force morale.[12]

Another incident related to Tractable was the capture by the Germans of an officer of the 8th Reconnaissance Regiment who had accidentally directed his scout car into their lines on the evening of 13 August. The officer was shot dead, but a copy of a 2nd Division instruction outlining the entire corps plan was found on his body. When Simonds learned what had happened, he angrily claimed that this individual act of carelessness had compromised surprise and enabled the enemy to make quick adjustments to his dispositions that undoubtedly resulted in casualties to Allied troops the following day. Simonds also apparently believed that it delayed the capture of Falaise for more than twenty-four hours. Yet according to Hubert Meyer of the 12th SS, no redeployment of import took place as there was insufficient time to react.[13] The uncomfortable fact thus remains that roughly 300 tanks and four brigades of infantry supported by massive artillery and air resources failed to overcome the *Hitlerjugend* and two reinforced infantry regiments (many of whose men had not been under fire before).

At the same time, it must be said that while the Canadians faced many fewer tanks, the killing power of Tigers, Panthers, and Jagdpanzers IVs in good defensible terrain with excellent fields of fire was formidable indeed. Antitank screens by 75-millimeter and 88-millimeter guns, despite the Luftwaffe's outright refusal to place the III Flak Corps under Army Group B, also took a fearsome toll. Simonds's expectation that the operation should have accomplished what it set out to do foundered on the banks of the Laison unfortunately.

In the view of the 7th Brigade's commander, Brigadier Foster, the attack formation employed in Tractable was one of the strangest anyone ever dreamed up. To Foster, what looked good to Simonds's precise engineering mind on paper seldom worked in practice once the human element was added. Yet Foster's conclusion that the attack formation had hardly a hope of succeeding as planned appears challengeable. Lining up formations in parade-square fashion was, of course, a luxury that could not possibly have been attempted without absolute air superiority. On the other hand, it solved the potentially disastrous movement problem of getting hundreds of armored vehicles to the start line in good order. Not to have expected huge amounts of dust to generate mass confusion and associated control problems seems an extraordinary oversight, but the misreading of the fordability of the Laison surely remains the fundamental reason why Tractable failed. There was simply no time left for recovery. Even then, like Totalize, it cracked a well-prepared German defense with relative ease on the first day. Dietrich further reported that Kraemer's I Panzer Corps defenses had been so shattered by the Tractable attack that a breakthrough to Falaise could hardly be prevented.[14]

Tractable suffered from difficulties in getting artillery forward, and at 1810 hours, Simonds had to order his artillery commander to get guns into the valley below Soignolles. While bombing errors likely contributed to this problem, artillery insistence on having gun areas cleared of Germans may also have been a factor. An additional impediment resulted from the tardy transference of command following Booth's incapacitation, about which Montgomery had warned Canadians earlier. Since the armored regiments of the 4th Brigade had continued to progress, an extra hour or two of firm direction from brigade level could have made all the difference from the standpoint of artillery coordination alone. Though lower echelons are often easier to blame than higher command for operational failures like Tractable, one can hardly fault the performance of units like the Canadian Scottish, which incurred 132 casualties, but managed without intimate tank support to throw the *Hitlerjugend* off Point 168. The performance of many other infantry and even armored units in Tractable does not seem to suffer by comparison.

On 13 August, Montgomery had directed Crerar and Bradley to strike for Trun and Chambois to backstop the pocket that was developing from the retreat of German forces at Falaise. Two days later, as the 2nd Canadian Infantry Division advanced on Falaise, Simonds ordered the 1st Polish Armored Division, which had that morning mopped up bombed-out Quesnay Woods and Potigny, to seize crossings over the River Dives around Jort and Vendeuvre with a view to taking Trun. The same day, Hitler declared Falaise a fortress and authorized Panzer Group Eberbach and Hausser's Seventh Army to begin withdrawing eastward. At 2100 hours that day, Dietrich's Fifth Panzer Army also ordered the XXXXVII Corps to withdraw behind the Dives along a line running from Houlgate on the Channel to Morteaux-Couliboef, from which Kraemer's I Panzer Corps would hold the line along the Ante stream to Falaise.

On 16 August, the *Leibstandarte* began pulling back, crossing the Orne at Putanges. On the same date, Simonds ordered the 2nd Canadian Infantry Division to clear Falaise and the 4th Canadian Armoured Division to strike eastward to gain crossings over the Ante in the area of Damblainville and Morteaux-Couliboef. As Haislip's regrouped XV Corps was well on its way to the Seine and threatening a longer encirclement, Kluge on 16 August ordered a general German withdrawal from the Falaise pocket.[15]

Meanwhile, Gerow's U.S. V Corps took over the divisions that Haislip left at Argentan and attacked north toward Chambois on 17 August. The next day, Field Marshal Walter Model, sent to replace Kluge, ordered the Seventh Army and Panzer Group Eberbach to be extricated from the pocket. He directed remnants of the 12th SS *Hitlerjugend* and 21st Panzer Divisions, under the II Panzer Corps, to hold the northern wall of the escape corridor, while the XXXXVII Panzer Corps secured the southern wall with what was left of the 2nd and 116th Panzer Divisions. Once the weakened 2nd SS Panzer Division *Das Reich* and the 9th SS Panzer Division *Hohenstaufen* passed through the Falaise gap, they were to be regrouped under the II SS Panzer Corps to launch a breakback attack toward Trun and Chambois to assist Hausser's Seventh Army in breaking out of the pocket. The 1st SS Panzer Division *Leibstandarte*, 10th SS Panzer Division *Frundsberg*, and the I SS Panzer Corps were to pull back to the Seine, while the *Panzer Lehr* Division and the 17th SS Panzergrenadier Division *Götz von Berlichingen* went into refit east of Paris. By 17 August, however, the 1st Polish Armored Division had turned Meyer's right flank and penetrated the depth of the disintegrating German defense. That afternoon, the 4th Canadian Armoured Division crossed the Dives at Morteaux-Couliboef and advanced on Trun.[16]

On 18 August, Hitler's fortress Falaise finally fell to the 2nd Canadian Infantry Division after two days of intense house-to-house fighting and a last-ditch stand by sixty *Hitlerjugend* under Krause, only a few of whom got away. The fall of Falaise reduced the gap between Canadian and American forces to some twelve miles, but as the main German escape route lay north of Chambois, it seemed clear that the 2 Canadian Corps would have to cork the bottleneck. After the capture of Trun that afternoon, Simonds ordered the 4th Division to push on to Chambois, which was also now the objective of the 1st Polish Armored and U.S. 90th Infantry Divisions. That evening, the 1st Polish Armored Division blocked all eastern exits from Chambois by seizing Point 262 north, Point 252, and Point 262 south on heights around Coudehard and Mont Ormel. Caught in the inexorable crush of Allied forces only loosely linked up in Chambois by the evening of 19 August, the Germans fought back with determination and skill. Under cover of darkness in the early hours of 20 August, Bittrich's II SS Panzer Corps attacked from Vimoutiers toward Trun and St. Lambert-sur-Dives to link up with Hausser's forces. Sandwiched in Model's Eastern Front–style operation, the completely isolated 1st Polish Division hung on grimly until finally relieved by the 4th Canadian Armoured Division the following day.[17]

Between St. Lambert and Chambois up "Dead Horse Alley," the Germans ultimately managed to extricate possibly one-third of their forces—by one estimate as many as 157,800 men—largely because formations such as the *Das Reich* kept various routes open; the highly respected 2nd Panzer Division did so for up to six hours. Another reason this happened related to the nature of the terrain. Unlike the region of the Caen plain, the rising countryside around Trun east of the Dives consisted of thickly wooded hills interspersed with hamlets, small fields, and numerous orchards, all ringed by valleys, streams, and winding sunken lanes. Like the area of Villers–Bocage, it was less than ideal tank country, but it was through here that the Canadian and Polish armored divisions and their insufficient infantry complements fought a series of desperate offensive and defensive actions against a cornered and wounded enemy. The horrific carnage and stench of dead horses and humans were overwhelming as Allied air strikes and artillery fire wreaked havoc on retreating German forces. The Waffen SS reportedly died hard in this *Götterdämmerung* and had no compunction about shooting any German soldiers they saw trying to surrender. Although none of them came out as coherent fighting divisions, they do seem to have broken out in greater strength than commonly thought. The *Hitlerjugend* paraded ten panzers and 12,000 troops after the battle, the *Das Reich* the same number, the *Leibstandarte* about 10,000, the *Hohenstaufen* 15,000, the *Frundsberg* 10,000, and the *Götz von Berlichingen* 6,000.[18]

By nightfall on 21 August, with Patton already on the Seine, the Falaise gap was closed for good, and the endless controversy about why so many Germans managed to escape began. The Waffen SS formations survived to fight another day, but the crushing defeat inflicted upon them and the rest of the German army in Normandy was catastrophic in the extreme. Ironically, in this hour when the sky was falling, Waffen SS *Oberstgruppenführern* headed both German armies in the West. Yet while their men fought tenaciously, the collective actions of those breaking out from the pocket ultimately turned into an escape and evasion operation. One SS man said he ran like a rabbit and was chased like one.

In many ways, it was a rout worse than Dunkirk, where Montgomery at least marched out with a cohesive division. The Fifth Panzer Army was hardly worth the name panzer, and most Waffen SS divisions were in tatters. Meyer retreated with a company of his men and stragglers, but finally passed through the chaos with under a dozen. The *Leibstandarte*'s commander, *Brigadeführer* Wisch, was severely wounded by shell fire and had to be packed out by half-track. The seriously wounded Hausser suffered a similar fate, evacuated by a beaten horse-drawn army. Wünsche made his way out with two or three others only to be captured in late August and sent into a British prisoner of war camp until 1948. Eberbach was captured in his pajamas by fast-moving British troops on 31 August. Meyer was captured in early September, having surely experienced the bitter agony of abject defeat along with the most battle-hardened Waffen SS. Mohnke survived the ordeal better than most and went on to take over the remains of the decimated 1st SS Panzer Division *Leibstandarte*, which he rebuilt, trained, and indoctrinated before taking it into action. Old habits die hard, and the subsequent *Leibstandarte* killing of some 300 American prisoners and 111 Belgian civilians in the Malmedy area massacres during the Battle of the Bulge occurred under his command.[19] But that is another story about which much is already known.

Conclusion

The Waffen SS formations that fought the Allies in the Norman summer of 1944 did not really leave the field of battle with heads held high. While conducting an impressive breakback operation into the Falaise pocket and stalwartly helping hold open the closing jaws of Allied pincers, they in the end slunk through the gap like so many whipped dogs. That wounded commanders like Hausser and Wisch had to be evacuated by vehicle could only have accentuated the hopelessness of the situation and exacerbated feelings of abject defeat. Hitler's dream of his concentrated Waffen SS spearheading a massive counterattack to throw the Allies back into the sea had of course evaporated much earlier. Arguably, it started with the piecemeal attack forced on Kurt Meyer by the Canadian advance on Carpiquet airfield on 7 June. Meyer's local success threw the Canadians back for more than a month, but they fought him to a standstill and left his 25th Regiment decisively committed in line. Forced into a defensive posture, he could not easily extricate his formation for another attack. As pointed out by the principal operations staff officer of the 12th SS Panzer Division, Meyer's action ultimately turned out to be counterproductive in the long run as it greatly reduced the chance of mounting a full-strength attack by the entire 20,000-man division later. In fact, as much as it would have liked to do so, the *Hitlerjugend* never managed to launch a full-scale divisional attack in Normandy.

At a higher level, continuous attempts by *Obergruppenführer* Dietrich and Geyr von Schweppenburg to launch multidivision corps counterattacks foundered as Montgomery continually beat them to the punch with his "colossal cracks." The attack by the II SS Panzer Corps, with the 9th SS *Hohenstaufen* and 10th SS *Frundsberg* under its command, looked more like two distinct division attacks than a properly coordinated corps attack. In typical Waffen SS fashion, it was launched far too hastily off the line of march without the necessary corps-coordinated artillery preparation and support that might have produced success.

This repeated the pattern of the relief of the Kamenetz-Podolsk pocket on the Eastern Front, where Hausser's II SS Panzer Corps was hurriedly rushed from France and committed piecemeal. The operation proved a partial success, albeit with heavy casualties, but the premature commitment of the II SS Panzer Corps in Epsom dashed any realistic hope of launching a decisive counterstroke against the Allies. Both Rommel and Geyr von Schweppenburg had wanted to use the II SS Panzer Corps in a coordinated night counterattack with Dietrich's I SS Panzer Corps striking north along the Anglo-American boundary toward Bayeux and the sea. Epsom forced the Germans to abandon these plans, from which point Waffen SS formations replayed their Eastern Front defensive role, dashing here and there to blunt enemy advances by counterattack, but always reacting to Allied initiatives. Instead of being used to exploit success, they were squandered in reactive responses.

A critical difference was that on the Eastern Front up to the Battle of Kursk, the Germans enjoyed Stuka support within a *blitzkrieg* combination of arms that proved stronger than the sum of its parts. Loss of air superiority, however, weakened the *blitzkrieg* and left the Germans in Normandy to fight offensively mainly by night under less favorable conditions. Movement by day remained perilous.

Long dependence on Stuka support had meanwhile led to the neglect and deterioration of German artillery, which was never able to match the overwhelming power of Allied indirect fire. The direct fire of infantry guns, assault guns, and panzers—as powerful as the last were—was no substitute for the concentrated indirect fire of artillery in offensive operations. As Helmut Ritgen of the *Panzer Lehr* Division observed, German artillery was too weak. It was also difficult to coordinate artillery support for widely dispersed battle groups fighting independently of each other. The German tendency to fight in such fragmented fashion rather than as complete divisions appears to have been forced by the unfavorable air situation coupled with the pronounced superiority of their Panthers and Tigers. Superficially combined arms of panzer, infantry, engineers, and mobile artillery, German battle groups lacked the key ingredient of massed and concentrated artillery support in the offensive. Whereas the artillery of an Anglo-Canadian division was commonly used as a seventy-two-gun battery to concentrate fire on one spot, German artillery was dispersed piecemeal throughout battle groups somewhat in the manner of the old, smaller British Jock columns. Thus, without air or any effective indirect fire artillery support, German battle groups were left to depend principally on maneuvering the direct firepower of their superior panzers and assault guns supported by infantry and engineers.

The fire-brigade reputation of the Waffen SS and the perception that they were good also resulted in divisions being habitually parcelled out bit by bit to deal with operational emergencies in unfamiliar terrain, often at the last minute with little time for orientation, reconnaissance, or liaison with friendly forces in the area of crisis. The 2nd SS Panzer Division *Das Reich*, with half the manpower and the bulk of the panzers facing the Americans, failed to play any decisive role in the U.S. sector since it was, from the beginning, fed in piecemeal to help plug gaps and shore up sagging German defense lines. Weidinger's *Das Reich* battle group deployed first to the British sector during Operation Epsom, then farther west to the 353rd Infantry Division around La Haye-du-Puits on 5 July. Another *Das Reich* battle group served with the battered *Panzer Lehr* until 18 July. The 17th SS Panzergrenadier Division, with no tanks on establishment, also had to be reinforced with panzers from the *Das Reich*.

During Epsom, Frey's 1st SS Panzergrenadier Regiment of the 1st SS Panzer Division *Leibstandarte* had also been attached to the 12th SS Division, whereupon Meyer ordered it to attack immediately with two just-arrived battalions. He ignored Frey's pleas to delay the attack until the rest of his troops and artillery arrived. Meyer's promise of 12th SS artillery support never materialized, and Frey ended up attacking without any artillery liaison whatsoever. Not surprisingly, this hurriedly and badly mounted attack failed.

Although the longer gun ranges and heavier armor of their superior panzers provided the Germans with enormous advantages in hitting power and withstanding enemy fire, the perceived imperviousness of these weapons encouraged an undue recklessness in already-aggressive Waffen SS crews. Meyer's carelessly mounted attacks on Bretteville from 8 to 10 June completely shattered against in-depth Canadian antitank defenses and devastating artillery fire.

Amply demonstrated by Wittmann at Villers-Bocage, the effectiveness of the Tiger, even at short range, was nonetheless enough to excuse some crews for thinking they could sally forth with impunity. While the Firefly ended this impunity, the real strength of the Tiger and even Panther continued to lie in their ability to defend. Hardly any Allied ground fire could knock out Panthers and Tigers that were properly sited in hull-down positions, but they could destroy anything on the Allied side. The Tiger could destroy any Allied tank at 2,500 meters, while the Panther could do the same at 2,000 meters and the Mark IV panzer at 1,500. Conversely, the Sherman could only penetrate a Mark IV frontally at 1,000 meters, but not kill a Tiger unless it closed to 100 meters or hit the rear or side plates. Range advantages of this order in open country also enabled the Germans to shoot laterally across their defensive fronts, taking Allied targets in enfilade with devastating results. This capability in particular, often overlooked when just measuring gun ranges in head-on comparisons, made the

Waffen SS formidable opponents in the defense and largely explains why they so decisively repelled Canadian attacks in Operations Windsor, Atlantic, and Spring.

All German successes in Normandy were defensive, and their offensive wins were limited to local battle group actions. Tigers and Panthers were best employed in hull-down positions firing at long range, but they were not well suited to distant or sustained offensive operations that called for extended movement. Despite a highly efficient armored-maintenance system of repair and recovery carried out as far forward as possible—which stood in direct contrast to the rear rally–based British repair system—the Germans experienced difficult in keeping their high-maintenance panzers running. Most Tigers broke down because of mechanical failure emanating from such problems as suspension and gear-box defects. Although the Panther could outmaneuver the Sherman in wet or muddy terrain, mechanical problems increasingly plagued it the more it moved. In fact, mechanical breakdown constituted the greatest single cause of German panzer losses, slightly edging out gunfire. Maneuver was the kiss of death for German panzers in the summer of 1944. For this reason and associated logistical concerns related to geography, the German counterattack at Mortain, though perhaps brilliant in theoretical conception, should have been avoided as no real capacity for operational-level maneuver existed.

In any case, the exceedingly clumsy deployment of Waffen SS formations for the Mortain counterattack contributed to the failure of the operation, which can only be described as a fiasco. Originally slated to deliver the main thrust, the 1st SS Panzer Division *Leibstandarte*, because of route congestion, was still twenty kilometers from its attack position on the evening of 6 August. The 2nd Panzer Division never received the *Leibstandarte* Panthers originally assigned for its midnight attack. Only at 0200 hours on 7 August did forty-three Panthers and several Mark IVs, a panzergrenadier battalion, and the reconnaissance battalion of the *Leibstandarte* join the 2nd Panzer Division's attack, which was already in progress.

The *Leibstandarte* never fought as a division, but rather participated as a number of dispersed battle groups. One battle group (a panzer-grenadier battalion, artillery battalion, Nebelwerfer battery, and four or five assault guns) never even took part in the Mortain attack. Hausser instead subordinated this force to the 84th Infantry Division to help stem the Allied attack south of Vire between 7 and 10 August. Some elements of the 2nd SS Panzer (Mark IV) Regiment did not even move west from the area of Brettteville-sur-Laize until late on 7 August and then took three days to reach the Domfront area. The rest of the *Leibstandarte*, consisting of two battalions of the 2nd SS Panz-ergrenadier Regiment, twenty assault guns, and the pioneer battalion, still remained five kilometers east of Mortain when the attack began.

Although faulty Waffen SS deployments were not always of their own making, they almost always had their fighting reputations enhanced by the mistakes of Allied commanders and troops. Meyer's 7 June attack on the 9th Canadian Infantry Brigade would never have succeeded had supporting artillery been forward as it should have been. The poor defensive deployment of the Royal Winnipeg Rifles at Putot left them vulnerable to 12th SS counterattack, and their sub-sequent assault on the south hangars at Carpiquet foundered for lack of adequate tank support.

Conversely, had O'Connor at the 8 Corps not stripped Roberts's 29th Armoured Brigade of the intimate support of its companion 159th Infantry Brigade, there might also have been a better outcome in Operation Goodwood. The 8 Corps' attack foundered mainly because O'Connor insisted that the spearhead 11th Armoured Divi-sion clear the villages of Cuverville and Demouville with its infantry brigade. O'Connor unfortunately dismissed Roberts's suggestion to reallocate the clearance task to the 51st (Highland) Division on the eastern flank of the 2 Canadian Corps.

When leading tanks of the 29th Brigade came under devastating fire from German assault guns in Le Mesnil-Frementel and Le Poirier, the 159th Infantry Brigade, which could have dealt with them, remained committed to clearing Cuverville and Denouville. With insufficient infantry to capture the fortified hamlet of Cagny, which contained 88-millimeter guns and was rapidly reinforced by the Germans, Roberts could only bypass what became a key center of resistance that stalled the subsequent advance of the Guards Armoured Division. The resulting traffic congestion held up the 7th Armoured Division, which was earmarked to advance on the left of the 11th Armoured. Much of the credit for defeating the Goodwood attack deservedly accrued to the 21st Panzer Division, especially Luck's battle group and Becker's assault guns.

The Canadian decision to exploit their success in Operation Atlantic, which supported Goodwood, provided a better opportunity for the Waffen SS to shine. Instead of realizing that Goodwood forced Dietrich to commit his *Leibstandarte* reserve and the German high command to divert the 2nd and 116th Panzer Divisions to the Caen area, Simonds imprudently decided to launch a hasty attack to take Verrières Ridge. In this instance, all German defensive advantages in Nebelwerfer and long-range panzer and assault-gun fire came into play, forcing Canadian soldiers to break and run from completely untenable positions.

For reasons not entirely the fault of Simonds, this pattern repeated itself in Operation Spring, with divisional attacks launched against the strongest concentration of panzers in the West and the largest number of Waffen SS formations on either the Eastern or Western Fronts. In Spring, the Waffen SS manifested the height of its defensive prowess in Normandy. Yet even here, while the Germans showed that they could capitalize on Allied mistakes and even humiliate attacking troops, it was more than evident that they were able to defend only with limited local counterattacks. They possessed little capability to attack and prevail. The Canadians, on the other hand, remained capable of launching extremely powerful multidivision corps attacks, which the Allies as well as the Germans had come to realize were more productive than single-division attacks against defensive systems.

In Operation Totalize, the 2 Canadian Corps shattered the German line, but then held back for self-inflicted reasons rather than enemy reactions. The best time to have launched a second attack upon the Germans was when they were reeling and disorganized, unable to immediately recover owing to severe disruption and turmoil. Clearly, this fleeting moment should have been seized upon by continuing to press the attack. Simonds's decision to pause for six hours to wait for a second bomber strike guaranteed a loss of momentum. Every passing minute allowed the Germans time to catch their breath and regroup. The pause actually invited the Germans to mount the very counterattacks that Simonds feared and, by initially striking deep into the German defensive depth, had hoped to avert. Had his armored divisions attacked mid-morning rather than in the afternoon, they would have encountered far less cohesive defense and beaten serious German counterattacks to the punch. When they finally attacked at 1355 after bomber strikes between 1226 and 1355—roughly the period of German counterattacks north of the bomb line—they stalled.

In contrast, Worthington Force actually demonstrated just what might have been accomplished by an aggressively handled armored force headed in the right direction. At 0200 hours, it drove deeply into the German defense to reach what it thought was its objective by 0700 hours. Had Worthington Force been unleashed in daylight at 1100 hours on 8 August, it might well have found its way to its intended objective by 1600 or even earlier. In any case, its presence even on the wrong objective caused momentary concern, at least until Wünsche's panzers wiped it out. Again, the Waffen SS demonstrated a commendable defensive capacity for capitalizing on enemy mistakes, which in turn made them look better than they perhaps were. One suspects that had the 12th SS *Hitlerjugend* been equipped with Shermans or Cromwells, all their good camouflage techniques, fire discipline, tactical skill, and even fanatical will would hardly have produced similar success.

Among the most common problems the Allies faced was congestion resulting from massing forces for battle, which the Germans also encountered on their march to the abortive attack on Mortain. Mixing up one's own forces produced a friction that prevented concentrating maximum combat power where it was needed most. On 7 June, congestion robbed the 9th Canadian Infantry Brigade of artillery support, just as it hurt the British in Epsom, where Dempsey unnecessarily decided to fall back. Yet in keeping with the generally proven military adage that the more you use, the fewer you lose, it was still better technique to employ the sledgehammer of a corps attack rather than the battle group pin prick so characteristic of Waffen SS operations in Normandy. All too often, perhaps to avoid such congestion, Allied company attacks were made that should have been carried out by battalions, and battalion attacks made that should have been carried out by brigades. Most glaringly, this is what happened in the case of Tilly, considered a two-company objective until eventually captured by two battalions. The clearance of St. Andre and St. Martin in Totalize should also have been given to a brigade rather than single battalions.

In Operation Cobra, the most successful corps attack delivered in Normandy, this did not occur since the initial breach was made by three infantry divisions. Although stiffer resistance than expected denied them their objectives, they penetrated the fragmented German line. On the afternoon of 25 July, in spite of the risk of congestion and reports describing conditions as chaotic, Collins unleashed a fourth mobile infantry division. His later decision to commit his 3rd Armored Division turned out to be vital to the success of Cobra, even though based on bad information. On the morning of 26 July, the 1st Infantry Division encountered German reinforcements that, tellingly, included two panzer companies of the 2nd SS Panzer Division *Das Reich*. Meanwhile, the advance of Middleton's supporting VIII Corps triggered panic in the 17th SS Panzergrenadier Division *Götz von Berlichingen*, which was defending near Périers, where SS men broke under the onslaught and streamed to the rear.

On the American front, the Waffen SS offered comparatively little resistance, though *Das Reich* companies were among the few—including the pulverized *Panzer Lehr*, 3rd Parachute, and 353rd Infantry Divisions—to pose effective resistance after 25 July. Had the *Das Reich* arrived sooner in Normandy, the Germans might have stood a better chance. Had Kluge heeded the advice of his Army Group B chief of staff and transferred the 1st SS Panzer Division *Leibstandarte* to the American front before the fall of St. Lô, the German position would have been strengthened, bearing in mind that the *bocage* restricted the long-range fire of Tigers and Panthers.

Kluge refused because his focus centered on the Caen sector, where he still planned to use both the I and II Panzer Corps in a major attack against Anglo-Canadian forces. Goodwood put an abrupt end to his attack plans, but not his fears of a breakthrough in that area. On the day of Cobra, he went to the Caen area, where Operation Spring opened, as he continued to believe that a renewal of a British offensive there would have far more serious consequences than an American breakthrough in the *bocage*. In fact, Montgomery intended to launch a 12 Corps attack west of the Orne on 28 July, with a subsequent push by the 8 Corps east of the Orne toward Falaise on 30 July. These operations were to be preliminary to another Goodwood-style offensive. Operation Spring nonetheless helped reinforce Kluge's fatal conviction during the first critical hours of Cobra that the American attack farther west was diversionary.

Cobra precipitated the collapse of the German front in Normandy. Hitler's hopes of reversing the tide of the war with his Waffen SS divisions remained elusive. Indeed, the bulk of these units were in the wrong place to deal with Cobra, and they lacked the operational and logistical capacity to cut the Americans off at Avranches. Given the situation on the Caen front, the Mortain offensive was also akin to putting one's head in a noose. By this time, too, the Waffen SS had lost its offensive edge, and its sheer ferocity, reckless courage, and aggressive risk-taking were no longer sufficient to produce success. Despite medals lavished upon the Waffen SS by Hitler, bravery was not the province of either side in Normandy, and casualty lists showed that the Allies were prepared to die in number—a willingness that had been characteristic of the Waffen SS from the start.

On a tactical level, the Waffen SS remained markedly proficient, reflecting good low-level leadership, hard realistic training, personal dedication, and—always—superior machines of war. The swashbuckling attitude of yore also continued to shine through as individual panzer commanders sought ace status.

Were they, then, just soldiers like any other? Probably many were—Wünsche most immediately comes to mind—and the longer they served at the front, the more like the army they became. Yet the Waffen SS at large possessed a streak of nihilism that ran all the way back to the concentration camps of Dachau, Sachsenhausen, Buchenwald, and Belsen. Waffen SS field formations routinely exchanged personnel with these centers even after they became extermination camps. The decision to establish the *Totenkopf* division and incorporate the *Totenkopfverbände* into the Waffen SS unavoidably produced this outcome. Although some German army and Allied units committed atrocities in Normandy, the Waffen SS evinced a distinct proclivity for doing so, which remains a dark stain on the otherwise commendable fighting record of a unique force that vainly tried to save what God abandoned.

Characteristics of Weapons

ALLIED AND GERMAN TANK/ASSAULT GUN COMPARISON							
Type	Crew	Weight (tons)	Armor (mm front/side) Turret	Hull	Caliber & Length (calibers[1])	Speed (mph)	Range (miles)
Cromwell	5	28	64/51	64/32	75/40	36	170
Churchill	5	39	150/95	140/95	6pdr/75mm	15	56
Sherman	5	31	76/51	50/38	75/40	26	150
Firefly	4	33	76/51	50/38	76.2/58	25	100
Mark IV	5	28	50/50	80/30	75/48	25	150
Panther	5	45	110/45	60/40	75/70	30	150
Tiger I	5	56	100/80	100/60	88/56	24	87
Tiger II	5	68	180/80	150/80	88/71	24	68
Jagdpz IV	4	23	80/40	50/30	75/48	26	130
Jagdpz IV	4	24			75/70		
Jagdpanther		45	100/50	60/40	88/71	28	150
Stug III	4	24	80/30	50/30	75/48	25	96
M10 TD	5	30	37/	/12	3-inch	25	180

Note: Tanks were constantly improved and armor upgraded on various models; for example, the Panther F had a 120/60 turret. Tanks weights shown here in British tons (2,200 pounds) are often given in U.S. short tons (2,000 pounds) and metric tons (1,000 kilograms), which approximate British tons.

1. Caliber means bore size (e.g., 75-millimeter). Barrel length is expressed as "calibers" (plural). For example, L/40 means the barrel is 40 calibers long—that is, 40 times the caliber. Caliber is an actual measurement, whereas calibers is a ratio (40:1). A gun of 75-millimeter caliber whose barrel is 40 calibers would be 3,000 millimeters (3 meters) in length.

ALLIED AND GERMAN TANK/ANTITANK GUN AMMUNITION COMPARISON

Gun Vehicle		Ammunition	Muzzle Velocity (meters/second)	Armor Penetration in mm at 30° Angle (100/500/1,000/1,800 meters)

ALLIED

75mm Sherman/Cromwell

Gun	Vehicle	Ammunition	Muzzle Velocity	Armor Penetration
		APBCM61	625	74/68/60/47
6 pdr	Towed	APBCM86	904	93/87/80/67 (2,698 lbs; crew, 4–5)
		APDS	1,158	143/131/117/92
17 pdr	Towed	APCBCMk8	884	149/140/130/110 (7,000 lbs; crew, 6)
	Firefly	APDS	1,204	221/208/192/160
57mm	U.S. TD	APCM86	822	—/ 81/64/50
3-inch	M10 TD	APCM62	793	109/ 99/89/73 (Achilles 17pdr)
76mm	Sherman	APCM62	793	109/99/89/73
90mm	U.S. TD	APCM82	807	140/129/122/114

GERMAN

KwK 40 (75mm)

L/48	Mark IV	PzGr39AP	790	106/96/85/66
	PaK 40	PzGr40	990	143/120/97/77 (3300 lbs; crew, 6)

KwK42 (75mm)

L/70	Panther	PzGr39AP	925	138/128/118/100
	PzJager	PzGr40/42	1,120	194/174/150/127

KwK36 (88mm)

L/56	Tiger I	PzGr39AP	773	120/112/102/88
	Flak36/37	PzGr40	930	171/156/138/123 (5 ton)

KwK43 (88mm)

L/71	Tiger II	PzGr39AP	1,000	203/187/165/137
	Jagdpanther	"	"	"

DIVISIONAL ARTILLERY GUNS AND HOWITZERS

Caliber	Range (meters)	Rate of Fire (per minute)	Gun Weight (kilograms)
GERMAN			
105mm	10,600	4–6	2,040
Wespe SP (crew of 5, 12 tons, 25 mph, 87 miles range)			
150	13,325	4	5,512
Hummel SP (crew of 6, 26 tons, 26 mph, 134 miles range)			
152	16,500	4	7,128
Nebelwerfer 41 (6 barrels, 150mm)	6,700	36/battery-salvos in 10 secs/min reload	
Nebelwerfer 42 (5 barrels, 210mm)	7,850	"	
ANGLO-AMERICAN			
Sexton SP			
25pdr	12,250	3	1,800 (6-man crew)
5.5 inch	18,200	—	(10-man crew)
75 how	8,700	3	1,340
Priest SP (25 tons, 25 mph, 125 miles range)			
105 how	11,200	3	2,250 (7-man crew)
155 how	16,100	1	5,700

Figures based largely on Ritgen, *Western Front*, 299–305; Horst Scheibert, *Sturmgeschutz 40 L/43 & L48—The Long Gun Version* (West Chester, PA: Schiffer, 1991); Chandler and Collins, *D-Day Encylopedia*, 56–65, 70–84B.

Rank Comparisons

Rank	Translation	SA Equivalent	*Heer* Equivalent	U.S. Equivalent	British Equivalent
neraloffiziere					
ichsführer-SS	National Leader	Stabschef-SA	Generalfeld-marschall	General of the Army	Field Marshal
erstgruppenführer om 1942)	Supreme Group Leader	(none)	Generaloberst	General	General
ergruppenführer	Senior Group Leader	Obergruppenführer	General	Lieutenant General	Lieutenant-General
uppenführer	Group Leader	Gruppenführer	Generalleutnant	Major General	Major-General
gadeführer	Brigade Leader	Brigadeführer	Generalmajor	Brigadier General	(None)
bsoffiziere					
erführer	Senior Leader	Oberführer	(None)	(None)	Brigadier
ndartenführer	Regiment Leader	Standartenführer	Oberst	Colonel	Colonel
ersturmbannführer	Senior Storm Unit Leader	Obersturmbannführer	Oberstleutnant	Lieutenant Colonel	Lieutenant-Colonel
rmbannführer	Storm Unit Leader	Sturmbannführer	Major	Major	Major
ppenoffiziere					
uptsturmführer	Chief Storm Leader	Sturmhauptführer	Hauptmann/ Rittmeister	Captain	Captain
ersturmführer	Senior Storm Leader	Obersturmführer	Oberleutnant	First Lieutenant	Lieutenant
tersturmführer	Junior Storm Leader	Sturmführer	Leutnant	Second Lieutenant	Second Lieutenant

SS Rank	Translation	SA Equivalent	*Heer* Equivalent	U.S. Equivalent	British Equivalent
Unterführer					
Sturmscharführer (Waffen-SS)	Storm Squad Leader	Haupttruppführer	Stabsfeldwebel	Sergeant Major	Regimental Sergeant Maj
Hauptscharführer	Chief Squad Leader	Obertruppführer	Oberfeldwebel	Master Sergeant	Sergeant Maj
Oberscharführer	Senior Squad Leader	Truppführer	Feldwebel	Platoon Sergeant	Staff Sergean
Scharführer	Squad Leader	Oberscharführer	Unterfeldwebel	Staff Sergeant	Sergeant
Unterscharführer	Junior Squad Leader	Scharführer	Unteroffizier	Sergeant	Corporal
Mannschaften					
Rottenführer	Section Leader	Rottenführer	Obergefreiter	Corporal	Lance-corpor
Sturmmann	Storm Trooper	Sturmmann	Gefreiter	Private First Class	Private
Obermann (from 1942) Oberschütze (Waffen-SS, from 1942)	Senior Trooper Senior Rifleman	(None)	Obersoldat (etc.)	(None)	(None)
Mann	Trooper				
Schütze (Waffen-SS)	Rifleman	Mann	Soldat (etc.)	Private	Private

Notes

INTRODUCTION

1. *Wenn alle Brüder schweigen: Großer Bildband über die Waffen SS* (Osnabrück, Germany: Munin-Verlag, 1985), 15–16.
2. George H. Stein, *The Waffen SS: Hitler's Elite Guard at War, 1939–1945* (Ithaca: Cornell University Press, 1966), 15–17. This work is indispensable in any study of the Waffen SS.
3. John Keegan, *Waffen SS: The Asphalt Soldiers* (New York: Ballantine, 1970), 140–43.
4. Stein, *Waffen SS*, 138–39, 163–64, 171–96; Keegan, *Waffen SS*, 93–109, 156–59; Bruce Quarrie, *Lightning Death: The Story of the Waffen-SS* (Sparkford, England: Patrick Stephens, 1991), 79, 91–95, 122–24. In all, some 130,000 Western Europeans served in the Waffen SS: 50,000 Dutch, 20,000 Flemings, 20,000 Walloons, 20,000 French, 6,000 Norwegians, 6,000 Danes, and 1,200 Swiss, Swedes, and Luxembourgers.
5. Jorge Rosado and Chris Bishop, *Wehrmacht Panzer Divisions 1939–45* (London, England: Amber Books, 2010), 23–35, 182–87; National Archives of Canada, General H. D. G. Crerar Papers, vol. 2, Remarks to Senior Officers, Cdn Army Operation "Totalize," by GOC-in-C First Canadian Army, 051100 August 1944.
6. Stein, *Waffen SS*, 252–54.
7. Charles W. Sydnor Jr., *Soldiers of Destruction: The Death's Head Division, 1933–1945* (Princteon, NJ: Princeton University Press, 1977), 177. This excellent work is absolutely indispensable to understanding the true nature of the Waffen SS.

CHAPTER 1: WHO WERE THE WAFFEN SS?

1. Stein, *Waffen SS*, xv–xxx, xxxiii, 4–6.
2. Himmler divided the German police system into two branches: the uniformed regular police (*Ordnungspolezei* or Orpo), which included national, rural, and local police forces; and the civilian-clothed security police (*Sicherheitspolezei* or Sipo),

which included the state criminal police (Kripo) and the state security police (Gestapo). Stein, *Waffen SS*, xxxvii–xxxviii; Keegan, *Waffen SS*, 34.

3. Keegan, *Waffen SS*, 26–31, 34–37; *Wenn alle Brüder schweigen*, 36; Quarrie, *Lightning Death*, 25, 29–30; Charles Messenger, *Hitler's Gladiator: The Life and Times of Oberstgruppenfuehrer and Panzergeneral-Oberst der Waffen-SS Sepp Dietrich* (London, England: Brassey's, 1988), 52–53; James J. Weingartner, *Hitler's Guard: The Story of the Leibstandarte SS Adolf Hitler* (Nashville, TN: Battery, 1996), 2–7; Stein, *Waffen SS*, xxxvii–xxxviii, 242.

4. Keegan, *Waffen SS*, 45–46, 49, 51, 53; Stein, *Waffen SS*, xxx, 7–11; Messenger, *Hitler's Gladiator*, 63; Weingartner, *Hitler's Body Guard*, 9–15, 20–21.

5. Quarrie, *Lightning Death*, 34–42; Weingartner, *Hitler's Body Guard*, 24–27. According to Quarrie, *Lightning Death*, 34–35, rank was based on the *Sturm* (company) of several *Truppen*, with three *Sturm* constituting a *Sturmbann* (battalion). Three *Sturmbann* made a *Standarte*, a number of which formed a brigade or *Gruppe* (a term dropped in favor of *Division* to prevent confusion).

6. *Wenn alle Brüder schweigen*, 15; Stein, *Waffen SS*, xxxi, 9, 15–21; Otto Weidinger, *Comrades to the End: The 4th SS Panzer-Grenadier Regiment "Der Führer" 1938–1945* (Atglen, PA: Schiffer, 1998), 14–15; Weingartner, *Hitler's Guard*, 16–19, 22–24, 27, 30–31.

7. Sydnor, *Soldiers of Destruction*, 16–21, 115; Keegan, *Waffen SS*, 62; Stein, *Waffen SS* 26, Messenger, *Hitler's Gladiator*, 71, 89; Weingartner, *Hitler's Guard*, 30–31

8. Stein, *Waffen SS*, 27–29; Richard Giziowski, *The Enigma of General Blaskowitz* (London, England: Leo Cooper, 1997), 146–74; Messenger, *Hitler's Gladiator*, 73–75; Weingartner, *Hitler's Guard*, 32–36.

9. Sydnor, *Soldiers of Destruction*, 22, 33–36, 52; Stein, *Waffen SS*, 30–31, 36; Messenger, *Hitler's Gladiator*, 76.

10. Stein, *Waffen SS*, 32–36, 40, 48–49, 258–263; Sydnor, *Soldiers of Destruction*, 36–37, 56, 119–20; Messenger, *Hitler's Gladiator*, 71.

11. Sydnor, *Soldiers of Desruction*, 59–63, 68–72, 112; Stein, *Waffen SS*, 50–55, 58–59.

12. *Wenn alle Brüder schweigen*, 69–71; Sydnor, *Soldiers of Destruction*, 106; Stein, *Waffen SS*, 55–57, 60–65; Keegan, *Waffen SS*, 63–65; Weidinger, *Comrades to the End*, 23–33, 34–42.

13. Ian Sayer and Douglas Botting, *Hitler's Last General: The Case against Wilhelm Mohnke* (London: Bantam, 1989), 32–87, 94–135; Weingartner, *Hitler's Guard*, 41; Messenger, *Hitler's Gladiator*, 78–86, 210; Keegan, *Waffen SS*, 63–64. This early prisoner exchange saw some survivors return to Britain. According to Sayer and Botting, *Hitler's Last General*, 87, the War Office reproached one for telling the story directly to the press.

14. Sydnor, *Soldiers of Destruction*, 86, 95, 104–5; Stein, *Waffen SS*, 67–69

15. Sydnor, *Soldiers of Destruction*, 90–96; Keegan, *Waffen SS*, 64–65; Stein, *Waffen SS*, 76–78; *Wenn alle Brüder schweigen*, 91. After being sentenced to death by a British Military Court on 25 October 1948, Knochlein was hanged for the Le Paradis murders.

16. *Wenn alle Brüder schweigen*, 69–71; Sydnor, *Soldiers of Destruction*, 99; Stein, *Waffen SS*, 70, 82–88.

17. Sydnor, *Soldiers of Destruction*, 100.

18. Sydnor, *Soldiers of Destruction*, 95, 106–8; Stein, *Waffen SS*, 89.

19. Sydnor, *Soldiers of Destruction*, 97, 106–7; Keegan, *Waffen SS*, 67; Stein, *Waffen SS*, 72–73, 89–90.

20. Keegan, *Waffen SS*, 67–69; Sydnor, *Soldiers of Destruction*, 110–20, 132–33; Stein, 23–24, 94–110; Messenger, *Hitler's Gladiator*, 88–89.

21. *Wenn alle Brüder schweigen*, 120, 126–27; Quarrie, *Lightning Death*, 6; Stein, *Waffen SS*, 113–18; Weingartner, *Hitler's Guard*, 49–56; Messenger, *Hitler's Gladiator*, 89–95, 215–16.

CHAPTER 2: PERDITION ON THE EASTERN FRONT

1. Charles Messenger, *The Art of Blitzkrieg* (London: Ian Allan, 1991), 179, 183; Keegan, *Waffen SS*, 76; Richard J. Evans, *The Third Reich at War* (New York: Penguin, 2009), 218–30; Richard Overy, *Russia's War: Blood upon the Snow* (New York: Penguin Putnam, 1997), 111; Quarrie, *Lightning Death*, 76–77.

2. Evans, *Third Reich at War*, 175–86; Anthony Beevor, *Stalingrad* (New York: Viking, 1998), 14-17, 54–61; Gerhard L. Weinberg, *A World at Arms: A Global History of World War II* (Cambridge, England: Cambridge University Press, 1994), 299–305.

3. Beevor, *Stalingrad*, 60–61, 84–85, Evans, *Third Reich at War*, 44–46, 561; Overy, *Russia's War*, 194–201

4. Sydnor, *Soldiers of Destruction*, 140–46.

5. Sydnor, *Soldiers of Destruction*, 147–53; Weidinger, *Comrades to the End*, 70.

6. Sydnor, *Soldiers of Destruction*, 153–63, 179. The German 37-millimeter antitank gun would not penetrate T-34 armor and the 50-millimeter only at ranges under 5,000 yards. Ibid., 182.

7. Sydnor, *Soldiers of Destruction*, 164–66, 186–211; Quarrie, *Lightning Death*, 81–83.

8. Weidinger, *Comrades to the End*, 64–79

9. John Keegan, *Rundstedt* (New York: Ballantine, 1974), 122–23; Messenger, *Art of Blitzkrieg*, 183–89; Messenger, *Hitler's Gladiator*, 102; Weidinger, *Comrades to the End*, 80–89; Quarrie, *Lightning Death*, 73.

10. Weidinger, *Comrades to the End*, 89–100; Quarrie, *Lightning Death*, 83–85.

11. Weidinger, *Comrades to the End*, 102–16; Quarrie, *Lightning Death*, 86–88.

12. Messenger, *Hitler's Gladiator*, 96–99, 102; Weingartner, *Hitler's Guard*, 59–61.

13. Messenger, *Hitler's Gladiator*, 100–102; Weingartner, *Hitler's Guard*, 61–63.

14. Messenger, *Hitler's Gladiator*, 101–4; Weingartner, *Hitler's Guard*, 62-67. By 21 November, the *Leibstandarte* had lost 5,281 men out of 9,994.

15. Messenger, *Hitler's Gladiator*, 107; Weingartner, *Hitler's Guard*, 71. Kraas rose to become the last commander of the 12th SS.

16. Messenger, *Hitler's Gladiator*, 104, 106–9; Weingartner, *Hitler's Guard*, 67–70.

17. Messenger, *Hitler's Gladiator*, 109–10; Quarrie, *Lightning Death* 75, 118–28; Stein, *Waffen SS*, 130–32, 191–93; Keegan, *Waffen SS*, 109, 143, 159. *Standartenführer* Otto Kumm rejected such categorization in his *Prinz Eugen: The History of the 7 SS Mountain Division "Prinz Eugen"* (Winnipeg, Canada: J. J. Fedorowicz Publishing, 1995), 267–73. Quarrie stated that Kumm tried to make the *Prinz Eugen* professional, but failed.

18. Quarrie, *Lightning Death*, 121–22, 124, 126; Stein, *Waffen SS*, 204–5; Weingartner, *Hitler's Guard*, 13, 77–78; Keegan, *Waffen SS*, 90–91, 143. Götz von Berlichingen was made famous in Johann von Goethe's *Sturm und Drang*.

19. Messenger, *Hitler's Gladiator*, 111–16; Weingartner, *Hitler's Guard*, 74–77.

20. Messenger, "Dietrich, Josef (Sepp)," *D-Day Encylopedia*, 182–83; Messenger, *Hitler's Gladiator*, 71; Weingartner, *Hitler's Guard*, 2–4, 12–13, 67–70, 78–79; Eversley Belfeld and H. Essame, *The Battle for Normandy* (London, England: Pan, 1983), 167–68. Messenger's balanced *Hitler's Gladiator* is the definitive biography of Dietrich.

21. Messenger, *Hitler's Gladiator*, 117; John A. English, *On Infantry* (New York: Praeger, 1981), 82, 105–6, 108–10, 143.

22. Quarrie, *Lightning Death*, 107–17; Sydnor, *Soldiers of Destruction*, 243–48; Keegan, *Waffen SS*, 87; Kenneth Macksey, *Panzer Divison: The Mailed Fist* (New York: Ballantine, 1972), 117–19; Richard Overy, *Why the Allies Won* (London: Pimlico, 1996), 92–96.

23. Sydnor, *Soldiers of Destruction*, 226–27, 248–49; Quarrie, *Lightning Death*, 103

24. Sydnor, *Soldiers of Destruction*, 192, 248, 253; Quarrie, *Lightning Death*, 81; James F. Dunnigan, ed., *The Russian Front* (London, England; Arms and Armour, 1978), 114–15; Macksey, *Panzer Division*, 107, 126–27; Weinberg, *World at Arms*, 423–24.

25. Messenger, *Hitler's Gladiator*, 119–20; Weidinger, *Comrades to the End*, 214–18, 255–56, 268; Quarrie, *Lightning Death*, 130–40; Stein, *Waffen SS*, 275–76.

26. Ibid; Michael Reynolds, *Sons of the Reich: The History of II SS Panzer Corps in Normandy, Arnhem, the Ardennes, and on the Eastern Front* (Havertown, PA: Casemate, 2002), 3–13.

CHAPTER 3: FIRST CLASHES WITH THE WAFFEN SS IN NORMANDY

1. Keegan, *Waffen SS*, 115; Quarrie, *Lightning Death*, 146; and Roman Johann Jarymowycz, *Tank Tactics: From Normandy to Lorraine* (Boulder: Lynne Reinner, 2001), 100, 141.

2. Weinberg, *World at Arms*, 629, 665; Overy, *Why the Allies Won*, 141.

3. Richard Hargreaves, *The Germans in Normandy* (Barnsley, England: Pen & Sword, 2006), xiv, 7, 10; Weinberg, *World at Arms*, 609–11, 623; Overy, *Why the Allies Won*, 98; David M. Glantz, "Soviet Military Strategy during the Second Period of the War (November 1942–December 1943): A Reappraisal," *Journal of Military History* 1 (January 1996): 149.

4. Weinberg, *World at Arms*, 1,076.

5. Overy, *Why the Allies Won*, 141–44, 153; Weinberg, *World at Arms*, 612–14, 628–29.

6. Joseph Balkoski, *Beyond the Beachhead: The 29th Infantry Division in Normandy* (Mechanicsburg: Stackpole Books, 1999), 66, 104–5; Overy, *Why the Allies Won*, 145, 150, 152, 167, 227; Helmut Ritgen, *The Western Front 1944: Memoirs of a Panzer Lehr Officer* (Winnipeg, Canada: J. J. Fedorowicz, 1995), 76.

7. Carlo D'Este, *Decision in Normandy: The Unwritten Story of Montgomery and the Allied Campaign* (London: Collins, 1983), 507.

8. Jarymowycz, *Tank Tactics*, 97, 99–100, 104–5, 277. Only fourteen Tiger IIs—King Tigers—fought in Normandy. Owing to mechanical defects, only six reached the *Panzer Lehr* Division. Fireflies using super APDS shot could not penetrate the frontal armor of the Tiger II but could defeat side and rear armor on the hull and turret. Ibid., 280. The Sturmgeschütz III assault gun sported a 75-millimeter StuK 40 L/48 gun, and the Jagdpanzer IV, mounted on a Mark IV panzer chassis, had the deadly 75-millimeter PaK 39 L/48 gun.

9. The 6-barrelled 150mm Nebelwerfer 41 had a range of 6,700 meters; the five-barrelled 210-millimeter Nebelwerfer 42, 7,850 meters. Ritgen, *Western Front*, 305.

10. Michael Reynolds, *Steel Inferno: 1 SS Panzer Corps in Normandy* (New York: Sarpedon, 1997), 31. The Wasps resembled the U.S. 105-millimeter Priest.

11. Jarymowycz, *Tank Tactics*, 258–64; Charles M. Baily, "Armor and Tracked Vehicles," *D-Day Encyclopedia*, 56–65.

12. Ibid.; John A. English, *The Canadian Army and the Normandy Campaign* (New York: Praeger, 1991), 207, 258, 312; Omar N. Bradley, *A Soldier's Story* (New York: Henry Holt, 1951), 322–23; and Russell A. Hart, *Clash of Arms: How the Allies Won in Normandy* (Boulder: Lynne Reinner, 2001), 307. The Americans were quick to notice the British advantage in the sabot round. An APDS round for the 6-pounder antitank gun came into service in late 1943. Jarymowycz, *Tank Tactics*, 283.

13. Hubert Meyer, *The History of the 12. SS-Panzerdivision Hitlerjugend* (Winnipeg, Canada: J. J. Fedorowicz, 1994), 1–9; English, *Canadian Army*, 212; ; Jarymowycz, *Tank Tactics*, 98; Craig W. H. Luther, *Blood and Honor: The History of the 12th SS Panzer Division "Hitler Youth," 1943–1945* (San Jose, CA: Bender, 1987), 57–59.

14. Meyer, *History of the 12. SS-Panzerdivision*, 40–45, provides an excellent detailed account of this first encounter. See also John A. English, "3d Infantry Division (Canadian)," *D-Day Encyclopedia*, 553–56; English, *Canadian Army*, 209; D'Este, *Decision in Normandy*, 118–19, 139–40; Col. C. P. Stacey, *Official History of the Canadian Army in the Second World War, The Victory Campaign: The Operations in North West Europe, 1944–1945* (Ottawa: Queen's Printer, 1966), 128, 131 (hereafter cited as *Victory Campaign*); Terry Copp, *Fields of Fire: The Canadians in Normandy* (Toronto, Canada: Toronto University Press, 2003), 63–71; Reginald H. Roy, *1944: The Canadians in Normandy* (Ottawa: Macmillan, 1984), 25; Marc Milner, "Stopping the Panzers: Reassessing the Role of 3rd Canadian Infantry Division in Normandy, 7–10 June 1944," *Journal of Military History* 74, no. 2 (April 2010), 503–13. Brig. P. A. S. Todd, who commanded the 3rd Canadian Division's artillery, told me at the Canadian Land Forces Command and Staff College that there was no excuse for not having the guns within range.

15. Sayer and Botting, *Hitler's Last General*, 155–59; Roy, *1944*, 30; Ian J. Campbell, *Murder at the Abbaye: The Story of Twenty Canadian Soldiers Murdered at the Abbaye d"Ardenne* (Ottawa, Canada: Golden Dog, 1996), 70–77, 104–13, 138–51, 174; Howard Margolian, *Conduct Unbecoming: The Story of the Murder of Canadian Prisoners of War in Normandy* (Toronto, Canada: Toronto University Press, 1998), ix–x, 57–74; Stacey, *Victory Campaign*, 129; Reynolds, *Steel Inferno*, 19, 29.

16. Ralph Allen, *Ordeal by Fire* (Toronto, Canada: Popular Library, 1961), 406, quoting from Goebbels' diary, February–March 1943.

17. Copp, *Fields of Fire*, 71; Max Hastings, *Overlord: D-Day and the Battle for Normandy* (New York: Simon and Schuster, 1984), 212; Stein, *Waffen SS*, 292; Keegan, *Waffen SS*, 145. This is not to say that all German army elements were stainless. The Allies protested alleged war crimes committed by the 752nd and 997th Infantry Regiments. In southern France, in June 1944, the 11th Panzer Division killed 125 resistance fighters at a cost of 4 wounded. In a separate operation, a German battalion killed 325 resistance fighters, but in neither case were any prisoners taken. Hart, *Clash of Arms*, 381, 399.

18. As told to me during conversation with Meyer in his home in Leverkusen, Germany.

19. D'Este, *Decision in Normandy*, 147; Hargreaves, *Germans in Normandy*, 70.

20. Overy, *Why the Allies Won*, 164.

21. D'Este, *Decision in Normandy*, 111, 115–19, 147, 151–59. Army Group G under Blaskowitz in southern France got the 9th, 11th, and 2nd SS Panzer Divisions.

22. D'Este, *Decision in Normandy*, 163; Messenger, *Hitler's Gladiator*, 125; Meyer, *History of the 12. SS-Panzerdivision*, 54–57; Milner, *Stopping the Panzers*, 516–17.

23. Stacey, *Victory Campaign*, 135–36; Meyer, *History of the 12. SS-Panzerdivision*, 49–52; English, *Canadian Army*, 209; Copp, *Fields of Fire*, 68–70; Reynolds, *Steel Inferno*, 75.

24. Sayer and Botting, *Hitler's Last General*, 160–67, 183, 186, 194, 229; Margolian, *Conduct Unbecoming*, 82–89, 90–102.

25. Meyer, *History of the 12. SS-Panzerdivision*, 51, 54–59; Reynolds, *Steel Inferno*, 76–82; Milner, *Stopping the Panzers*, 517–20.

26. John A. English, *Marching through Chaos: The Descent of Armies in Theory and Practice* (Westport, CT: Praeger, 1996), 104.

27. Meyer, *History of the 12. SS-Panzerdivision*, 60–61; D'Este, *Decision in Normandy*, 166–168; Milner, "Stopping the Panzers," 52; Reynolds, *Steel Inferno*, 81–85.

28. Stacey, *Victory Campaign*, 139–40; Meyer, *History of the 12. SS-Panzerdivision*, 67–69; English, *Canadian Army*, 213–14; Reynolds, *Steel Inferno*, 81–87; Sayer and Botting, *Hitler's Last General*, 141–43, 152–53, 167–69, 205–9, 216–17, 235–36, 240–87. Mohnke ended the war in Hitler's Berlin bunker and went into Soviet captivity until his release in 1955. The loss of his foot in Yugoslavia probably saved his life as it meant he never set foot in the Soviet Union and therefore, with no accusations levelled against him, escaped the lot of other SS prisoners. The Russians obviously prized him as a source of information on Hitler and his Reich for propaganda purposes and with the threat of extradition hanging over his head, Mohnke proved most cooperative. Sayer and Botting, *Hitler's Last General*, 315–20.

29. Margolian, *Conduct Unbecoming*, 123–24.

CHAPTER 4: TIGER SHOCK AND "COLOSSAL CRACKS"

1. D'Este, *Decision in Normandy*, 172–74; Public Records Office, Kew, 70473, WO 285/9-11, Dempsey Diary (DD), 12 Jun 44.

2. D'Este considers it a wise decision, but Reynolds called it incomprehensible. D'Este, *Decision in Normandy* 176; Reynolds, *Steel Inferno*, 110. The 7th Armoured also had some Fireflies.

3. In the fall of 1942, Tiger units were given 500 series numbers. Being separate from the army, the Waffen SS started with 501, but in spring 1944, Heavy SS Panzer Battalion 501 was redesignated as 101 (to the I SS Panzer Corps) and 502 as 102 (to the II SS Panzer Corps). In October 1944, the 101 became the 501. Helmut Ritgen letter to author, 2 November 1990; Jarymowycz, *Tank Tactics*, 106.

4. D'Este, *Decision in Normandy* 174–98; Quarrie, *Lightning Death*, 148–49; Reynolds, *Steel Inferno*, 96–111; Hastings, *Overlord*, 157–64; DD, 13-14 Jun 44. See also John A. English, *Patton's Peers: The Forgotten Allied Field Army Commanders of the Western Front, 1944–1945* (Mechanicsburg, PA: Stackpole Books, 2009), 58–59; and English, *Canadian Army*, 205–6.

5. Reynolds, *Steel Inferno*, 83–84, 98, 102, 113–16; D'Este, *Decision in Normandy*, 232; Stacey, *Victory Campaign*, 147; Quarrie, *Lightning Death*, 149–50.

6. Stephen Ashley Hart, *Montgomery and "Colossal Cracks": The 21st Army Group in Northwest Europe, 1944–45* (Westport, CT: Praeger, 2000), 103, 114; English, *Patton's Peers*, 59–60.

7. D'Este, *Decision in Normandy*, 235; Reynolds, *Steel Inferno*, 117–24; Meyer, *History of the 12. SS-Panzerdivision*, 100–113.

8. Reynolds, *Steel Inferno*, 128–31; Meyer, *History of the 12. SS-Panzerdivision*, 121–24; Copp, *Fields of Fire*, 80–83.

9. Reynolds, *Steel Inferno*, 131–35; Weidinger, *Comrades to the End*, 303–6; Meyer, *History of the 12. SS-Panzerdivision*, 123–24.

10. Reynolds, *Steel Inferno*, 132–37; Reynolds, *Sons of the Reich*, 18–31; Meyer, *History of the 12. SS-Panzerdivision*, 125–27, 129. Bittrich had served as a lieutenant in the German air force and been twice wounded in World War I. On rejoining the interwar German armed forces, he was part of a secret air force team that taught flying to Russians. When Hitler came to power, Bittrich joined the newly formed Luftwaffe, but in the 1930s, he switched to the Waffen SS, where promotion was faster. Bittrich, who said he was never a robot and never intended to become one, grew disenchanted with Hitler's military approach and openly said so. Cornelius Ryan, *A Bridge Too Far* (New York: Simon and Schuster, 1974), 110–11.

11. DD, 19–30 Jun and 1 Jul 44; D'Este, *Decision in Normandy*, 235–44; Stacey, *Victory Campaign*, 147–49; Weidinger, *Comrades to the End*, 306–8; Meyer, *History of the 12. SS-Panzerdivision*, 127–29.

12. English, *Canadian Army*, 160–63.

13. Copp, *Fields of Fire*, 79–87, 293; Reynolds, *Steel Inferno*, 138–44; Ritgen, *Western Front 1944*, 67–71; Stacey, *Victory Campaign*, 150; D'Este, *Decision in Normandy*, 244.

14. Copp, *Fields of Fire*, 86–87, 293; Ritgen, *Western Front 1944*, 85–86; Reynolds, *Steel Inferno*, 141; Stacey, *Victory Campaign*, 149.

CHAPTER 5: A TOUGH BUSINESS

1. Stacey, *Victory Campaign*, 153–55; Roy, *1944*, 45–50; English, *Canadian Army*, 214–16.

2. Reynolds, *Steel Inferno*, 145–46; Meyer, *History of the 12. SS-Panzerdivision*, 134–35.

3. Stacey, *Victory Campaign*, 153–55; Roy, *1944*, 45–50.

4. Meyer, *History of the 12. SS-Panzerdivision*, 136–37.

5. English, *Canadian Army*, 216.

6. Meyer, *History of the 12. SS-Panzerdivision*, 137–40; English, *Canadian Army*, 217; Copp, *Fields of Fire*, 99–100.

7. English, *Canadian Army*, 217.

8. Ibid.; Stacey, *Victory Campaign*, 157–60, Roy, *1944*, 51.

9. Reynolds, *Steel Inferno*, 152; Copp, *Fields of Fire*, 103.

10. English, *Canadian Army*, 219.

11. Stacey, *Victory Campaign*, 160; Copp, *Fields of Fire*, 103; Reynolds, *Steel Inferno*, 154

12. English, *Canadian Army*, 219–21.

13. Stacey, *Victory Campaign*, 160–61; Copp, *Fields of Fire*, 103–4.

14. English, *Canadian Army*, 221; Stacey, *Victory Campaign*, 162; Reynolds, *Steel Inferno*, 154.

15. Which is how one of *Sturmbannführer* Hans Seigel's men at a Caen reunion of 12th SS Panzer Division *Hitlerjugend* described the fighting around Buron. See also DD, 7–9 Jul 44; English, *Canadian Army*, 217–22; D'Este, *Decision in Normandy*, 305–6, 309–18; and Stacey, *Victory Campaign*, 153–64.

16. Alexander McKee, *Caen: Anvil of Victory* (London, England: Macmillan, 1964), 198–204; Meyer, *History of the 12. SS-Panzerdivision*, 52–53, 139–40; Sayer and Botting, *Hitler's Last General*, 202–4, 213–15; Tony Foster, *Meeting of Generals* (Toronto, Canada: Methuen, 1986), 334–35. Ritgen tells the same story of Luxenburger, but incorrectly attributes his capture to Canadians. He is more correct in stating that a German major also escaped. Ritgen, *Western Front*, 39.

17. Jonathan F. Vance, "Men in Manacles: The Shackling of Prisoners of War, 1942–1943," *Journal of Military History* 59 (July 1995): 483–504; Tim Cook, "The Politics of Surrender: Canadian Soldiers and the Killing of Prisoners in the Great War," *Journal of Military History* 70 (July 2006): 637–65; Robert Graves, *Good-bye to All That* (London, England: Jonathan Cape, 1929), 234–37; Stacey, *Victory Campaign*, 558; Hastings, *Overlord*, 183, 248–51; Balkoski, *Beyond the Beachhead*, 218; Campbell, *Murder at the Abbaye*, 152–55; Giziowski, *Enigma of General Blaskowitz*, 456–57.

18. Sydnor, *Soldiers of Destruction*, 305; Stein, *Waffen SS*, 291, 293–94; Ryan, *A Bridge Too Far*, 43, 110–12, 424–25; Dennis Showalter, *Hitler's Panzers: The Lightning Attacks that Revolutionized Warfare* (New York: Berkley Caliber, 2009), 332; Sayer and Botting, *Hitler's Last General*, 153, 160–61, 182–83. At Arnhem, Bittrich sent a bottle of brandy to the commander of the British 1st Airborne Division after a wounded evacuation parley. Hitler's hanging of Gen. Erich Hoepner as a conspirator in the 20 July plot fanned Bittrich's outspoken criticism of the *Führer*'s military leadership and he was saved from reprisal only by his professional competence. Suspected of war crimes, Bittrich spent eight years in prison after the war. He was convicted in 1953 by a French military tribunal for ordering the killing of resistance fighters, but a civil court later acquitted him in June of the same year. Ryan, *A Bridge Too Far*, 111, 424–25; Showalter, *Hitler's Panzers*, 371. Bremer was locked up by the French until 1948.

19. Reynolds, *Steel Inferno*, 158–64; Reynolds, *Sons of the Reich*, 37–43; Meyer, *History of the 12. SS-Panzerdivision*, 151–53; Hastings, *Overlord*, 263–68.

20. Ibid.

21. Copp, *Fields of Fire*, 102–3, 296; Reynolds, *Steel Inferno*, 155, 166–67; Stacey, *Victory Campaign*, 163–64; Hargreaves, *Germans in Normandy*, 119–21, 134; Weingartner, *Hitler's Guard*, 101–3.

CHAPTER 6: TANK CHARGE TO CONSERVE INFANTRY

1. D'Este, *Decision in Normandy*, 242–44, 260–63; Stacey, *Victory Campaign*, 149, 163, 166; Meyer, *History of the 12. SS-Panzerdivision*, 153–54; Hart, *Montgomery and "Colossal Cracks"*, 49–61, 64, 145; DD, 10 Jul 44; and Belfield and Essame, *Battle for Normandy*, 144–45.

2. Hart, *Montgomery and "Colossal Cracks"*, 70, 145; D'Este, *Decision in Normandy*, 354–59; DD, 12 Jul 44. For original source references too lengthy to repeat here, see English, *Patton's Peers*, 63–66.

3. Stacey, *Victory Campaign*, 165–69; English, *Patton's Peers*, 66–69; Martin Blumenson, *Breakout and Pursuit, United States Army in World War II, The European Theater of Operations* (Washington, DC: Department of the Army, 1961), 189; D'Este, *Decision in Normandy*, 355–57; Hart, *Montgomery and "Colossal Cracks"*, 68–69, 86, 99.

4. D'Este, *Decision in Normandy*, 294, 354, 362–67, 396; English, *Patton's Peers*, 67–68; English, *Canadian Army*, 182, 208; Hart, *Montgomery and "Colossal Cracks"*, 81–82,

86, 139, 147, 314–15; Omar N. Bradley and Clay Blair, *A General's Life* (New York: Simon and Schuster, 1983), 274–75.

5. English, *Patton's Peers*, 68–69.

6. Reynolds, *Steel Inferno*, 170–71; British Army Staff College Camberley booklet "Battlefield Tour—Operation Goodwood 18th–19th July 1944"; Col. Hans von Luck, *Panzer Commander: Memoirs* (New York: Praeger, 1989), 150–51.

7. Reynolds, *Steel Inferno*, 171–72; Meyer, *History of the 12. SS-Panzerdivision*, 155–56.

8. D'Este, *Decision in Normandy*, 357–58, 370–72, 377, 389–90; English, *Patton's Peers*, 69–71; Chester Wilmot, *The Struggle for Europe* (London: Fontana/Collins, 1974), 409–11; and DD, 12–13 and 18 Jul 44. Good staff work, especially tight movement control, was the only, if not entirely satisfactory, solution to the bridgehead congestion problem.

9. Reynolds, *Steel Inferno*, 175–79; Meyer, *History of the 12. SS-Panzerdivision*, 157–58; Luck, *Panzer Commander*, 152–60.

10. Reynolds, *Steel Inferno*, 179–82; D'Este, *Decision in Normandy*, 373–85; Stacey, *Victory Campaign*, 169–70; English, *Patton's Peers*, 69–71; DD, 18–19 Jul 44.

11. Reynolds, *Steel Inferno*, 182–84.

12. Reynolds, *Steel Inferno*, 178–80; Wilmot, *Struggle for Europe*, 413,416; Copp, *Fields of Fire*, 144.

13. D'Este, *Decision in Normandy*, 367, 374, 385–88; English, *Patton's Peers*, 71–72; Hart, *Clash of Arms*, 316.

14. Stacey, *Victory Campaign*, 168–71; English, *Canadian Army*, 222–25.

15. Stacey, *Victory Campaign*, 169–73; Meyer, *History of the 12. SS-Panzerdivision*, 158; Roy, *1944*, 68–74; English, *Canadian Army*, 225–26; Copp, *Fields of Fire*, 137–40.

16. English, *Canadian Army*, 227–28; Copp, *Fields of Fire*, 147.

17. English, *Canadian Army*, 228; Stacey, *Victory Campaign*, 175; Reynolds, *Steel Inferno*, 185.

18. English, *Canadian Army*, 228–29

19. Ibid.

20. Stacey, *Victory Campaign*, 176; English, *Canadian Army*, 230.

CHAPTER 7: COBRA SPRING

1. Stacey, *Victory Campaign*, 183–85; Wilmot, *Struggle for Europe*, 447–49; Charles B. MacDonald, *The Mighty Endeavor: American Armed Forces in the European Theater in World War II* (New York: Oxford, University Press, 1969), 298.

2. John S. D. Eisenhower, *The Bitter Woods: The Battle of the Bulge* (New York: Da Capo), 40–43; Hargreaves, *Germans in Normandy*, 35;

3. Quarrie, *Lightning Death*, 146–49; Weingartner, *Hitler's Guard*, 103–4. Ostendorf had been Hausser's chief of staff at Kursk. For information on Rhino tanks, see James Jay Carafano, *After D-Day: Operation Cobra and the Normandy Breakout* (Boulder: Lynne Rienner, 2000), 213.

4. James Lucas, "Ostendorff, Werner" and "17th SS Panzer Grenadier Division," *D-Day Encyclopedia*, 412–13, 505–6; Hargreaves, *Germans in Normandy*, 68–69.

5. Ibid. The 17th's motto was *Leck mich am Arsch* after Berlichingen's famous remark *Er kann mich im Arsche lecken* in Goethe's play *Götz von Berlichingen*.

6. Hargreaves, *Germans in Normandy*, 69, 78–79; Lucas, "Ostendorff," 506; Hastings, *Overlord*, 189; MacDonald, *Mighty Endeavor*, 284; Antonio J. Munoz, *Iron Fist: A Combat History of the 17. SS Panzergrenadier Division "Götz von Berlichingen"* (New York: Axis Europa, 1999), 7. Just before Cobra, one battle group of the 17th SS had

only 1,000 rounds per machine gun and 30 rounds per rifle—less than two days' combat at average consumption rates. Hart, *Clash of Arms*, 403.

7. G. H. Bennett, *Destination Normandy: Three Regiments in Normandy* (Westport, CT: Praeger Security International, 2007), 121–28; Martin K. A. Morgan, *Down to Earth: The 507th Parachute Infantry Regiment in Normandy, June 6–July 15, 1944* (Atglen, PA: Schiffer Military History, 2004), 138–259.

8. Whereas the old Waffen SS rejected men for the slightest imperfections, they now needed men and even inducted Alsatians of dubious loyalty. Max Hastings, *Das Reich: Resistance and the March of the 2nd SS Panzer Division through France, June 1944* (London: Michael Joseph, 1981), 13.

9. Giziowski, *Enigma of General Blaskowitz*, 279–82; Hastings, *Das Reich*, 73, 80–120; Weidinger, *Comrades to the End*, 278–82.

10. Sydnor, *Soldiers of Destruction*, 26, 281–82; Hastings, *Das Reich*, 21–22.

11. Hastings, *Das Reich*, 80–81. To the Germans, who had formally accepted the surrender of France in 1940, they were simply terrorists and *franc-tireurs* not protected by the Geneva Convention. Arguably, however, by occupying Vichy France the Germans had violated the surrender terms.

12. Hastings, *Das Reich*, 120–28, Stein, *Waffen SS*, 276.

13. Hastings, *Das Reich*, 144–81; Weidinger, *Comrades to the End*, 283–301. Diekmann was killed by a shell splinter on 30 June and so never stood trial, but twenty-one of his men were found and indicted—two were hanged and the remainder were given stiff prison sentences. Another forty-two were sentenced to death in absentia. Quarrie, *Lightning Death*, 151–52.

14. Hastings, *Das Reich*, 180–86, 210–18; Weidinger, *Comrades to the End*, 319; Lucas, "Lammerding, Heinz," *D-Day Encyclopedia*, 337.

15. Weigley, *Eisenhower's Lieutenants*, 112, 155–59; Ritgen, *Western Front 1944*, 98–106.

16. Geoffrey Perret, *There's a War to Be Won: The Unites States Army in World War II* (New York: Ballantine, 1991), 317–18; Weigley, *Eisenhower's Lieutenants*, 125–28; Weidinger, *Comrades to the End*, 314.

17. Weigley, *Eisenhower's Lieutenants*, 129–34; Ritgen, *Western Front 1944*, 85–89.

18. Weigley, *Eisenhower's Lieutenants*, 138–43; Perret, *There's a War to Be Won*, 325–26; Reynolds, *Steel Inferno*, 208; Hastings, *Overlord*, 293.

19. Carafano, *After D-Day*, 86–89; Bradley, *Soldier's Story*, 330–41; Eisenhower, *Bitter Woods*, 40–43.

20. Carfano, *After D-Day*, 109–17; Eisenhower, *Bitter Woods*, 43–45; Weigley, *Eisenhower's Lieutenants*, 154; Hastings, *Overlord*, 303.

21. Carafano, *After D-Day*, 203; Weigley, *Eisenhower's Lieutenants*, 155–59; Messenger, *Hitler's Gladiator*, 136; Hargreaves, *Germans in Normandy*, 168–69; Reynolds, *Steel Inferno*, 209.

22. Carafano, *After D-Day*, 218–26, 232; Weigley, *Eisenhower's Lieutenants*, 162; Weidinger, *Comrades to the End*, 319–23; Hargreaves, *Germans in Normandy*, 170, 173; English, *Patton's Peers*, 289. Baum commanded a *Totenkopf* battalion in the Demyansk pocket and subsequently became one of the most brilliant field commanders in the Waffen SS, rising to *Brigadeführer* at age thirty-three. One of the most highly decorated German soldiers of World War II, he received the Knight's Cross with Oak Leaves, Swords, and Diamonds. Baum commanded a *Leibstandarte* rifle company at Wormhoudt, but was clearly not involved in the murder of prison-

ers. Sydnor, *Soldiers of Destruction*, 215; Sayer and Botting, *Hitler's Last General*, 20, 38, 104, 126–29.

23. Weigley, *Eisenhower's Lieutenants*, 159–60; Carafano, *After D-Day*, 232–45.

24. Weigley, *Eisenhower's Lieutenants*, 167–68; Carafano, *After D-Day*, 245–53; Hargeaves, *Germans in Normandy*, 172–73.

25. Weidinger, *Comrades to the End*, 303–14; Ritgen, *Western Front 1944*, 85, 95; Hastings, *Das Reich*, 212–14; Weigley, *Eisenhower's Lieutenants*, 163; Will Fey, *Armor Battles of the Waffen-SS* (Winnipeg, Canada: J. J. Fedorowicz, 1990), 116–19. Ritgen respected Wislency's field performance, but his troops apparently achieved notoriety in Gascony fighting the French resistance. Hastings, *Das Reich*, 83.

26. Wilmot, *Struggle for Europe*, 448; English, *Canadian Army*, 240–41; Weingartner, *Hitler's Guard*, 104–5; Weigley, *Eisenhower's Lieutenants*, 167.

27. English, *Canadian Army*, 241–42.

28. Ibid.; Jarymowycz, *Tank Tactics*, 125, 130–33, 141–42, 144. The twenty-three-ton Jagdpanzer IV sported a 75-millimeter L/48 or 70 gun on the Mark IV chassis. The forty-five-ton Jagdpanther had an 88-millimeter L/71 gun on a Panther chassis. Ritgen, *Western Front 1944*, 301.

29. English, *Canadian Army*, 244.

30. Ibid.; Jarymowycz, *Tank Tactics*, 133; Reynolds, *Steel Inferno*, 194–95.

31. English, *Canadian Army*, 246; Jarymowycz, *Tank Tactics*, 143–44; Reynolds, *Steel Inferno*, 194–95.

32. English, *Canadian Army*, 246.

33. Ibid., 247–48; Ritgen, *Western Front 1944*, 80–82; Jarymowycz, *Tank Tactics*, 134–35, Copp, *Fields of Fire*, 175–76; Reynolds, *Steel Inferno*, 195–96.

34. English, *Canadian Army*, 242–44, 250–51; Reynolds, *Steel Inferno*, 191, 193; Copp, *Fields of Fire*, 178.

35. Jarymowycz, *Tank Tactics*, 137.

36. Stacey, *Victory Campaign*, 194–95; English, *Canadian Army*, 248–49; Jarymowycz, *Tank Tactics*, 130, 142.

CHAPTER 8: A MURDER OF PANZERS

1. Copp, *Fields of Fire*, 179–80; English, *Patton's Peers*, 72; DD, 25–29 Jul 44; BAOR Battlefield Tour, Operation Bluecoat: 8 Corps Operations South of Caumont 30–31 July 1944, Spectator's Edition (1947), 1–14; Hart, *Montgomery and "Colossal Cracks"*, 39, 82, 98, 139–40; D'Este, *Decision in Normandy*, 422; and Hart, *Clash of Arms*, 317, 335.

2. Hastings, *Overlord*, 345–46; English, *Patton's Peers*, 72.

3. English, *Patton's Peers*, 73; DD, 30 Jul–3 Aug 44; Field Marshal The Viscount Montgomery of Alamein, *Normandy to the Baltic* (London, England: Hutchinson, 1946), 89–94; BAOR Bluecoat, 17–22; Belfield and Essame, *Battle for Normandy*, 208–9; D'Este, *Decision in Normandy*, 422–24; Stacey, *Victory Campaign*, 203–4; Weigley, *Eisenhower's Lieutenants*, 168–69. Reynolds recounts in detail the battle-group delaying actions of the Waffen SS. Bittrich knew that he stood no chance of pushing O'Connor's 8 Corps back. Reynolds, *Sons of the Reich*, 58–77.

4. English, *Canadian Army*, 255–56; Reynolds, *Steel Inferno*, 200–202; Stacey, *Victory Campaign*, 205–7; Roy, *1944*, 144–46.

5. Ibid.

6. Reynolds, *Steel Inferno*, 204–6; Copp, *Fields of Fire*, 198–99.

7. English, *Patton's Peers*, 102–3; Perret, *There's a War to Be Won*, 333–34; D'Este, *Decision in Normandy*, 408–13.

8. Weingartner, *Hitler's Guard*, 108–9; Jarymowycz, *Tank Tactics*, 152, 276–78.

9. Wilmot, *Struggle for Europe*, 460–75; Weidinger, *Comrades to the End*, 320, 323–24; D'Este, *Decision in Normandy*, 414–15; Weingartner, *Hitler's Guard*, 108; Hastings, *Overlord*, 333, 337; Reynolds, *Steel Inferno*, 209–11.

10. Reynolds, *Steel Inferno*, 213–14; Weidinger, *Comrades to the End*, 323–26; Quarrie, *Lightning Death*, 125–26; Hastings, *Overlord*, 336; Jarymowycz, *Tank Tactics*, 152, 154, 160. Hastings says that the *Das Reich* fought half-heartedly at Mortain. Hastings, *Overlord*, 336, 373.

11. Weigley, *Eisenhower's Lieutenants*, 196–98; Reynolds, *Steel Inferno*, 214–18.

12. Reynolds, *Steel Inferno*, 222–23; Weigley, *Eisenhower's Lieutenants*, 202–7; Hastings, *Overlord*, 337–38. See Hart, *Clash of Arms*, 263, 257, 404, for actual number of vehicles knocked out by air attack.

13. Wilmot, *Struggle for Europe*, 462–69; Reynolds, *Steel Inferno*, 214, 222–23.

14. English, *Patton's Peers*, 103–5; D'Este, *Decision in Normandy*, 408–21; Weigley, *Eisenhower's Lieutenants*, 202–3; Eisenhower, *Bitter Woods*, 50–55; Perret, *There's a War to Be Won*, 333–39; USMA West Point Archives, Thomas R. Goethals Papers, Extracts from Telephone Journal Seventh German Army, 8–9 August 1944.

CHAPTER 9: SURRENDER INVITES DEATH

1. National Archives of Canada (NAC), General H.D.G. Crerar Papers, Vol. 2, Remarks to Senior Officers, Cdn Army Operation "Totalize" by GOC-in-C First Cdn Army 051100, August 1944; Paul Douglas Dickson, *A Thoroughly Canadian General: A Biography of General H. D. G. Crerar* (Toronto: University Press, 2007), 298; Sayer and Botting, *Hitler's Last General*, 170–71. Much of this chapter has been based on English, *Canadian Army*, 262–88, and English, *Patton's Peers*, 1–50.

2. NAC, Record Group (RG) 24, Vol. 10,808, Operation Totalize Appreciation by Lieutenant General G. G. Simonds, 1 August 1944.

3. Stacey, *Victory Campaign*, 211–13, 216–18; English, *Canadian Army*, 268–69; British Army of the Rhine (BAOR) Battlefield Tour Operation Totalize: 2 Canadian Corps Operations Astride the Road Caen-Falaise, 7–8 August 1944, Spectator's Edition (1947), 12–13.

4. English, *Canadian Army*, 263–66, 269–70; Copp, *Fields of Fire*, 191–94; BAOR Totalize, 1–16.

5. English, *Canadian Army*, 265–67, 269–73; and BAOR Totalize, 6–15.

6. English, *Canadian Army*, 269–70, 285; Meyer, *History of the 12. SS-Panzerdivision*, 170.

7. Reynolds, *Steel Inferno*, 230; Meyer, *History of the 12. SS-Panzerdivision*, 167–68; English, *Canadian Army*, 269–70.

8. English, *Patton's Peers*, 15–16.

9. English, *Canadian Army*, 273–74; BAOR Totalize, 17–22; RG 24, Vol. 10,800, "Immediate Report" on Operation "Totalize," 7–9 August 1944; Stephen Hart, *Road to Falaise* (Stroud, England: Sutton, 2004), 41–47. Brigadier Wyman, commanding the 2nd Armoured Brigade, signaled at 0615 hours that the forward area was securely held and that the situation appeared to be entirely suitable for further

operations to begin. Jody Perrun, "Best Laid Plans: Guy Simonds and Operation Totalize, 7–10 August 1944," *Journal of Military History* 1 (January 2003): 164–65.

10. Brig. Gen. E. A. C. (Ned) Amy, "Normandy: 1 Squadron Canadian Grenadier Guards, Phase 2 Operation Totalize 7/8 August 1944," unpublished paper dated 21 February 1993; RG 24,Vol. 10, Simonds Draft of Lessons, 1 July 1944; and English, *Patton's Peers*, 17–19.

11. Dwight D. Eisenhower (DDE) Library, Abilene, Kansas, J. Lawton Collins Papers, Box 5, Operation Cobra, Chapter I:VII Corps Operations (24–31 Jul 44); Carafano, *After D-Day*, 185–86, 192–203, 221, 262–63; Weigley, *Eisenhower's Lieutenants*, 155–64; D'Este, *Decision in Normandy*, 404; Eisenhower, *Bitter Woods*, 45.

12. English, *Patton's Peers*, 19–20.

13. Reynolds, *Steel Inferno*, 233–35; Meyer, *History of the 12. SS-Panzer Division*, 171–76; English, *Canadian Army*, 277. The debate over who killed Wittmann continues. What is known is that Trooper Joe Elkins, a Firefly gunner in the 1st Northamptonshire Yeomanry, knocked out the rearmost Tiger of Wittmann's attacking four at 1240 hours. The second Tiger than veered right and returned fire, but the Firefly reversed to a new position and knocked it out at 1247. Elkins then finished off the third Tiger at 1252. The 1st Northamptonshire Yeomanry's war diary provides evidence of this. The Canadian claim that Sherbrooke tanks got Wittmann cannot be substantiated since the Sherbrooke war diary was destroyed; it is based only on the recollections of a veteran who, since 1989, convinced himself that he got Wittmann from a forward position west of the Caen-Falaise highway. He was likely not as far forward as he recalls, however, since the bomb line ran north of Gaumesnil. The Canadian claim is thus based on a very thin reed. Moreover, that deadeye Elkins got three Tigers indicates that he could well have gotten a fourth (Wittmann's). Like the second Tiger, Wittmann could also have veered to the right, allowing Elkins to score a left rear hit. Hart, *Road to Falaise*, 155–58; Meyer, *History of the 12. SS-Panzerdivision*, 335–36.

14. Reynolds, *Steel Inferno*, 238.

15. English, *Canadian Army*, 277–78.

16. Reynolds, *Steel Inferno*, 236–37: Meyer, *History of the 12. SS-Panzerdivision*, 173; English, *Canadian Army*, 278.

17. Stacey, *Victory Campaign*, 225; English, *Canadian Army*, 278–79.

18. Ibid.

19. Meyer, *History of the 12. SS-Panzerdivision*, 177–78; Stacey, *Victory Campaign*, 225–28; English, *Canadian Army*, 280.

20. English, *Canadian Army*, 282; Meyer, *History of the 12. SS-Panzerdivision*, 179–80. In discussion with the author, Meyer disputed that the Canadians captured the hill, but they certainly gained and held the commanding top.

21. English, *Canadian Army*, 282–83; Meyer, *History of the 12. SS-Panzerdivision*, 180–81.

22. At 0710 hours, Simonds ordered both armored divisions to feed forward. RG 24, Vol. 10,797, COS 2 Cdn Corps Handwritten Telephone Notes, 8 August 1944; English, *Patton's Peers*, 20–22; CP, Vol. 21, Crerar to Stacey, 3 December 1958.

23. Ibid.; English, *Canadian Army*, 279–80.

24. Meyer, *History of the 12. SS-Panzerdivision*, 170–80; English, *Patton's Peers*, 19, 21–23.

CHAPTER 10: INTRACTABLE ENEMY

1. Meyer, *History of the 12. SS-Panzerdivision*, 181; Stacey, *Victory Campaign*, 248; Wilmot, *Struggle for Europe*, 476–81; Reynolds, *Steel Inferno*, 262–63.

2. Wilmot, *Struggle for Europe*, 475–76, 482; D'Este, *Decision in Normandy*, 425–27; Terrence Poulos, *Extreme War* (New York: The Military Book Club, 2004), 52–54.

3. D'Este, *Decision in Normandy*, 427, 443–48; Belfeld and Essame, *Battle for Normandy*, 225.

4. English, *Canadian Army*, 292–93; Stacey, *Victory Campaign*, 236.

5. English, *Canadian Army*, 294–95.

6. Ibid., 295

7. Meyer, *History of the 12. SS-Panzerdivision*, 183–84; Reynolds, *Steel Inferno*, 250–51; Stacey, *Victory Campaign*, 248, Copp, *Fields of Fire*, 225–26.

8. Meyer, *History of the 12. SS-Panzerdivision*, 184–85; Maj. Gen. George Kitching, *Mud and Green Fields: Memoirs* (Langely, Canada: Battleline, 1986), 216–20.

9. English, *Canadian Army*, 296.

10. Ibid.; Reynolds, *Steel Inferno*, 252; Meyer, *History of the 12. SS-Panzerdivision*, 185.

11. Meyer, *History of the 12. SS-Panzerdivision*, 185–87; Reynolds, *Steel Inferno*, 252; English, *Canadian Army*, 297; Copp, *Fields of Fire*, 230.

12. English, *Canadian Army*, 297–98; Copp, *Fields of Fire*, 229.

13. Meyer, *History of the 12. SS-Panzerdivision*, 184.

14. Hargreaves, *Germans in Normandy*, 198–99; English, *Canadian Army*, 298–99.

15. Stacey, *Victory Campaign*, 249–50; Meyer, *History of the 12. SS-Panzerdivision*, 187–88; Reynolds, *Steel Inferno*, 255, 259, 266; Copp, *Fields of Fire*, 232.

16. Meyer, *History of the 12. SS-Panzerdivision*, 192–94; Reynolds, *Steel Inferno*, 26; Stacey, *Victory Campaign*, 255; Jarymowycz, *Tank Tactics*, 192.

17. Stacey, *Victory Campaign*, 255, 261–62; Meyer, *History of the 12. SS-Panzerdivision*, 188–91, 196–202; Reynolds, *Steel Inferno*, 216–19, 271–72; English, *Canadian Army*, 299–300.

18. Wilmot, *Struggle for Europe*, 485–88; Jarymowycz, *Tank Tactics*, 198, 202; Hargreaves, *Germans in Normandy*, 217–18; Roy, *1944*, 306

19. Reynolds, *Steel Inferno*, 276–80; Meyer, *History of the 12. SS-Panzerdivision*, 201–3; Ritgen, *Western Front 1944*, 128–30; Weidinger, *Comrades to the End*, 328–32; Sayer and Botting, *Hitler's Last General*, 242–43, 248–87.

Bibliography

PRIMARY SOURCES
Government Records, Personal Papers, and Manuscript Collections
Dwight D. Eisenhower (DDE) Library, Abilene, Kansas: DDE Collection, Pre-Presidential Papers: 1916–1952, Principal File, J. Lawton Collins Papers.
National Archives of Canada (NAC): Record Group 24, National Defence 1870–1981, and H.D.G. Crerar Papers.
Public Record Office (PRO), London: Cabinet Office Historical Section files, Dempsey Papers (WO285).

Memoirs, Journals, and Accounts
Alanbrooke, Field Marshal Lord. *War Diaries 1939–1945*. Eds. Alex Danchev and Daniel Todman. London: Weidenfeld & Nicolson, 2001.
Bradley, Omar N. *A Soldier's Story*. New York: Henry Holt, 1951.
Bradley, Omar N., and Clay Blair. *A General's Life: An Autobiography by General of the Army Omar N. Bradley*. New York: Simon and Schuster, 1983.
Fey, Will. *Armor Battles of the Waffen-SS*. Winnipeg, Canada: J. J. Fedorowicz, 1990.
Gavin, General James M. *On to Berlin: Battles of an Airborne Commander, 1943–1946*. New York: Bantam, 1981.
Graves, Robert. *Good-bye to All That*. London: Jonathan Cape, 1929.
Horrocks, Sir Brian, with Eversley Belfield and Major-General H. Essame. *Corps Commander*. Toronto: Griffen House, 1977.
Kitching, Major General George. *Mud and Green Fields: Memoirs*. Langley, Canada: Battleline, 1986.
Kumm, Otto. *Prinz Eugen: The History of the 7 SS Mountain Division "Prinz Eugen."* Winnipeg, Canada: J. J. Fedorowicz, 1995.
Luck, Colonel Hans von. *Panzer Commander: Memoirs*. New York: Praeger, 1989.
Meyer, Hubert. *The History of the 12. SS-Panzerdivision "Hitlerjugend."* Trans. H. Harri Henschler. Winnipeg, Canada: J. J. Fedorowicz, 1994.

Montgomery of Alamein, Field Marshal The Viscount. *Memoirs*. London: Collins, 1958.
———. *Normandy to the Baltic*. London: Hutchinson, 1946.
Ritgen, Helmut. *The Western Front 1944: Memoirs of a Panzer Lehr Officer*. Winnipeg, Canada: J. J. Fedorowicz, 1995.
Weidinger, Otto. *Comrades to the End: The 4th SS Panzer-Grenadier Regiment "Der Führer" 1938–1945*. Trans. by David Johnston. Atglen, PA: Schiffer Military History, 1998.
———. *Das Reich I: 1934–1939*. Trans. Bo Friesen. Winnipeg, Canada: J. J. Fedorowicz Publishing, 1990.
———. *Das Reich II: 1940–1941*. Trans. by Bo Friesen. Winnipeg, Canada: J. J. Fedorowicz Publishing, 1995.

Official Histories
Blumenson, Martin. *Breakout and Pursuit, United States Army in World War II , The European Theater of Operations*. Washington, DC: Department of the Army, 1961.
Stacey, C. P. *Arms, Men and Governments: The War Policies of Canada 1939–1945*. Ottawa, Canada: Information Canada, 1974.
———. *Official History of the Canadian Army in the Second World War*, vol. 3, *The Victory Campaign: The Operations in North West Europe, 1944–1945*. Ottawa, Canada: Queen's Printer, 1966.

SECONDARY SOURCES
Books
Allen, Ralph. *Ordeal by Fire*. Toronto, Canada: Popular Library, 1961.
Balkoski, Joseph. *Beyond the Beachhead: The 29th Infantry Division in Normandy*. New York: Dell, 1989.
Beevor, Anthony. *Stalingrad*. New York: Viking, 1998.
Belfield, Eversley, and H. Essame. *The Battle for Normandy*. London, England: Pan, 1983.
Bennett, G. H. *Destination Normandy: Three Regiments in Normandy*. Westport, CT: Praeger Security International, 2007.
British Army Staff College Camberley booklet *Battlefield Tour—Operation Goodwood 18th–19th July 1944*.
Campbell, Ian J. *Murder at the Abbaye: The Story of Twenty Canadian Soldiers Murdered at the Abbaye d'Ardenne*. Ottawa, Canada: Golden Dog, 1996.
Carafano, James Jay. *After D-Day: Operation Cobra and the Normandy Breakout*. Boulder, CO: Lynne Rienner, 2000.
Chandler, David G., and James Lawton Collins, Jr., eds. *The D-Day Encyclopedia*. New York: Simon and Shuster, 1994.
Cooper, Matthew. *The German Army, 1933–1945: Its Political and Military Failure*. Chelsea, MI: Scarborough House, 1991.
Copp, Terry. *Cinderella Army: The Canadians in Northwest Europe 1944–1945*. Toronto, Canada: Toronto University Press, 2006.
———. *Fields of Fire: The Canadians in Normandy*. Toronto, Canada: Toronto University Press, 2003.
Deighton, Len. *Blitzkrieg: From the Rise of Hitler to the Fall of Dunkirk*. London, England: Jonathan Cape, 1979.
D'Este, Carlo. *Decision in Normandy: The Unwritten Story of Montgomery and the Allied Campaign*. London, England: Collins, 1983.

Dickson, Paul. *A Thoroughly Canadian General: A Biography of General H. D. G. Crerar.* Toronto, Canada: Toronto University Press, 2007.

Dunnigan, James F., ed. *The Russian Front.* London, England: Arms and Armour, 1978.

Eisenhower, John S. D. *The Bitter Woods: The Battle of the Bulge.* New York: Da Capo, 1995.

English, John A. *The Canadian Army and the Normandy Campaign: A Study of Failure in High Command.* New York: Praeger, 1991.

———. *Marching through Chaos: The Descent of Armies in Theory and Practice.* Westport, CT: Praeger, 1996.

———. *On Infantry.* New York: Praeger, 1981.

———. *Patton's Peers: The Forgotten Allied Field Army Commanders of the Western Front, 1944–45.* Mechanicsburg, PA: Stackpole Books, 2009.

Evans, Richard J. *The Third Reich at War.* New York: Penguin, 2009.

Foster, Tony. *Meeting of Generals.* Toronto, Canada: Methuen, 1986.

Giziowski, Richard. *The Enigma of General Blaskowitz.* London, England: Leo Cooper, 1997.

Hargreaves, Richard. *The Germans in Normandy.* South Yorkshire, England: Pen & Sword, 2006.

Hart, Russell A. *Clash of Arms: How the Allies Won in Normandy.* Boulder, CO: Lynne Rienner, 2001.

Hart, Stephen Ashley. *Montgomery and "Colossal Cracks": The 21st Army Group in Northwest Europe, 1944–45.* Westport, CT: Praeger, 2000.

———. *Road to Falaise.* Stroud, England: Sutton, 2004.

Hastings, Max. *Das Reich: Resistance and the March of the 2nd SS Panzer Division through France, June 1944.* London, England: Michael Joseph, 1981.

———. *Overlord: D-Day and the Battle for Normandy.* London, England: Pan, 1984.

Jarymowycz, Roman Johann. *Tank Tactics: From Normandy to Lorraine.* Boulder, CO: Lynne Rienner, 2001.

Keegan, John. *Rundstedt.* New York: Ballantine, 1974.

———. *Waffen SS: The Asphalt Soldiers.* New York: Ballantine, 1970.

Lackenbauer, P. Whitney, and Chris M.V. Madsen, eds. *Kurt Meyer on Trial [A Dsocumentary Record].* Kingston, Canada: Canadian Defence Press, 2007.

Lucas, James. *Hitler's Commanders: German Bravery in the Field 1939–1945.* London, England: Cassell, 2000.

Luther, Craig W. H. *Blood and Honor: The History of the 12th SS Panzer Division "Hitler Youth," 1943–1945.* San Jose, CA: Bender, 1987.

MacDonald, Charles B. *The Mighty Endeavor: American Armed Forces in the European Theater in World War II.* New York: Oxford University Press, 1969.

Macksey, Kenneth. *Panzer Divison: The Mailed Fist.* New York: Ballantine, 1972.

Margolian, Howard. *Conduct Unbecoming: The Story of the Murder of Canadian Prisoners of War in Normandy.* Toronto, Canada: Toronto University Press, 1998.

McKee, Alexander. *Caen: Anvil of Victory.* London, England: Macmillan, 1964.

Messenger, Charles. *The Art of Blitzkrieg.* London, England: Ian Allan, 1991.

———. *Hitler's Gladiator: The Life and Times of Oberstgruppenfuehrer and Panzergeneral-Oberst der Waffen-SS Sepp Dietrich.* London, England: Brassey's, 1988.

Mitcham, Samuel W. *The Panzer Legions: A Guide to the German Army Tank Divisions of World War II and Their Commanders.* Westport, CT: Praeger, 2000.

Morgan, Martin K. A. *Down to Earth: The 507th Parachute Infantry Regiment in Normandy.* Atglen, PA: Schiffer, 2004.

Munoz, Antonio J. *The East Came West: Muslim, Hindu, and Buddhist Volunteers in the German Armed Forces, 1941–1945.* New York: Axis Europa, 2002.

———. *Iron Fist: A Combat History of the 17. SS Panzergrenadier Division "Götz von Berlichingen."* New York: Axis Europa, 1999.

Overy, Richard. *Russia's War: Blood upon the Snow.* New York: Penguin Putnam, 1997.

———. *Why the Allies Won.* London, England: Pimlico, 1996.

Perret, Geoffrey. *There's a War to be Won: The United States Army in World War II.* New York: Ballantine, 1991.

Poulos, Terrence. *Extreme War: The Military Book Club's Encyclopedia of the Biggest, Fastest, Bloodiest, and Best in Warfare.* Garden City, NY: The Military Book Club, 2004.

Quarrie, Bruce. *Lightning Death: The Story of the Waffen-SS.* Sparkford, UK: Patrick Stephens, 1991.

Reid, Brian A. *No Holding Back: Operation Totalize, Normandy, August 1944.* Toronto, Canada: Robin Brass, 2005.

Reynolds, Michael. *The Devil's Adjutant: Jochem Peiper, Panzer Leader.* New York: Sarpedon, 1997.

———. *Sons of the Reich: The History of II SS Panzer Corps in Normandy, Arnhem, The Ardennes and on the Eastern Front.* Havertown, PA: Casemate, 2002.

———. *Steel Inferno: 1 SS Panzer Corps in Normandy.* New York: Sarpedon, 1997.

Rosado, Jorge, and Chris Bishop. *Wehrmacht Panzer Divisions, 1939–1949.* London, England: Amber, 2010.

Roy, Reginald H. *1944: The Canadians in Normandy.* Ottawa, Canada: Macmillan, 1984.

Ryan, Cornelius. *A Bridge Too Far.* London, England: Book Club Associates, 1975.

Sayer, Ian, and Douglas Botting. *Hitler's Last General: The Case against Wilhelm Mohnke.* London, England: Bantam, 1989.

Showalter, Dennis. *Hitler's Panzers: The Lightning Attacks that Revolutionized Warfare.* New York: Berkley Caliber, 2009.

Stein, George H. *The Waffen SS: Hitler's Elite Guard at War, 1939–1945.* Ithaca, NY: Cornell University Press, 1966.

Sydnor, Charles W. *Soldiers of Destruction: The Death's Head Division, 1933–1945.* Princteon, NJ: Princeton University Press, 1977.

Ullrich, Karl. *Wie ein Fels im Meer: 3. SS-Panzerdivision "Totenkopf" im Bild.* Osnabrück, Germany: Munin-Verlag, 1985.

Walther, Herbert. *Die 12. SS-Panzer-Division HJ: Eine Dokumentation in Wort und Bild.* Friedberg, Germany: Podzum-Pallas-Verlag, 1987.

Weigley, Russell F. *Eisenhower's Lieutenants: The Campaign of France and Germany, 1944–1945.* Bloomington, IN: Indiana University Press, 1981.

Weinberg, Gerhard L. *A World at Arms: A Global History of World War II.* Cambridge: University Press, 1994.

Weingartner, James J. *Hitler's Guard: The Story of the Leibstandarte SS Adolf Hitler.* Nashville, TN: Battery, 1996.

Wenn alle Brüder schweigen: Grosser Bildband über die Waffen SS. Osnabrück, Germany: Munin-Verlag, 1985.

Wilmot, Chester. *The Struggle for Europe.* London, England: Fontana/Collins, 1974.

Theses, Manuscripts, and Studies

British Army of the Rhine Battlefield Tour, Operation Totalize: 2 Canadian Corps Operations Astride the Road Caen-Falaise 7–8 August 1944. Spectator's Edition, 1947.

British Army of the Rhine Battlefield Tour, Operation Bluecoat: 8 Corps Operations South of Caumont 30–31 July 1944. Spectator's Edition, 1947.

Articles

Amy, Brig. Gen. E. A. C. (Ned). "Normandy: 1 Squadron Canadian Grenadier Guards, Phase 2 Operation Totalize 7/8 August 1944." Unpublished paper dated 21 February 1993.

Cook, Tim. "The Politics of Surrender: Canadian Soldiers and the Killing of Prisoners in the Great War." *Journal of Military History* 70 (July 2006): 637–65.

Glantz, David M. "Soviet Military Strategy during the Second Period of War: A Reappraisal." *Journal of Military History* 60 (January 1996): 115–50.

Milner, Marc. "Stopping the Panzers: Reassessing the Role of 3rd Canadian Infantry Division in Normandy, 7–10 June 1944." *Journal of Military History* 74 (April 2010): 491–522.

McNorgan. M. R. "Between Strawberry and Raspberry: An Examination of the Action Fought at Le Mesnil-Patry on June 11, 1944." *The Rifleman: The Journal of the Queen's Own Rifles of Canada.* Toronto: Regimental Headquarters, 1997.

O'Keefe, David R. O. "Double-Edged Sword Part 1: Ultra and Operation Totalize, Normandy, August 8, 1944." *Canadian Army Journal* 12 (Winter 2010): 85–93.

Perrun, Jody. "Best Laid Plans: Guy Simonds and Operation Totalize, 7–10 August 1944." *Journal of Military History* 1 (January 2003): 137–173.

Vance, Jonathan F. "Men in Manacles: The Shackling of Prisoners of War, 1942–1943." *Journal of Military History* 59 (July 1995): 483–504.

Index